The Best American Short Plays

2010–2011

The Best American Short Plays

2010–2011

edited with an introduction by
William W. Demastes

APPLAUSE THEATRE & CINEMA BOOKS
An Imprint of Hal Leonard Corporation

The Best American Short Plays 2010–2011
Edited with an intoduction by William W. Demastes

Copyright © 2012 by Applause Theatre & Cinema Books (an imprint of Hal Leonard Corporation)

Published in 2012 by Applause Theatre & Cinema Books
An Imprint of Hal Leonard Corporation
7777 West Bluemound Road
Milwaukee, WI 53213

Trade Book Division Editorial Offices
33 Plymouth Street, Montclair, NJ 07042

Printed in the United States of America
Book interior by UB Communications

ISBN 978-1-55783-835-3 [cloth]
ISBN 978-1-55783-836-0 [paper]
ISSN 0067-6284

www.applausebooks.com

contents

Introduction
Love, the Strange Attractor
William W. Demastes

Do any of us long for anything more desperately, hungrily, achingly than we long for love? And is there anything that scares us more? Falling in love is heaven, falling out is hell, and the unrequited sort is an unbearable blend of both. We vow time and time again never to fall into a trap that, statistically speaking, more often ends poorly than well. Heartbreak outdistances happily-ever-after no matter how you try to spin the evidence.

Medicine can't inoculate against it, psychology can't cure it, science can't dissect it, and reason can't fathom it. So sometimes we choose just to ignore it. Tom Stoppard reminds us (in *Arcadia*) that love is the attraction that Newton left out when he created that orderly world view that we all pretend to live in. But love is in the system and erupts onto the scene often when we're least prepared for its unexpected arrival. Maybe we should quarantine it as we do malware in our electronics. Being the truly rational creatures that we are, surely we should simply find ways to avoid this most irrational of human attractions as we work to create secure and comfortable lives for ourselves and our "loved" ones. Create a good firewall....

But we don't. We accept the fact that "the course of true love never did run smooth" (thank you, Mr. Shakespeare) and pursue it against all good reason. We shadow those we love, hoping for any sign of attention, seeing even pity, sometimes even downright contempt, as a sort of sign of love. In perhaps one of the greatest short plays ever written (*The Zoo Story*), Edward

Albee reveals that love and hate sometimes spawn from the same emotions. And, sad to say, "neither kindness nor cruelty, by themselves, independent of each other, creates any effect beyond themselves." It is "the two combined, together, at the same time, [that] are the teaching emotion."

The following short plays, in an incredible variety of ways, demonstrate Albee's point. These best short plays of the 2010–2011 season were selected from among a large group of very high-quality works (it was a very good year) whose primary nexus involved matters of love in one form or another. What it says about the beginning of the second decade of this no-longer-new century (if anything) is a matter of speculation I leave for the reader. What it says about love is pretty apparent: it's a subject that occupies a good deal of our time, interest, and energy, often despite our better intentions. These plays show people trying to build firewalls in order to avoid the teaching emotion, only to learn that love can't be quarantined. They show people learning hard lessons by way of the teaching emotion, coming back to life despite repeated efforts to spare themselves the pain and suffering. They show people lovingly trying to prevent others from suffering through the teaching emotion, only to discover that the lessons are non-transferable: we need to learn them on our own, and meddling invariably causes more problems than it solves.

Love finds a way despite all our efforts to negotiate, reject, or control it. And in the end, even against our better judgment and despite evidence to the contrary, it is pretty hard to argue that life really would be better without love in the picture.

Those early first fumblings in love can be the most painful, poignant, and funny (at least for other people). Lorin Howard's *The Subtext of Texting* puts a contemporary spin on these early romantic contacts by reminding us how the advent of new technologies like texting generates a new language of love not quite sorted out. Howard confesses that she is the desperate character in the play, "feverishly obsessing over what is said in a series of cryptic, no-frills texts after precisely seven months of the beginning of a relationship that actually began online." Text-speak is a whole new language whose subtleties and innuendoes appear to have gender-specific responses. Howard reports that when she asks whether or not this staged relationship will end happily, "inevitably, the girls respond with a resounding 'yes.' The boys are less optimistic and think that 'the end' is the end of the relationship." The play is about communication and how it looks in 2011. And Howard confirms, "Yes, this is a love story."

Poignant describes Vincent Delaney's *The Request*, which also revolves around contemporary technology, but in this case technology creates a completely unexpected by-product in the virtual realm of Facebook and Internet: "immortality." Delaney recalls being inspired by an eerie discovery that a Facebook page had outlived a deceased friend by several years. Says Delaney, "The strangeness of this made me think about the odd permanence we're all creating online, and how little control we really have over it. I wonder if we should be more careful." With this experience as inspiration, Delaney plays on the hauntings of past loves and lovers that we all experience in our lives, this time with a uniquely contemporary, sadly modern twist.

John Franceschini's *It's Only a Minute a Guy* takes on the anxieties of a recently divorced woman and her reluctant adventure with another recent phenomenon: speed dating. Franceschini says, "It's difficult to restart your social life after a divorce. Accept the fact you'll churn through a lot of flotsam before you can connect with a genuine soul mate. The secret is to believe it will happen and keep trying."

Thread Count is perhaps the most romantic piece in this volume, triggered by an instantaneous spark of inspiration: Lisa Soland summarizes: "I was in the mall shopping. I had just stepped onto the escalator to go down a floor, when I turned and looked back just in time to see a male salesclerk opening up and tossing a bedspread across a display bed. A female customer stood across from him and she was reaching across the bed to catch and help to lower the comforter neatly onto the bed. In that single moment, I had the entire play." The play is its own *Miracle on 34th Street*, bringing together an uppity sales clerk and North Dakota widow and generating a not-quite love-at-first-sight encounter that is wacky and romantic at the same time.

Actually, some might consider Craig Pospisil's *Dissonance* the most romantic play in this volume. By no means a conventional boy-meets-girl play, it involves a former musician and the daughter of a just-deceased music teacher. These two characters, loosely inspired by actual friends of Pospisil, are joined together in the most unlikely of circumstances, generating a harmony of their own, which, we learn, necessarily involves a certain degree of dissonance to succeed. The first drafting of this play occurred, says Pospisil, while "I was on my honeymoon, of all places."

Creatures by Janet Allard is an inspired little project generated as a response to the writing prompt "A secret has just been revealed: What happens next?" The comic incongruities that result—a werewolf is a central character—remind us of the compelling and essential nature of secrets even among those we love. Secrets of identity, how we hide who we are, and when we choose, or are forced to reveal, who we are. And what happens when we do. Says Allard, "I find this really compelling."

The Coyote Stratagem by G. Flores has a title whose reference is to the tactics of Wile E. Coyote in the Warner Bros. Roadrunner cartoons. The play warmly documents a specific instance of immature behavior that—if we really think about it—is manifest in many of even the most healthy relationships. Flores observes about his play that "it isn't quite a condemnation of the immaturity of a lot of American men (a trait that I suffer from as well), but it certainly is a critique of our childlike reaction to adult problems."

Arlene Hutton's *Chocolates on the Pillow* is another take on the theme of deception in romance, benign and otherwise. This one involves a first-time (last time?) bed-and-breakfast getaway where, as Hutton notes, her two characters "are playing roles in a clichéd land of faux Victorian decor with fluffy towels, fancy soaps, chocolates, and sherry. Do they really want to go antiquing and hiking or are they talking about these things because that's what they think they should be doing? From the very first lines it's clear that they are not listening to each other and although we're rooting for them, we're not hopeful that this weekend will be everything they want it to be." Disturbingly, a pet teddy bear takes on something of a life of its own as observer and critic, increasing the characters' self-awareness that they have taken on roles in this relationship that aren't necessarily who they really are.

And Yet . . . by Steve Feffer takes Shakespeare's famous sonnet on love unvarnished ("My mistress' eyes are nothing like the sun") and utilizes video technology to probe the mysteries of performed behavior in love relations. "Acting" is a central component to all human behavior but seems even more intensified and concentrated when love is involved. Inspired by the sonnet, Feffer reports: "I knew immediately that I wanted the play to speak to how these mediatized images were getting in the way of the main character seeing his love. . . . I like how that struggle comes through in Sam's effort to communicate both with the audience in his direct address and with Shayna as a TV." Yes, a television is a character in the play. Hyper self-conscious as we all are today about the mediating influences of technology, Feffer's play takes a unique approach by literalizing the idea that our lives are like television.

Is honesty always the best policy? If so, then why does love inspire so much deception and such strange behavior? John Bolen, in *A Song for Me, or Getting the Oscar*, confronts this issue by making the obvious point. At least it's obvious to those of us who are willing to be honest about the subject: "How could any relationship survive unfiltered when verisimilitude will serve much better, and get us kissed at night?" Bolen adds, "We have to be selective with our truths, for our spouses really do not want to know that those jeans make their asses look fat." The attendant problem, of course, is determining how much truth is a good thing, because complete mendacity surely can't be the correct strategy.

Forcing the truth to be known and struggling to live with that truth is the subject of Gabriel Rivas Gomez's *Scar Tissue*, a play "about hearts in disrepair, both literally and figuratively." Gomez explains: "It is dirty. It is ugly. It is vicious. And, at its core, it is a story about love. And loss. It is a story about what damages and eventually repairs the heart. The rest is just a vehicle." Best intentions gone awry infiltrate lives of good people, leaving regret amid honest confrontations with the complexities that comprise truth.

Regret and honesty also inform Brent Englar's *Snowbound*. Englar observes that the play is a "conversation turned to art, philosophy, and eventually God," which is simultaneously dramatized in a manner that, in the end, defends love and forgiveness as gifts that defeat hatred and urges for vengeance. *Eleanor's Passing* by John Patrick Bray has a similar elegiac quality to it. Described by Bray as "a subtle look at three friends who decide to stick together until the end, whenever that may be," it is a reflection upon life and living by a new-made widower and his aging friends.

Kimberly La Force's *A Marriage Proposal* has a negotiated quality to it that doesn't occur (at least not so directly) in the other plays. Here it involves a single mother and hard-working illegal immigrant, both of whom need something other than love from a relationship. The play unfolds as a frank view on the romantic versus practical nature of marriage. Economic necessity rarely finds its way into discussions where love and romance should dominate, but it is a consideration that does take center stage when people are weighed down by the struggle of day-to-day survival. Necessity can be a powerful force. But even then, many of us still tend to stand by our romantic inclinations.

Taking a far lighter look on matrimonial matters, *Till Death Do Us* by Gene Fiskin was inspired by the conclusion that men and women view things differently when it comes to weddings. Says Fiskin: "This play was a brief tongue-in-cheek exploration of those differences."

But if women have more romantic notions about marriage, life after marriage sometimes entails a female conversion to far more pragmatic matters, including keeping the lid on dreamy, idealistic husbands. *A Number on the Roman Calendar* by David Johnston looks back to an earlier millennial happening (AD 1000) and follows a poor but loving couple through their thoughts and actions on the undoubted eve of the end of the world. Upon reflection, I think that this play, too, could be among the most romantic in this collection.

There are no women available to qualify the thoughts and actions of the two men in *Six Dead Bodies Duct-Taped to a Merry-Go-Round* by Lindsay Marianna Walker and Dawson Moore. But women in the background do inspire these men to bizarre acts of self-expression. What the play captures is, as Moore observes, "nothing more complicated than a couple of seemingly disparate people finding each other's humanities."

Moore's description also aptly describes Michael Ross Albert's *Starfishes*, involving a lonely youth's encounter with an equally lonely prostitute in a desolate lighthouse along the Nova Scotia coastline. Albert reports, "As I worked on the play and discovered what it really wanted to be, a goofy sex farce turned into a play about loneliness. It is a love story about two people, both cut off from the rest of the world, finding hope in one another."

St. Matilde's Malady by Kyle John Schmidt has its own prostitutes. In fact, it's set in a "pre-industrial" brothel and, as Schmidt says, "speaks to the ambivalent nature of love," though his interest involves "not falling in love (which is always easy), but love in a continuum (which is never easy)." Schmidt adds: "This kind of love is like a debilitating, contractible disease: restricting freedom, limiting action, and containing a brutality that verges on criminality. However, this chronic sickness is not only sought after but undertaken with joy and excitement."

Lobster Boy by Dan Dietz confronts "the inability to feel pain, a profound sense of guilt . . . and lobsters." It's a mesmerizing work that captures much of Albee's "teaching emotion" gone horribly wrong. How do you teach fear? Is it love or is it hate that inspires someone to give the life-preserving gift of fear to someone who doesn't come by it naturally?

Ending on a light note, *You're Invited!* by Darren Canady is both funny and telling. Love in our culture has become something of a commodity that we tend to think has monetary value. Buying love is recognized by many as prostitution, of course, but it curiously seems that money spent on sons and daughters signals familial balance and order, especially in middle-class suburbia where keeping up with the Joneses has become a money-hemorrhaging marathon that has lost sight of its ultimate goal. Let's not forget, Canady reminds us, that love preexists in our children and simply needs to be nurtured in the simplest of ways.

Love. What a word.

The Subtext of Texting

Lorin Howard

Lorin Howard

Lorin Howard, a Los Angeles native, has been involved in all aspects of theater. With a BA in theater arts and English and a MA in psychology, and after years of teaching elementary and preschool, Howard, an award-winning actor, continues to involve herself in theater.

Howard has studied and taken workshops/private coaching with Jeff Corey, Darryl Hickman, Tom Schlesinger, Richard Krevolin, and Cecilia Fannon of the Tony Award–winning South Coast Repertory Company. She has expanded on her theatrical experience as an actor, producer, and director to focus on playwriting. Howard has written and produced plays that have been performed on the Los Angeles and Orange County theater circuit, in Michigan, New York, and Seattle, in addition to shows developed for children's theater. Her short plays have garnered numerous awards.

··· production history ···

The Subtext of Texting was produced at the Mysterium Theatre, Santa Ana, California, by New Voices Playwrights Theatre in September 2011. Concurrently, it had its New York premiere (October 2011) in Ticket 2 Eternity's production of "Disjointed Love Shorts" at the TheatreLab NYC. It was produced in 2011 at the Hudson Guild Theatre, New York City, by Variations Theatre Group, making its New York debut twice in the same season.

characters

> **CORI**, early to mid-thirties
> **GREG**, mid-thirties
> **MADDY**, mid-thirties

setting

Split stage: CORI's house and GREG's office. Morning. The present.

• • •

[CORI *enters with her cell phone connected to a charger and an extension cord. An impeccably dressed* GREG *talks to someone on his land line.*]

CORI [*Checks cell for calls, text messages, etc.*] Five days! It's been five days since the last text. I'm done. It's over. We are so finished.

GREG [*On his land line.*] I was in Chicago. I think I was actually at O'Hare, waiting for my boarding call. I'm thinking about how much I miss her and suddenly I remember just how much—

CORI I miss him.

GREG I miss her.

CORI Did he lose interest?

GREG Maybe I said something wrong.

CORI Maybe he found someone else.

GREG I don't even know if she's still into me.

CORI He could be lying in a hospital bed with amnesia or on the side of the road in a pool of blood.

GREG We've never gone this long without contact.

CORI I'd never know if he got into an accident, because no one he knows, knows me.

GREG It's not like her.

CORI Not hearing from him is not like him.

GREG Who stopped texting whom first? I don't even remember.
[*To the person on land line.*]
Yeah, Buddy. Catch you later.

[*Hangs up the phone.*]

CORI Okay, so oops! He sent the last text. But I'm not about to send the next one. He's the guy. It's his turn. It's protocol after a long hiatus.

GREG [*To himself.*] So you're standing on principle. How's that workin' for ya', Greg? Worth the angst of not knowing?
[*Texting.*]
How's my girl?

CORI [*The phone pings.*] He called me his girl. He's alive. Thank God he's not wandering aimlessly in and out of skid row soup kitchens, mumbling something about a lost shopping cart.
[*Beat.*]
I'm over here suffering and all you can say is, "How's my girl?"

GREG She isn't answering. Her texts are usually instantaneous. This can't be good.
[*Texting.*]
Talk to me, baby....

[*Ping!*]

CORI Then pick up the friggin' phone and call me—baby. It takes more energy to text than it does to dial!

GREG Is she trying a new strategy? Maybe I'll try a new strategy.
[*Texting.*]
Going out of town next weekend. Need to see you soon.

[*Ping!*]

CORI   Who's he going out of town with?

GREG   [*Texting.*] A short trip with my business partners.

[*Ping!*]

CORI   And what's "soon"? Tonight? Tomorrow? Friday morning? You think I don't have a life? Do you expect me to drop everything and just pick up where we left off?

GREG   Why can't we just pick up where we left off? We've been together for seven months and—

CORI   We haven't seen each other in two weeks.

GREG   Let's not lose the momentum because someone is too hardheaded to answer a text. She could very well be the One—even if she is stubborn as hell, and if I give up now, I might never know.
[*Texting.*]
You better not be seeing someone else. Winky face.
[*Ping!*]
Okay, that was just plain dumb. I sound desperate and threatening.

CORI   He's agonizing. That makes me so happy.

GREG   She probably figures I have no other options. Loser.

CORI   He's so hot, he could probably date any girl he wants. I better step it up a notch if I don't want to lose him.
[*Texting.*]
No one else. Only have eyes for you.
[*Ping! She rereads the text.*]
Diarrhea of the mouth! I should have stopped at "No one else." But no. I have to embellish. I hate when I do that! "Only have eyes for you." What was I thinking?

GREG   I think she's still crazy about me. She's being evasive—not responding to my vulnerability, but at least she's responding.

[*Texting.*]

BTW, miss you, baby. XOXOXO

[*Ping!*]

CORI   He misses me. He still cares. BTW, if you miss me so much, ask me out on a date. A movie, dinner, a lecture on the economy. Anything!

[*Texting.*]

Miss you too, baby. XOXOXO

[*Ping!*]

GREG   She misses me. Yes! How do I respond to that? Something original. Not overly personal, but enough to show her how much she means to me....

[*Texting.*]

Need to see you—all caps—SOON.

[*Ping!*]

CORI   What's with the "SOON"? Drive fifteen minutes and you can see me really soon. I'll even meet you halfway—sooner! How do I say all that in a text without sounding too eager?

[*Texting.*]

I'd love to see you too. Soon. LMK.

[*Ping!*]

GREG   LMK? I don't know that one.

CORI   Shoot! I used the "L" word. Why did I say, "I'd love to see you soon"?

GREG   LMK? Leave me...? Let—me...?

CORI   I should have said, "I'd like to see you soon." Tourette's!

GREG   Know! Let me know!

[GREG's *land line rings. There is a knock on* CORI's *door. He answers the phone.*]

Hello.

CORI   Come in!

[MADDY *enters.*]

Maddy, what're you doing here?

MADDY   Came to pick up my gym bag. And you. And you're not ready.

CORI   I'm not going.

MADDY   You couldn't have called to tell me?

CORI   I texted you.

MADDY   No...

CORI   Didn't I?

MADDY   No.

CORI   Last night I had four glasses of Pinot Grigio for dessert. Then I texted you, put the phone down, and fell asleep. When I woke up this morning, I found my phone in the meat compartment of the refrigerator with a dead battery. I guess I forgot to hit "send." Sorry.

MADDY   You had four glasses of wine—alone?

CORI   You say it that way and it sounds like I should be in rehab. Actually it was four mugs. And half a jar of Nutella. He texted me this morning. Finally.

MADDY   And you're going out with him tonight, so you have to start getting ready at nine o'clock in the morning?

CORI   Not exactly. I'll probably never see him again. We're on a one-way ticket to Nowhere Fast. The beginning of a vague recollection.

MADDY   You're breaking up with him?

CORI   Not exactly. He just doesn't seem as interested in me as he used to be.

MADDY   He says he adores you. At least, according to all the texts you read to me.

CORI   Ten minutes of texting, then radio silence for 120 hours. How does that translate into adoration? I screwed something up and I don't even know what.

MADDY   Nah. The honeymoon's over. That's all.

CORI   That's all? That's tragic!

GREG   [*Hangs up; returns to cell.*] I don't want to screw this up. I'll say something romantic, but not too sweet; passionate, but not too graphic. Just enough to keep her engaged.

[*Texting.*]

I want to kiss and slowly caress every part of your beautiful body; to make intense love to you for—all caps—HOURS. Need to be one with you for—all caps—LIFETIMES.

[*Ping!*]

I did not just say that in a text.

CORI   He said he wants to make love to me. For hours!

MADDY   In a text. Let me see that. No. That's borderline sexting. He's seducing you with his words.

CORI   And this is a problem—why?

MADDY   Honey, he's a man.

CORI   No, I think he's different.

MADDY   Put him on the spot. Call him and say, "My place or yours?"

CORI   Way too pushy. I'd never do that.

MADDY   You've already slept with him. What difference does it make?

GREG   I was way too pushy. I probably offended her with the verbal foreplay, and makeup sex isn't even on the table.

CORI   The sex. That's what's wrong with our relationship.

MADDY   No chemistry?

CORI   No. *Great* chemistry. But that's the extent of our connection. I'm nothing but a booty call. Now that he's already sampled the goods, there's no incentive for an enduring relationship. We have nothing to say to each other and nothing in common. I've decided I can't see him anymore.

MADDY   You couldn't see him any less. Where is my gym bag?

CORI   I don't even know his religion.

MADDY   Do you even care?

CORI   Not really.

MADDY   I thought you loved being with him.

CORI   What's not to love?

MADDY   Then love him.

CORI   Look at how miserable I am.

MADDY   So break up with him.

CORI   I don't want to.

MADDY   Just make a decision! You're playing games and you're giving me a pain-in-the-ass headache. I'm going to yoga class. Where the hell is my bag?

CORI   I'm playing games? He's leading me down a garden path so he can seduce me in the flower bed. Look under the sink in my bathroom.

GREG   I crossed the line. How can she take me seriously if she thinks our entire love affair is based on an affair without love?
[*Texting.*]
Want to kiss your sweet lips. To look into your eyes, to feel your heartbeat.

[*Ping!*]

CORI   I knew it. He's my soul mate.

MADDY   Tell him talk is cheap.

CORI   My soul mate? In a text? I don't think so.

MADDY   If he's your soul mate, wouldn't he just "get" you?

CORI You can't hear someone's inflection when it's only words.

MADDY [*Finds the gym bag.*] So add an expressive emoticon.

GREG I sound like a 1960s Hallmark card. I've got to convince her of how committed I am to be with her without making her nauseous.
[*Texting.*]
Cori, are we okay? XO

MADDY [*Goes through gym bag.*] Did you take my sports bra?

CORI Mine were all dirty and you always keep an extra. Look in the clothes hamper.

MADDY Wear one of your dirty sweaty bras? That's disgusting!

CORI [*Looking for the text.*] What's taking so long?

MADDY He texted you twenty seconds ago. Ten seconds ago he was your soul mate. How much more do you want from the guy?

GREG [*Ping!*] Damnit!
[*Texting.*]
Of course we're okay, Mom. I meant, "Are you okay?"
[*After a moment, GREG's phone pings. Reads message aloud.*]
I'm fine, darling. My ankles are swollen, but I'll live. XO to you too, dear. PS Who is Cori?
[*Texting.*]
Shit!
[*Texting.*]
Cori, are we okay? XO

[*Ping!*]

CORI XO? XO—really? There are supposed to be eight XOs. What happened to the other six? See? His interest is waning.

MADDY You're ridiculous! Give me the damn phone—and find my bra!
[*Grabs the phone and texts.*]

Greg, put your money where your mouth is. Show me how much you want me.

CORI You did not! If you hit "send," I swear, I'm never speaking to you again.

[*Taking phone back.*]

You didn't send it, did you?

MADDY Only one way to find out.

GREG All right, taking a huge risk and upping the ante.

[*Texting.*]

Luv you, baby.

[*Ping!*]

CORI You sent my text, didn't you?

MADDY My text. Why?

CORI He's never said he loves me before.

MADDY He still hasn't.

CORI Sure he has.

MADDY No. He typed, "L - U - V - U comma baby." That's totally different than saying, "I love you, Cori."

CORI It's textbook text-speak, Maddy. Shorthand? What should I tell him? What would you say?

MADDY No response is a response.

CORI I want him to know that I feel the same way. If I wait too long, he'll give up on me. If I text him too soon, he'll think I have nothing better to do with my time than wait around for his texts.

MADDY Ever thought of telling him the truth?

CORI I'm scared I'll say something stupid that I'll end up regretting.

MADDY You say smart things that you end up regretting. Especially when you're under the influence—

CORI I haven't been drinking.

MADDY Under the influence of pheromones. Come with me to class and clear your head. Then make a decision.

CORI No, thanks. Pheromones plus endorphins equals a really deadly combination.

[CORI *paces, stares at the phone, looks at her watch, looks in the mirror, jots something down, etc.* MADDY *looks everywhere for her bra.* GREG *paces, stares at the phone, types on the computer, looks at his watch, etc. This segment goes on in total silence.*]

GREG [*Texting.*] Are you still there?

[*Ping!*]

CORI Should I answer him? Tell me what to do.

MADDY [*Starts to exit.*] Answer him. Don't answer him, but don't look to me for your answers. Talk to you later.

GREG I wonder if I said too much. Maybe she's feeling smothered....

CORI I hate ignoring his texts.

MADDY All this insanity because of a man you barely know.

[*Ping!*]

Let him wait.

CORI A gorgeous man. With a body to die for, and who kisses like—

MADDY What do you really know about him? Not his looks or his tongue technique. What do you know about the man?

CORI I know that...Well, he's...I mean, he always says that...I guess we don't talk so much....What happens next?

MADDY One of you calls the other and makes a real, in-person, grown-up date.

[*Ping!*]

Or not.

CORI Texting is safe. There's not as much of an investment. He takes me at face value and I'm enough just the way I am.

MADDY   He doesn't know you "just the way you are," and how can he take you at face value, when he never sees your face?

[*Ping!*]

CORI   He said he loves me.

MADDY   Give him a chance to prove it.

CORI   What if he doesn't like me when he gets to know who I really am?

MADDY   At least you'll know where you stand.

CORI   I'm scared, Maddy. I don't want it to end. Not yet.

MADDY   That's the first really real thing you've said all morning.

CORI   Let's go to the gym.

[*She leaves the phone behind. They exit.*]

GREG   I know it doesn't make any sense, but I'm really falling in love with you, Cori. I only wish I could find the right words to tell you. . . .

[*Texting.*]

Have a great day.

[*Ping!*]

• • •

The Request

Vincent Delaney

Vincent Delaney

Vincent Delaney's plays have been produced and developed at the Guthrie Theater, Actors Theatre of Louisville, TACT, Seattle Rep, ACT, Alabama Shakespeare Festival, Florida Stage, InterAct, the Children's Theatre Company, the Magic, Woolly Mammoth, Pittsburgh Public, New Century Theatre Company, the Lark, and Orlando Shakespeare Festival, among others. Awards include a McKnight fellowship, a Jerome commission, the Heideman, a Bush fellowship, the Virtual Theatre Project New Play Award, and the Nathan Miller Award. He is a core alumnus of the Playwrights Center and a proud member of the Seattle Rep Writers Group. Delaney's plays are published by Smith and Kraus, Samuel French, Heinemann, *Dramatics Magazine*, Theatre Forum, and Playscripts.com.

···production history···

The Request was recorded for podcast in October 2011, before a live audience at West of Lenin Theatre, Seattle. It was produced by the Sandbox Artist Collective, and directed by Leslie Law, with music by Jose Gonzales. The cast was as follows:

OWEN, K. Brian Neel

ROSA, Annette Toutonghi

JACK, Shawn Belyea

CUSTOMER, David Natale

BARISTA, Eric Ray Anderson

VOICE OF CAMILLE, Kathryn Van Meter

characters

OWEN

ROSA

JACK

CUSTOMER/BARISTA

VOICE OF CAMILLE

• • •

[*Night.* OWEN *and* ROSA *in bed. Sex. She's the aggressor.*]

OWEN   Oh. Oh God.

ROSA   Yeah?

OWEN   Oh my God.

ROSA   I've got more. More for you.

OWEN   What are you doing. Oh. What. Are you. Doing.

ROSA   Stop?

OWEN   No. Please don't.

ROSA   That's for you. For you.

OWEN   God yes.

ROSA   Good?

OWEN   Yes. Oh yes. Oh yes, yes. Rosa.

[*Beat. Panting.*]

ROSA   Did you like it?

OWEN   I think you broke me.

ROSA   Where are you going?

OWEN   [*Exiting.*] Water. Parched.

ROSA   I'm just going to check messages.

OWEN   [*From off.*] What?

ROSA   [*She opens her laptop.*] Just take me one sec.

OWEN   [*Returning.*] You're on the computer? Already?

ROSA   I'm just checking status updates.

OWEN   You're not supposed to go on Facebook after sex. Zuckerberg said so.

ROSA   Hey. Oh my God. Is that her?

OWEN   Who?

ROSA   That's her. No. She still has a profile?

OWEN   Weird.

ROSA   Did you know? Have you looked at this before?

OWEN   That would be sick. She's dead.

ROSA   She came up as a friend suggestion. God, her poor family. Why is this all still here?

OWEN   Let's go to sleep.

ROSA   Look, there's galleries. Summer 2008. Newport Beach.

OWEN   Please don't open those.

ROSA   Is that her? In the bikini?

OWEN   I think so, yes.

ROSA   Owen. You did sleep with her.

OWEN   Okay, it's her.

ROSA   She's gorgeous.

OWEN   She was okay. You're gorgeous.

ROSA   Her body is perfect.

OWEN   It's not, it's not perfect. It wasn't. This is really confusing.

ROSA   Is that you? Kissing her?

OWEN   Probably.

ROSA   She looks so happy. So do you.

OWEN   It was three years ago.

ROSA   It's so eerie. Everything is preserved. Do you want to read her last status update?

OWEN   No, this is perverse. Just turn it off.

ROSA   Here it is.
[*Reads.*]
Owen brought me flowers and now I'm sneezing. That is so sweet.

OWEN   I'm really tired.

ROSA   She loved you, didn't she?

OWEN   They need to close the profile. This is wrong.

ROSA   Maybe her family knows. Maybe they want it active.

OWEN   Why?

ROSA   She still has friends. A status. She's almost a person. It would be like killing her twice.

OWEN   You can be so odd sometimes.

[OWEN *at work. He's on a headset. Distracted. Across the stage, a customer on a telephone.*]

CUSTOMER   [*Into phone.*] You said this was a free scan. I wouldn't have to buy anything.

OWEN [*Into phone.*] Yes, sir, that's right.

CUSTOMER I'm looking at the screen, it says I still have infected files. It's sending me to a download page and asking for my credit card.

OWEN Sir.

CUSTOMER I'm not giving you my credit card. Hello. Are you there?

OWEN Sorry, what did you say?

CUSTOMER I said your site wants my credit card.

OWEN Sir, we don't request that information.

CUSTOMER My e-mail is hacked. Why would I give you my credit card number?

OWEN That's not our site. If you just click refresh—

CUSTOMER I'm on your site. I'm looking at your site. I'm supposed to get a free virus scan.

OWEN Yes, I can help you with that, if you'll just—

CUSTOMER I have been on the phone with you for thirty-five minutes, and I don't think you're even paying attention to me. Are you there?

OWEN [*Distracted.*] What?

CUSTOMER What the hell was your name? Orson? Oliver?

JACK [*Entering to* OWEN.] Hey, Owen. Whoa. Hot pics.

OWEN Jack, I'm on a call.

JACK Looks like it.

[JACK *whistles.*]

OWEN [*Into phone.*] Sir, let me help you create a system restore point.

CUSTOMER We did that half an hour ago! Who is that whistling on the line?

OWEN No one, sir. It's the connection.

CUSTOMER   Listen to me, you insolent prick. The only copy of my fantasy novel, six years of work, is on this laptop, and I can't access it. I want your supervisor.

JACK   Allow me.

[*Takes the headset.*]

This is Jack. I'm Owen's supervisor. Fantasy novels suck. Especially yours. Enjoy your viruses.

[JACK *hangs up.* CUSTOMER *exits.*]

So. What's her name?

OWEN   You shouldn't have done that.

JACK   It's a free virus scan. What do they expect? Damn, she is hot. Who is she?

OWEN   My old girlfriend. Camille.

JACK   Snooping the ex on Facebook. On company time. I like your style. Jesus, why do some girls show so much skin online? Sorry. You obviously still have feelings.

OWEN   No, she's, um. She died. Three years ago.

JACK   You're shitting me. This girl is dead? And still on Facebook?

OWEN   It's very odd.

JACK   It's all still here. Galleries, videos. Why didn't her family close it?

OWEN   I asked them not to.

JACK   Does Rosa know you did that?

OWEN   Sure. Sort of.

JACK   Camille was totally hot. Why'd you ever break up?

OWEN   She was raped and murdered.

JACK   I suck. I really totally suck. I am suckful.

OWEN   It's okay, you didn't know.

JACK   I'm an ass. I didn't know you were still with her when it happened. What are you doing?

OWEN Posting on her wall.

JACK Whoa. Whoa, whoa, whoa. This is not good. Hey. Come on, Owen. You should not be doing this.

OWEN I just said I missed her.

JACK She's dead. It's just an algorithm. Owen. Log off. Seriously, you need to get out of Facebook.

OWEN I know, I know.

JACK I mean it, log off. Fine, I'm going to do it for you. Move.

OWEN Wait. Jack. Do you see that?

[JACK *yelps.*]

JACK No. No, no, no, no. Fuck me.

OWEN She just liked my post.

JACK She did not. She did not like your post.

OWEN She did. She liked it.

JACK The break is over. Break is totally officially over.

OWEN What the hell, what the hell.

JACK It's a prank. Some asshole hacked her accounts. Some insensitive fuck is in her profile, and you need to unfriend her. Now.

OWEN I can't.

JACK Unfriend her. I mean it, right now.

OWEN I need to go.

JACK Owen! I really think this violates the terms of service!

[*A rooftop. Sound of seagulls.* OWEN's *phone rings. Across the stage,* ROSA *on her phone.*]

OWEN [*Into phone.*] Hi.

ROSA [*Into phone.*] Hey, it's me. Miss you.

OWEN Miss you too.

ROSA   They said you left work early.

OWEN   Yeah. It got to be too much.

ROSA   Where are you? I hear birds.

OWEN   Nowhere, I'm at home.

ROSA   You're not at home, 'cause I'm at home.

OWEN   I'm on the roof.

ROSA   What roof?

OWEN   Downtown. Parking garage. Where he cut her open.

ROSA   You're where?

OWEN   No one else was here. He held her down. She couldn't scream. He violated her. Then he started to separate her. All her pieces.

ROSA   Come home. Right now. Get off that roof. Get away from there.

OWEN   It took her so long to die. Bleeding. Spreading.

ROSA   Owen! Get off the rooftop!

OWEN   Can't. I'm reading her posts.

ROSA   You're what? That's the past, it's over.

OWEN   No. These are new posts.

ROSA   Come home. Please, Owen.

OWEN   She just sent me an audio file. That is so nice.

[*Sound. Clarinet. Gentle, simple. A song for* OWEN.]

ROSA   What was that?

OWEN   She's been practicing. She's really good now.

ROSA   Come home. Right now.

OWEN   I'm happy here, Rosa.

[*Voice of* CAMILLE.]

CAMILLE   Love. Love. Love you. Love.

ROSA Owen? Are you there? Owen?

CAMILLE Love you, Owen. Love you. Love you.

[*Music, clarinet. Lights change. Coffee shop. Upstage, a barista pouring coffee.*]

BARISTA Why don't you two have a seat. I'll bring your drinks right over.

ROSA Thank you.
[*To* OWEN.]
Sit down. I want you to relax.

OWEN Why?

ROSA This is my fault. I'm the one who started this.

OWEN Everything's fine.

ROSA How is everything fine?

OWEN Because it is.

ROSA We're going to log on. We're going to say good-bye. And you're going to unfriend her.

OWEN I don't think so.

ROSA Fine, then I'll log you on.

OWEN You know my password?

ROSA Of course I know your password.
[*Types.*]
There's her profile.

OWEN How do you know my password?

BARISTA [*Walking up.*] Okay, two extra-tall double-shot caffeine towers.

ROSA Thank you.

BARISTA Whoa. Good-looking woman. Friend of yours?
[*Beat.*]
I'll get back to work now.

[*Moves away.*]

ROSA   It was three years ago. You have to get past this. Look, nothing to be afraid of. Just videos and galleries and…um. Owen? What is that?

OWEN   New gallery.

ROSA   There's no new gallery.

OWEN   She said she'd post something new for me.

ROSA   Who is screwing around with this profile?

OWEN   Open it.

ROSA   No. This is someone's sick game. I'm unfriending her.

OWEN   NO. YOU WILL NOT.

ROSA   Let go of me.

OWEN   You will NOT take my GIRLFRIEND. You will NOT TAKE HER.

ROSA   Owen, she's dead. GIVE THAT BACK.

OWEN   I'm opening the gallery! These are my pics! She posted them for me!

ROSA   STOP IT.

OWEN   There. It's open. It's—it's.

ROSA   Oh God.

BARISTA   Everything okay over here? Oh. That is disgusting.

ROSA   Oh God, oh God, oh God, oh God.

BARISTA   I'm going to be sick.

OWEN   It's beautiful. Look at her face. Her lovely face.

BARISTA   Um, I don't think that is a face.

OWEN   She's so pretty. So gorgeous.

BARISTA   [*Shaken.*] I work here. I shouldn't have to see this. I'm a good person.

[*Barista exits.*]

OWEN   She's smiling at me.

ROSA   She's not smiling! That isn't even human, whatever it is! Give me the laptop. Right now.

OWEN   I can't.

ROSA   I'm e-mailing that asshole Zuckerberg. I can't believe Facebook would tolerate this. I want this account gone.

OWEN   It won't work.

ROSA   I'm logging you off, and I'm taking your laptop until this is over.

OWEN   I still have my iPad.

ROSA   What's wrong with you?

OWEN   She wants me back.

ROSA   She's dead. This is a prank. You're talking about a dead girl.

OWEN   Look at her pretty eyes.

ROSA   Stop it.

OWEN   She wants me back, Rosa.

ROSA   You're sick. You're sick, Owen. I'm leaving.

[*Rosa exits.*]

OWEN   [*Whispers.*] I love you. Always. Your eyes. Your pretty eyes.

[*Clarinet. Office sounds. The call center. JACK on his headset.*]

JACK   [*Into phone.*] I'm so sorry the software isn't working for you. Maybe it's because we didn't write it for dumb asses. Have a nice day.
[*Hangs up.*]
Hey, Owen. You look like crap.

OWEN   [*Entering.*] Yeah. Hey, Jack.

JACK   You okay?

OWEN   Tough night.

JACK   I tried to call you.

OWEN   I had to think things over.

JACK   Rosa's here. Been waiting for you.

ROSA   [*Entering.*] Hi.

OWEN   Hey.

ROSA   Figured I'd catch you at work. How are you?

OWEN   Really sorry.

ROSA   You never came home. I thought maybe—

OWEN   Rosa. I said some stupid things. I'm sorry. I'm really sorry.

ROSA   I'm sorry too. I am. I shouldn't have—

OWEN   No, it was me.

ROSA   I was so worried.

OWEN   It's my fault.

ROSA   Owen? Facebook contacted her parents. The profile is gone.

OWEN   Oh.

ROSA   I know we kind of killed her. Again. I'm so sorry.

OWEN   No. It's how it should be. She's gone.

ROSA   Are you sure?

OWEN   I was an idiot. I was so bad to you. I need to move on. I know I do. I really love you.

ROSA   I love you too. I love you so much.

OWEN   Listen, do you want to—it's so nice out, and . . .

JACK   Hey. You just got to work.

OWEN   You're right, never mind.

JACK   Screw it, go. These customers are all assholes anyway.

OWEN   Thanks, Jack. Come on. Let's get outside. Let's start over.

ROSA   [*Relieved.*] I was so worried. I was so scared.

OWEN It's over. It's the past. Come on, let's go for a walk.

ROSA Hold on, just give me one sec.

OWEN What is it?

ROSA I really should check messages.

OWEN What?

ROSA I just need to check updates. Super quick.

OWEN Can't it wait? Please.

ROSA One second. There, I'm done. Oh, look. I've got a friend request.

OWEN Who is it?

[ROSA *screams.*]

• • •

It's Only a Minute a Guy
a comedy

John Franceschini

John Franceschini

John Franceschini turned to playwriting following a career as a pharmacist. His plays have been produced in Florida, Texas, Virginia, Washington, Los Angeles, and Hollywood. Franceschini is a member of Orange County Playwrights Alliance and New Voices Playwrights Theatre.

···production history···

Produced: New Voices Playwrights Theatre's Summer Voices Festival, hosted by
Mysterium Theatre, Santa Ana, California, September 2011; Pend Oreille Playhouse
Community Theatre's One Act Play Festival, Newport, Washington, July 2011;
Stage Door Productions' Fourth Annual One Act Play Festival, Fredericksburg,
Virginia, May 2011, where it won the Audience Favorite Award; Three Roses Players'
The Writer Speaks '11: Evening 12, North Hollywood, California, March, 2011.
Staged Readings: Orange County Playwrights Alliance's Discoveries Series; For Love
or Money, hosted by Empire Theatre, Santa Ana, California, February 2011; Drama
West Productions, Drama West Fest, Los Angeles, California, November 2010.

characters

BETTY, recently divorced woman with insecurities about herself, is
reluctantly reentering the dating scene. She is a librarian.
(30–40s)

HENRY, low-key, friendly bartender at a speed-dating bar. He is a
poet. (30–40s)

Actor playing HENRY (wear different hats/scarves for each character)
doubles as:

JEFFERSON, nerd, believes the correct response to one question
can lead to marriage.

CODY McCOY, swaggering, egotistical, Texan.

SALEEM, Eastern mystic palm reader.

RONDOLFO, Latin American man seeking wealthy American
woman.

LARRY, guy with a Brooklyn accent who fancies himself as a
smooth-talking playboy.

time—place—setting

Current year, Los Angeles, Center City bar hosting a "one-minute speed-
dating event." (Set can be a barstool, two folding chairs, and a small table.)

*This is a work of fiction. Names, characters, places, and incidents either are the product of
the author's imagination or are used fictitiously, and any resemblance to actual persons,
living or dead, business establishments, events, or locales is entirely coincidental.*

• • •

[BETTY *is on her cell phone seated on a barstool.*]

BETTY   [*On cell phone.*] Hello, Linda, where are you? I've been waiting fifteen minutes. . . . Oh no, you had a flat? Did you get help? . . . That's good. . . . Don't worry about it. I wasn't sure I wanted to go through with this "one minute speed dating" thing anyway. . . I'll see if I can get my money back for the cover charge. . . . Talk to you later, bye.

[HENRY *walks over.*]

HENRY   Hello, my name is Henry; I'm your drink server. What can I get you?

BETTY   I don't want a drink, thank you. Do you know where I can get a refund for the cover charge?

HENRY   You just got here, didn't you?

BETTY   Yes, and now I'm leaving.

HENRY   The speed dating hasn't started yet. Having second thoughts?

BETTY   Yes . . . eh, no, my friend was supposed to meet me here, but she can't make it.

HENRY   Ah, flying solo then. Some people always get a little shaky trying it for the first time.

BETTY   [*Indignant.*] What makes you think it's my first time? I didn't say that.

HENRY   Hold on, I only meant you might enjoy yourself; it's only a one-minute date per guy.

BETTY   I've changed my mind. . . . I have a right to change my mind.

HENRY   Ah, a little low on self-confidence, I see. What's your name?

BETTY   [*Angry.*] I beg your pardon! Just tell me where I can get my money back!

HENRY   I'm guessing . . . Carol. Like the television star, Carol Burnett, from the sixties. Am I right?

BETTY [*Self-consciously.*] That's terrible; you think I'm that old! I mean, do I look it!? I put on makeup tonight and had my hair done. Oh, what am I saying!? Where's the manager!?

HENRY Hey, hey...no offense intended.

BETTY I wouldn't even be here tonight if it wasn't for that rat bastard of a husband, I mean ex-husband. Because of him, I have to get back in circulation, as my friend Linda puts it.

HENRY You mean, he's here tonight?

BETTY Certainly not! He's in the Bahamas with his child bride, who has the body of a stripper and IQ of sawdust.

HENRY You could use a drink, definitely.

BETTY Just tell me how I can get my twenty bucks back!

HENRY I think you're cute.... Laura?

BETTY What?

HENRY Your name, is it Laura?

BETTY No, it isn't. Do you play this name game with everyone who asks for a refund?

HENRY Relax; I'm on your side. Just trying to be supportive.

BETTY I don't need your help.

HENRY Almost everyone in here feels a little jittery at first.

BETTY How would you know?

HENRY I work here. Some guys come up to the bar and pop two quick drinks to bolster their courage. Then they hit the tables for their "one minute" date.

BETTY Really, two drinks just to talk with a woman?

HENRY No one wants to get rejected. So it's a liquid fortifier... instant bravery. Want to try it?

BETTY Why would you think I need a drink to talk with a man? I'm talking with you, aren't I?

HENRY   Now that wasn't bad, was it? You just did it.

BETTY   Did what?

HENRY   Have a "one minute" date with me. We talked for sixty seconds, or something like that.

BETTY   We did? Oh yeah, I guess we did.

HENRY   See, what did I tell you; no serious injuries of any kind, still in one piece, and you feel better about it, don't you?

BETTY   It was only a minute, wasn't it?

HENRY   I think you're ready for the tables. The way it works, you pick a table and the guys rotate around. A bell rings to start and a minute later it rings to end.

BETTY   Well, I already paid my money; I guess I could give it a go.

HENRY   That's the spirit. I cruise the tables for drinks. So I'll see you in a little while.

BETTY   Henry.

HENRY   Yes?

BETTY   My name is Elizabeth, but you can call me Betty.

HENRY   Thanks, Betty. See you soon.

[BETTY *sits at a table (or two facing chairs).*]

[*Bell rings.*]

[JEFFERSON *sits at the table.*]

JEFERSON   [*A nerdy personality.*] Hi, my name is Jefferson. What's yours?

BETTY   Elizabeth.

JEFFERSON   I'm thirty-seven and work as an actuarial. Do you know what that is?

BETTY   Yes, someone who calculates risks and rates for an insurance company.

JEFFERSON   Great! I always ask that question first. It helps me save time.

BETTY   How do you mean?

JEFFERSON   If you don't know what it is, then I know you don't know as much as I know.

BETTY   And if I didn't know?

JEFFERSON   You would be a risk, according to my tables.

BETTY   What kind of risk?

JEFFERSON   I calculated the probability of a successful first date leading to an engagement and marriage. All based on someone knowing the answer.

BETTY   You can't book a honeymoon suite based on an answer to one question. You have to know someone first; there has to be an attraction to start with and . . .

JEFFERSON   . . . Not necessarily. There are plenty of tests I plan to administer. First off, how many children do you want? I believe five is the right number. When a family vote comes up, there will never be a tie.

BETTY   Jefferson, may I ask you a question? Do you still live at home with your mother?

JEFFERSON   [*Self-consciously.*] How perceptive. Amazing you should know that.

BETTY   Jefferson, may I make a suggestion?

JEFFERSON   Oh, please do.

BETTY   Hold off on making a deposit on an engagement ring.

[*Bell rings.* JEFFERSON *leaves. Bell rings.* CODY McCOY *sits at the table.*]

CODY McCOY   [*Egotistical and swaggering personality. Texas twang.*] Howdy, little lady, my name is Cody "Two a Day" McCoy and the pleasure will be all yours.

BETTY   Excuse me!

CODY McCOY   What do your lovers call you while they chew on your ear?

BETTY   Good grief! Are you for real?

CODY McCOY   What line are you in?

BETTY   Line? What do you mean?

CODY McCOY   Gimmick, activity, work, you know… or do you sit and polish your nails all day?

BETTY   I most certainly don't polish my nails all day. I'm a librarian.

CODY McCOY   Burying? Is that some fancy name for an undertaker? I mean, why don't you just say I lay them to rest. With emphasis on the "lay." Get it?

BETTY   Oh, God. I need a Rolaids tablet. I feel an ulcer developing.

CODY McCOY   Want to know why they call me "Two a Day" McCoy?

BETTY   Not really.

CODY McCOY   I'll tell you… Viagra.

BETTY   Viagra?

CODY McCOY   That's right. I take two a day every day. Why, little filly, you can throw a saddle on old Cody and ride all day like the Pony Express into the sunset.

BETTY   Mr. McCoy, I think…

CODY McCOY   …Hey, since we're friends, just call me "Two a Day."

BETTY   Well, Mr. Two a Day, I think you are an insecure, coarse, and vulgar man.

CODY McCOY   Hold on now, you're a feisty one. I'm gettin' to likin' you. I can see a prairie home for the two of us.

BETTY   Before you get too far into your Wild West delusional dream, put a spur up your ass and get off my table.

[*Bell rings.* CODY McCOY *leaves.*]

Oh, why did I ever come here? This was a mistake.

[*Bell rings.* SALEEM *sits at the table.*]

SALEEM   [*Assumes a light Indian or exotic eastern accent.*] I am the know-all, see-all, feel-all . . . the great Saleem, mystic and psychic, speaking to you.

BETTY   Come again?

SALEEM   Wait, don't tell me . . . you are Alexandria from Egypt, a distant descendent of the great Cleopatra. A Sagittarius with three children.

BETTY   Mr. Saleem, I'm Elizabeth, a Leo from San Diego with no children.

SALEEM   In this life, perhaps, but not in another. Do not deny your heritage, child. Seek your galactic family to become whole again.

BETTY   What is it you do for a living?

SALEEM   Provide guidance for wandering souls lost in the cosmic dust of space.

BETTY   How do you do that?

SALEEM   Ah, for a modest sum spread over three equal installments, the great Saleem reads the lines on your feet, your hands, your forehead . . .

BETTY   [*Anxiously touching her forehead.*] Oh no, I don't have lines on my forehead . . . do I? Good grief, now I need to start using Botox!

SALEEM   I sense a heavy presence, the weight of many souls.

BETTY   [*Upset.*] I knew this dress would make me look fat. Oh my God, I'm a wreck tonight.

SALEEM   I'm picking up a vibration. . . .

BETTY   [*Sarcastically.*] . . . You really know how to make a woman feel good about herself, Saleem.

SALEEM   Your palm wishes to tell me something.

BETTY   What is it saying to you?

[BETTY *waves good-bye with her hand.*]

SALEEM   It's moving I cannot read the lines.

BETTY I'll read it for you. It's saying … GOOD-BYE!

[*Bell rings.* SALEEM *leaves.*]

I've got to get out of here. This is ridiculous.

[*Bell rings.* RONDOLFO *sits at the table.*]

RONDOLFO [*Light Latin accent.*] Hello, beautiful lady. I am Rondolfo from Buenos Aires in Argentina.

BETTY Oh, how exotic-sounding. I'm Elizabeth.

RONDOLFO You are single, no?

BETTY No, I mean, yes, I'm not married. I thought you had to be single to do this.

RONDOLFO *Sí*, this is true. But one must make certain with all the cheating going on today. Rondolfo only wants a single woman.

BETTY Are you married?

RONDOLFO Oh no, not at all, free as a bird, no attachments. My mother, she wants me to get married, raise a large family…

BETTY … You still live at home?

RONDOLFO *Sí*, but just until my parole is up.

[*Pause.*]

Then I want to live in a beach house. You own such a house, no? You have money, no?

BETTY Parole, what parole?

RONDOLFO A huge misunderstanding got me in trouble with the … what you call it … the FBI. I … how do you say it … am like a cheerleader. I make people happy. That's why I was arrested.

BETTY I don't believe it … they arrested you for that?

RONDOLFO *Sí*, this is true.

BETTY HEY, HOLD ON! … Were you dressed as a clown and did something with children!?

RONDOLFO No, no, no…I was doing…what you call it…

[*Raising both arms.*]

…"the wave," like in a sports stadium.

BETTY You mean, they arrested you just for doing that?

RONDOLFO *Sí*, I told everyone to raise their arms. It worked; everyone did…even the bank tellers.

[*Pause.*]

How did I know an FBI agent was in line? You like Rondolfo, no?

BETTY Good God, why is this happening to me?

[*Bell rings. RONDOLFO leaves.*]

Is it me? Is this the best I can do?

[*Bell rings. LARRY sits at the table.*]

LARRY [*Bronx accent.*] Wow, I'm picking up a wonderful aura from you. I felt it across the room and couldn't wait to get here.

BETTY Really? No, you're just saying that.

LARRY Larry never lies. I was just killing time with the other women until I could meet you. What's your name?

BETTY That's sweet, Larry. I'm Elizabeth.

LARRY I could feel your fingerprint on my heart. I wish we could spend more time together, perhaps dinner and a glass of wine.

BETTY Too soon, we don't know each other.

LARRY Our emotional paths are intertwined. How can you deny it?

BETTY I, eh, well, maybe one drink.

LARRY Wonderful. I want to absorb your complete essence, every atom of your being.

BETTY Gosh, you make it sound like you're delving into my soul.

[*LARRY's cell phone rings. He answers, turns slightly, and tries to cover his mouth.*]

LARRY Yo, Jimmy...you guys are goin' bowlin'?...I'm at the speed-dating bar.... Yeah, I'm feeding her the old lines. I think she's falling for it.... Wait a second, I want to make sure...

[BETTY *overhears the muffled conversation and is shocked.*]

[*To* BETTY.]

Hey, are we gonna hook up tonight or what?

BETTY Yeah, sure. First go to the bar and get a corkscrew because I wanta drill into your head to see what you're using for a brain!

[*Bell rings.* LARRY *leaves.*]

I swear I'm gonna' deck the next jerk that comes over here.

[HENRY *walks up to table.*]

HENRY How's it going, Betty? Want a drink?

BETTY Henry, you didn't tell me I'd get a front-row seat at the circus freak show.

HENRY Hey, if you're bummed out, my shift ends in ten minutes. I'll buy you a cup of coffee. We can call it our "one-minute date." Okay?

BETTY Thanks, but no thanks. My head is still spinning. I mean, are there no normal men around?

[HENRY *holds* BETTY's *hand.*]

HENRY [*Softly.*] Relax, soothe yourself. Feel the clearness of the lake, taste the blueness of the sky, cover yourself with the tranquility of butterflies....

BETTY ... What is that?

HENRY Something I made up.

[BETTY *jerks her hand away.*]

BETTY [*Irritated.*] More like something you plagiarized.

HENRY Don't you like it?

BETTY I would have if you didn't lie about it. I'm disappointed in you. You're just like the others.

HENRY   How do you mean?

BETTY   It's from one of my favorite poems written by Dobson. I read his book a hundred times. I know it by heart.

HENRY   Oh, bring it around sometime and I'll autograph it for you.

BETTY   Right, what name will you sign?

HENRY   My own.

BETTY   Wait . . . you don't mean . . . you're . . . HENRY . . . HENRY DOBSON!?

HENRY   In the flesh. . . . Now, can we have our coffee and a "one minute" date?

[BETTY *extends her hand and* HENRY *grasps it.*]

BETTY   Henry.

   [*Pause.*]

   Let's make it a two-minute date.

• • •

Thread Count
a romantic comedy in one act

Lisa Soland

Lisa Soland

Lisa Soland graduated from Florida State University with a BFA in acting and received her Equity card working as an apprentice at the Burt Reynolds Jupiter Theatre. Her plays *Waiting*, *Cabo San Lucas*, *Truth Be Told*, and *The Name Game*, along with the anthology *The Man in the Gray Suit & Other Short Plays*, are published by Samuel French, Inc. Her work can also be found in "best of" anthologies published by Samuel French, Smith & Kraus, Applause Books, and Dramatic Publishing. She has produced and/or directed over eighty productions and play readings, fifty-five of which have been original. Her production company, Rose's Name Game Productions, has been producing original works since 1993, with Soland still at the helm, and she continues to work as artistic director and teacher of the All Original Playwright Workshop, helping to inspire countless original play readings and productions across the country. *Thread Count* was first heard in public when given as a reading for Dramatists Guild Friday Night Footlights at the Academy for New Musical Theatre in North Hollywood, California, on May 25, 2007. Jeff Charlton played Fergus, Susan C. Hunter played Dot, and Phillip Sanchez played Tiny. On this same day, the playwright's mentor and beloved teacher, Charles Nelson Reilly, passed away. Soland would like to dedicate this publication to him.

—

··· production history ···

Thread Count was first produced as part of an evening of romantic comedies by Lisa Soland, entitled Meet Cute, at the Clayton Performing Arts Center by Pellissippi State College, Knoxville, Tennessee, on October 15, 2010. It was directed by Charles R. Miller, who also designed the set; the stage manager was Alex Spangler; and the technical director was David Crutcher. The lights were designed by Kate Bashore, and Patti Rogers designed the costumes. The cast, in order of appearance, was as follows:

FERGUS, Jacques DuRand

DOT, Biz Lyon

TINY, Matt Gulley

characters

DOT, a woman in her 40s/50s, from North Dakota

FERGUS, a man in his 40s/50s, originally from London

TINY, a super-sized maintenance man, any age, from Eastern Tennessee

scene

An upscale department store in New York City.

time

It is evening, following a hot summer day in August.

description

What could possibly instigate a love match between a NYC luxury linen sales clerk and a practical, down-to-earth woman visiting from North Dakota? Counting threads on a display bed in Macy's department store. Dot's path crosses Fergus's, weaving their lives together as tightly as the thread count on the linen he sells. When Macy's closes with the two of them inside, they are left to ponder the possibilities laid before them—a chance encounter or a brand-new life.

setting

We are in the linen section of an upscale department store in New York City. There is a display bed center stage, fully dressed with sheets, pillows, and a luxurious comforter. Also onstage are several display counters stocked high with various fine linens for purchase.

• • •

[*It is evening, following a hot summer day in August. FERGUS, a Macy's sales consultant, is rearranging various linens on a counter upstage of the display bed. DOT, a rural, small-town woman, enters stage left, looking heat-exhausted and fanning herself to no avail with a column of the newspaper. She searches for a cool place to rest her tired feet.*]

DOT Oh boy, do my eggs lake.

[*She sits on the end of the display bed.*]

FERGUS [*Folding.*] Legs ache. Not there.

DOT What?

FERGUS Not there. The sign clearly states, "Do not sit on the display beds."

DOT No, the thing you said just before you said "not there."

FERGUS Legs ache.

DOT Yours too? It's awful, this town. Too big. New York City is much too big for its britches.

FERGUS Madame, *please*. The display. You're bringing about wrinkles.

DOT Oh, jeez.

[*Once realizing what she's done, she quickly rises.*]

I'm sorry.

FERGUS [*He quickly removes the wrinkles in the display comforter.*] Quite all right. Quite all right.

DOT [*She reads the sign.*] "Display bed." I see. It's just that my legs...

FERGUS One moment and I'll be right with you.

DOT [*Somewhat to self.*] They said to wear cushy shoes, but these tennis shoes just aren't cutting it. I'm exhausted.

[*Looking for somewhere else to sit, but there is none.*]

FERGUS [*Completing the task at hand, he turns to her.*] All right then, how may I help you this evening?

DOT Yes, thanks a bunch.

[*Beat.*]

I seem to have gotten myself all turned around. Could you tell *me where I am?*

FERGUS [*To self.*] Ah, another one.

[*Beat.*]

You are in the luxury, fine linen department of Macy's, fifth floor.

DOT [*She finds the ceiling vent that is blowing cool air and opens the top of her dress in order to properly ventilate.*] Did you know this is the coolest floor in the building? And they say hot air rises, but it don't seem to be the case in New York City.

[*To self.*]

If I ever find that Empire State Building, I'll freeze my ass off.

FERGUS If you're here only to enjoy the temperature of the air, I must ask you to . . . skip along.

DOT Skip along? I couldn't crawl.

FERGUS I have other, more pressing work to do, madame.

DOT Oh, no, no.

[*Trying to find a legitimate reason to stay.*]

I've, uh . . . I've noticed that these, uh . . . several of these . . . quilts here . . .

FERGUS Comforters.

DOT Comforters, yes. They have something about *thread count* printed on them. Could you explain to me what that is?

FERGUS Thread count?

[*Surprised she does not know.*]

Yes, of course. Thread count is the number of horizontal and vertical threads woven into one square inch of fabric.

DOT   One square inch?

FERGUS   That is correct.

DOT   This quilt...comforter, says two hundred. Is that possible?

FERGUS   Oh, yes.

DOT   Two hundred up-and-down threads woven into one tiny little square inch?

FERGUS   If you're a textiles expert, one inch is quite large, actually. One can do an awful lot with one inch.

DOT   Oh, really?

FERGUS   You'd be surprised.

DOT   I'm sure you're right.

[*A package of linen falls to the floor and they both go to pick it up together, bumping heads. Due to the confusion, they don't hear the following announcement.*]

WOMAN   [*Voiceover.*] Macy's will be closing in ten minutes. Please decide on your purchases and make your way to the nearest cashier.

DOT   It feels soft.

FERGUS   Yes. Because they spin the cotton into very thin threads. Or in this case, silk—here, madame, tempt your largest organ with this one.

DOT   My largest organ?

FERGUS   Your *skin*, madame.

DOT   Oh, sure. Of course. My skin.
[*Feeling another of the comforters on the shelf.*]
Oh my. Oh my!

FERGUS   This is listed at four hundred.

DOT   Four hundred what?

FERGUS   Four hundred thread count.

DOT   Per square inch?

FERGUS   Yes.

DOT   That's twice as much as this one.

FERGUS   Yes, madame. That is correct.

DOT   That's ridiculous.

FERGUS   Well now, do not go attaching yourself to four hundred. The numbers continue on upward from there.

DOT   I've never heard of such a thing.

FERGUS   Can you feel the difference between the two? Though they say they can, most people cannot.

DOT   [*Feeling.*] Yeah, sure I can.

FERGUS   [*Surprised.*] Really?

DOT   This one is much softer.

FERGUS   Remarkable.

DOT   What does something like this cost?

FERGUS   It might be best that I not give you that information, madame.

DOT   "Not give me . . . ?" What are you talking about?

FERGUS   I'm suspecting it might be too much of a shock for you.

DOT   Oh, for Pete's sake. I'll be fine.

FERGUS   All right, then. Let me get you a chair.

[*Starts to exit.*]

DOT   [*Stopping* FERGUS.] There's no sense making that big of a deal about it. I may be from Podunk, North Dakota, but it's not like I just fell off the goat truck.

FERGUS   Turnip truck, madame.

DOT   Excuse me?

FERGUS [*Discarding the metaphor.*] Quite all right.

    [*Beat.*]

    Ready?

DOT Sure.

FERGUS [*Referring to the 400 thread count item.*] This comforter sells for six hundred and fifty dollars.

DOT [*Her eyes widen and she becomes physically unstable.*] Six hundred and . . . oh my. My oh my.

    [FERGUS *looks around nervously for a chair, then as a last resort, lowers* DOT *back onto the display bed.*]

    People can afford to spend that kind of cash on their *sheets*?

FERGUS Linen. Yes, madame.

DOT Something they *sleep* on?

FERGUS Sleep *with*, not *on*. One never sleeps *on* a down comforter.

DOT Sleep *with*.

FERGUS [*His refined sales pitch.*] Yes, madame. They can afford it and they choose to because of the difference they feel when they do. It's simply a better quality of life. And that's what we sell here in the luxury linen department at Macy's, madame—a better "quality of life."

DOT I see.

FERGUS I sell approximately twelve to fifteen of these a day.

DOT A day? No! At that rate?

FERGUS And this one here—this one you're *sitting on*—approximately five to six.

DOT Sitting on?

    [*She stands up.*]

    Oh, I'm sorry. I got a little dizzy.

FERGUS [*He quickly removes the wrinkles in the comforter.*] Quite all right. Quite all right.

DOT [*Taking notice of the display bed comforter.*] Well, now what's this here?

FERGUS Oh, madame. This is the crème de la crème.

DOT Crème...?

FERGUS Cream of the cream.

DOT Okay.

FERGUS Close your eyes and then, if you will, gently run your fingers over this precious silk.

DOT Oh, oh, oh. Wowwwww. That is heaven on earth.

FERGUS Heaven on earth?! You are a delight, my lady. Is this your first visit to the metropolis of New York?

DOT Yeah.

[*Busy feeling the comforter.*]

This feels like...well, it feels...Can I open my eyes now?

FERGUS Certainly.

DOT [*Opening her eyes, she looks at the tag.*] One thousand?! One thousand?!

[*Looking to* FERGUS.]

Per square inch?!

FERGUS Yes, madame.

DOT What the heck!

FERGUS It's true.

DOT I don't believe it! Impossible.

FERGUS How can I convince you, madame?

DOT [*Direct.*] Get me a magnifying glass.

FERGUS Are you quite serious?

DOT Yes. *Quite.*

FERGUS Madame, even if I had a magnifying glass...

DOT Do you?

FERGUS Yes.

DOT Get it.

FERGUS Even if I...There is no physical way anyone could count up to one thousand...

DOT I may be from Podunk, North Dakota...

FERGUS Podunk? Is that really the name...?

DOT No. I'm just saying that I can count better than...

FERGUS I wasn't insinuating that you can't count....It's your eyes, madame.

DOT My eyes?!

FERGUS Yes, you're eyes. They're...

DOT I'll have you know, I won first prize in the mile-long "spot your pigeon contest" for Spiritwood's Fifth Annual Bald Eagle Days Festival last summer.

FERGUS Spiritwood?

DOT North Dakota.

FERGUS What happened to Podunk?

DOT It's just one of those...sayings.

FERGUS Well, that's wonderful, congratulations, but this is thread, madame—very tiny and tightly bound up against one another. So no matter how nice your eyes may look...I mean, function, they can't possibly see such tiny, hardly-visible-to-the-naked-eye threads.

[*They have moved a bit closer to one another.*]

DOT Especially when they're so tightly bound up against one another?

FERGUS That is correct.

DOT [*Leaning in and serious.*] Get me the magnifying glass.

FERGUS [*Running off.*] You are no ordinary woman!

DOT [*To herself.*] Bet your tight ass, I'm not.

[*Overwhelmed by temptation,* DOT *gets into the bed and feeling the luxurious linen begins to roll from left to right as though on a cloud in heaven. She begins to make sounds implying great pleasure.*]

Ohh. Myy. Ohhh. Myyyyy. Ahhhhhh.

FERGUS [*Entering with magnifying glass, he sees her enraptured and clears his throat.*] Madame? Um . . . excuse me, madame. The sign.

DOT Oh yeah—the sign. I'm very sorry. I got carried away.

FERGUS And you almost carried me right with you.

DOT There's something very, very special about this fabric.

FERGUS [*His more refined sales pitch.*] Madame, I am not attempting a forward pass with this comment, in any way, shape, or form. In fact, what I am about to say is only to help further promote the deep appreciation of this product in which I am personally quite fond of. This type of fabric . . . well . . . some say that this thread count can actually help a woman . . .

DOT Help a woman . . . ?

FERGUS Yes. Help her . . .

[*Beat.*]

. . . along.

DOT I'm not sure I understand.

FERGUS Yes, well . . .

[*Changing the subject, he holds up the magnifying glass.*]

I've located the . . .

DOT Super.

[*She grabs the magnifying glass from him, gets up on all fours, focuses the glass on one small area, and begins to count.*]

One, two, three, four, five, six, seven, eight . . .

FERGUS Madame! Your shoes!

DOT   Thirteen. Oh. Sorry.

   [*She kicks off her shoes.*]

   Fourteen, fifteen, sixteen...

FERGUS   Careful with the magnifying glass. If you hold it in one place too long, you might just set the bed on fire.

DOT   ...twenty-six. That ain't how you set a bed on fire. Twenty-seven, twenty-eight, twenty-nine, thirty...

FERGUS   [*Picking up her shoes and neatly placing them beside the bed.*] Yes, I suppose you're right. One would have to be outside, with the sun positioned straight above, shining down heavily, making you sweat...

   [*Beat.*]

   Are you actually counting those?

DOT   [*Counting.*] Yes. Fifty, fifty-one, fifty-two...

FERGUS   You can see each individual thread?

DOT   [*Counting.*] Fifty-five. Yes. I have twenty/fifteen vision...

FERGUS   Twenty...

DOT   Twenty...

FERGUS   ...fifteen?

   [*Crawling up on the bed with her to try to see what she is seeing.*]

   Show *me*. Let *me* see.

DOT   [*Counting.*] Sixty. It's my gift. Sixty-one, sixty-two, sixty-three, sixty-four...

FERGUS   I can't see a thing....How can you possibly...?

DOT   [*Counting.*] Sixty-five. You're screwing up my concentration. If you're going to be up here with me, you're going to have shut your trap. Sixty-six, sixty-seven, sixty-eight, sixty-nine...

FERGUS   Oh, very sorry.

WOMAN   [*Voiceover.*] Macy's is now closed.

FERGUS [*Panicking.*] Oh no.

WOMAN [*Voiceover.*] Please make your way to the nearest cashier to arrange for your final purchases.

FERGUS [*He gets out of bed.*] No!

WOMAN [*Voiceover.*] Macy's will reopen tomorrow morning at ten a.m.

FERGUS I've yet to finish my closeout. Oh my. Look what you've done! I'm . . . madame, you have to exit my department right now.

[*He hands her her shoes.*]

DOT Ninety-five. No. Ninety-six, ninety-seven, ninety-eight . . .

FERGUS [*He nervously cowers.*] Oh. Okay. Well, try not to upset the display too much. I'll see if I can complete my close out, then . . .

[*Suddenly the lights go dim. Everything's going wrong.*]

Oh dear.

[*Noticing he has* DOT*'s shoes in hand, he puts them back down.*]

DOT One hundred twelve. Holy moly. I can't see a gosh darn thing. One hundred twelve. I need a flashlight. What's your name? What's your name?

FERGUS Fergus. Fergus.

DOT Well, I need a flashlight, Fergus Fergus.

FERGUS No, madame. Just one.

DOT That's right. Just one. I can't look up or I'll lose my place. One hundred twelve. Please, Fergus Fergus. Hurry.

FERGUS [*So he won't forget, while running off.*] Flashlight. Flashlight.

DOT [*Calling after him, but still remaining focused on comforter.*] No, just one!

[*Beat.*]

One hundred twelve. One twelve. One twelve.

[*She remains on the bed, with her eyes focused down on the square inch, holding the magnifying glass still. She gets an itch but is afraid to itch it. She finds her balance and reaches back and gets it.*]

FERGUS [*Over the loud speaker, he clears his throat.*] Testing. Testing. Excuse me, madame? I have located the requested item and am now on my way back over to your present location.

DOT [*Shouting to him.*] SUPER!

FERGUS [*Entering with flashlight.*] We actually had a torch in the return closet.

DOT Torch?! What the heck am I gonna do with a torch?

FERGUS A torch is...oh, never mind.

[*He hands her the flashlight.*]

DOT Flashlight.
     [*She turns it on.*]
     Return closet? Did someone return it?
     [*She is back to counting.*]
     One hundred thirteen, one hundred fourteen, one hundred fifteen...

FERGUS Well, if they did, it was to the wrong department.

DOT [*Counting, 120.*] People actually return these comforters once they buy them and bring them home?

FERGUS Similar to any other purchase, I suppose.

DOT [*Counting, 125.*] And then you have to give them back all that money?

FERGUS I'll have you know, our return policy at Macy's is the best on Broadway.

DOT [*Counting, 130.*] How could anyone return anything as heavenly as this?

FERGUS [*He gets up on the bed and shines the flashlight for her.*] I'm not sure. You'll have to ask my wife.

DOT [*Counting, 135.*] She returned one of these?

FERGUS Yes.

DOT [*Counting, 136.*] Which one?

FERGUS Me.

[*He sits on the bed alongside* DOT.]

DOT [*She stops counting, but does not lose her place. Compassionately.*] I set you up for that one, didn't I?

FERGUS Yes, madame. You . . . "opened the door," should I say.

DOT So is that where *you* live—the return closet?

[DOT *hands* FERGUS *the flashlight.*]

FERGUS [*He gets onto the bed and holds the flashlight for her.*] Oh no. I have a little place in Greenwich Village.

DOT Must be expensive.

FERGUS It wasn't when I bought it. I walk to work.

DOT Oh, super. I've always wanted to walk to work, but you can't do that in the country. Things are too far spread apart.

FERGUS I have always wanted things spread apart.
      [*Making himself more clear.*]
      I mean, living here in the city, one never gets to spend any time in the open air, you know—no time to truly breathe.

DOT What was her problem?

FERGUS Pardon?

DOT Your wife. Her problem? Her reason for leaving?

FERGUS [*With vulnerability.*] Oh. She claimed I lacked spontaneity.

DOT Spontaneity? You gotta be kidding me.

[*She returns to her counting, 137, 138, 139.*]

FERGUS Yes. I mean, no.
      [*Seeing that* DOT *has returned to her counting.*]

Listen, I'm willing to lend you this flashlight, but you're going to have to take over the job of keeping it erect. My arms are growing quite numb, and I have to go now and complete my official closeout for the day.

DOT One hundred fifty-four.

[*She stops counting.*]

I can't hold it and count at the same time.

FERGUS Didn't you have to hold a gun when you shot all those pigeons?

DOT I didn't shoot the pigeons; I just counted them, Fergus Fergus.

FERGUS No, madame. Just one. Just one Fergus. My last name is not the same as my first.

DOT Oh, sorry.

FERGUS Quite all right.

DOT I'm no murderer of pigeons. I just have good eyes.

FERGUS That, my dear lady, is a flat fact.

[*They find themselves quite close.*]

DOT Why, thank you, Fergus. That's very kind of you.

FERGUS [*He hands the flashlight back to her.*] Madame, let's just lay all this out on the bed...I mean, table. I understand we've done a bit of bonding here this evening, but the store is now closed....

DOT [*Returning to her counting.*] One hundred fifty-five, one hundred fifty-six, one hundred fifty-seven...

FERGUS [*Continuing.*] If I didn't have a spare set of closeout keys, we wouldn't...

DOT Closeout keys?

FERGUS [*Continuing.*] ...even be able to continue this very odd counting extravaganza of yours.

DOT   One hundred sixty-nine. One hundred sixty-nine. One hundred sixty-nine.

[*She stops counting.*]

FERGUS   So let me suggest that you set this work aside for the night, go back to your lovely hotel, and return, showered and shaved . . . I mean, freshly dressed and adorned at ten a.m., and I would be happy to oblige you in this adventure once again.

DOT   You're not from here, are you?

[*The next seven lines come quickly.*]

FERGUS   New York?

DOT   No, here here.

FERGUS   The United States?

DOT   Yes.

FERGUS   No.

DOT   No?

FERGUS   Yes.

       [*Beat.*]

       Quite right.

DOT   I didn't think so. I've been trying to place your accent for some time now. Australia?

FERGUS   [*He is pained but remains accommodating.*] No. No, madame.

DOT   Scotland?

FERGUS   [*Again pained but remains accommodating.*] Well, close. You're very close—England.

DOT   Oh sure, England!

       [*Beat.*]

       I almost went there once with the high school chorus. Oh jeez, that was quite a while back now.

FERGUS   Why almost?

DOT   We couldn't get a hold of the money, so they cancelled the trip.

FERGUS   That's disappointing. I myself have the heart of a singer, just not the vocal cords to go along with it.

DOT   That's a bunch of hogwash. Everyone can sing.

FERGUS   I do rather well in the shower, but in the presence of another person...my throat just seems to...compress.

DOT   [*Innocently trying to solve his problem.*] Have you ever tried singing in the shower to another person?

FERGUS   No. No, I haven't. I, uh...I tend to do the shower business alone.

DOT   I see.

FERGUS   [*Vulnerably.*] But regardless, it takes a certain amount of courage to sing in front of someone in any situation, don't you think? A sort of courage I admire but have myself never possessed.

DOT   Well, I think something like that depends on the certain someone you're with. You know? Not so much a change in you, but a change in your company.
[*Suddenly aware that she's lost count.*]
Oh, fiddlesticks! I forgot all about my counting.

FERGUS   You couldn't have made much progress. Let me recommend that you start over tomorrow.

[*He attempts to move her along.*]

DOT   [*She sits up on her knees.*] What do you mean "made much progress"? I was up to one hundred and sixty-nine.

FERGUS   One hundred and sixty-nine?!

DOT   I told you—it's my gift. Everyone has a gift...

FERGUS   Maybe not everyone.

DOT   ...and mine's good eyes.

FERGUS   Well, that is obvious. Quite obvious...madame.

DOT   Dot. You can call me Dot.

FERGUS   Dot. What a lovely…easy name to spell.

DOT   How can you see my eyes? Everything's so dark in here.

FERGUS   [*Growing poetic.*] It is not so dark that I cannot see your eyes.

DOT   Really? Sure you don't need the torch, Fergus?

[DOT *takes the flashlight and shines it down onto her face. There is a moment where* FERGUS *almost kisses her.*]

FERGUS   Dot?

DOT   Yes?

FERGUS   Have you ever seen the view from the Empire State Building at night?

DOT   I've never seen the Empire State Building. Is that even in this city?

FERGUS   Is that in this city?!

DOT   Well, where's it hiding? I've been looking for it all day and I'm just plain pooped out.

FERGUS   How could you, you of all people, not see the Empire State Building? It has pigeons all over it.

DOT   Yes, but even I can't see the lumber for the trees.

FERGUS   Forest.

DOT   What?

FERGUS   Forest for the trees.

[*Beat.*]

Listen. I just came up with a fantastic idea.

DOT   What, Fergus?

FERGUS   How 'bout *we*, you and I…?

[DOT *yawns and tries to hide it.*]

Oh, you're yawning.

DOT   I can stay awake. Go on.

FERGUS   I'll finish closing out, and then I was thinking that maybe you would allow me to escort you for a spectacular view of New York City from the top of the Empire State Building. If, that is, you have no other plans for this evening?

DOT   No, no. I just have to catch that thing-a-ma-jig back to Brooklyn.

FERGUS   "Thing-a-ma-jig." Madame...

DOT   Dot.

FERGUS   Dot, you are a delight.

[*He reaches for the flashlight on the bed, and their lips almost touch.*]

DOT   [*She gets nervous.*] Oh. Oh. Oh.

FERGUS   [*He stops.*] How 'bout you wait for me right here?

DOT   Right here.

FERGUS   And I'll finish up my work, lock up, and then escort you to a view you will never forget.

DOT   Super. I love to see things I know I won't forget. I'll wait right here for you, Fergus.

FERGUS   Right here?

DOT   Right here.

FERGUS   Fine.

[*He backs out of the room smiling.*]

DOT   [*Waving.*] Hurry up now.

FERGUS   Fine. Fine.

[*He trips going backward, falls, and quickly gets up.*]

DOT   Ooops.

FERGUS   I'm fine. Quite fine.

DOT   [*She rises and crosses in a bit as he goes.*] Fergus Falls! Did you know there's a town just outside of Fargo called Fergus Falls? 'Course I'd rather be here than there.

FERGUS Lovely. I'll be right back.

[*He exits.*]

DOT [*Looking after him.*] Fergus Falls.

[*She feels the comforter on the bed again, and notices the price.*]

Five to six of them a day?

[*Yawning.*]

Holy crap! You have got to be kidding me!

[*She runs her hands over the comforter once more.*]

"Quality of life."

[*Out of curiosity, she pulls back the comforter and looks beneath.*]

Sheets!

[*She touches them.*]

Oh, my word.

[*She crawls inside and pulls everything back on top of her. Silence.*]

FERGUS [*Entering.*] Dot? Dot, are you . . . here?

[*Discovering her, with compassion.*]

Oh, she's fallen asleep, poor thing.

[*Suddenly realizing what's happened.*]

Oh! She's fallen asleep. Dot! Dot! Wake up!

[*He tries to wake her.*]

There's no sleeping in the store. And . . . you're on display! Oh, what a night. What a night! Wake up. Dot? Wake up!

[*He tries to wake her again, but she is sleeping soundly.*]

This is unacceptable. You've pulled the comforter right on top of you and it's wrinkling and soiling. Wrinkling and soiling!

[*Beat.*]

Well, I'm just going to have to carry you out of here. Perhaps that won't be as difficult as it seems. Oh, Fergus, how do you get yourself into situations like this?

[*Beat.*]

What am I talking about? I never get myself into situations like this.

[*He manages to get her up and onto his back.*]

Ugh. Oh, oh, oh. She is quite dense, actually. Quite dense for a person with such a small name.

[*He staggers back and forth, not moving much of anywhere, then notices something shiny on her left, ring finger.*]

Oh. My. God.

DOT [DOT *begins to sing.*] "Baa, baa, black sheep, have you any wool? Yes, sir, yes, sir, three beds full."

FERGUS Dot?

DOT "One for the master, One for the dame..."

FERGUS Dot? Are you awake?

[*He drops her back onto the display bed and falls on the floor at the foot of the bed.*]

DOT "And one for the little boy who lives in Greenwich Village."

FERGUS I thought you said you could stay awake.

DOT [*She rolls on her side, facing downstage.*] I thought you said you weren't spontaneous.

FERGUS Oh, am I? You think?

DOT I would say you're *very* spontaneous. What was your wife's problem anyway?

FERGUS [*Come to think of it.*] Well, I'm not sure.

DOT People don't know what they got till they've lost it.

FERGUS Dot, I know tonight was just a...No permanent plans between us, certainly...No promises made and none broken.

DOT Cut to the chase.

FERGUS A moment ago, while I was stumbling around with you over my shoulder, I noticed that you...

DOT You had me over your shoulder?

FERGUS   Yes, I did.

DOT   Oh, I'm so sorry. I sleep like a rock.

FERGUS   [*Innocently.*] And you carry like one too.

DOT   I'm actually surprised I woke up at all.

FERGUS   Yes. Very lucky for me, I suppose.

DOT   It's usually the roosters that open my eyes.

FERGUS   Yes, yes. Roosters? I suppose that's true.
　　　　　　[*Beat.*]
　　　　　　I noticed that you had a ring on your left hand.

DOT   Oh, *that*.

[*She sits up.*]

FERGUS   [*Disappointed.*] Yes. That.

[*Beat.*]

DOT   Well, I lost my husband, Fergus. About eight years ago, and I still wear the ring.

FERGUS   Oh. I'm very sorry to hear that.

DOT   [*She stands.*] We were visiting my relatives in South Dakota and . . .

FERGUS   Before you continue, Dot, I just want to say that you are under no obligation to share this information with me. No obligation. Quite all right.

DOT   No, I'd like to. I don't get too many chances to talk about it. After the first five or six months, nobody wanted to listen anymore.

FERGUS   [*Sits on the end of the bed.*] I'm all ears.

DOT   [*Suddenly looking closely at the sides of his face, then innocently.*] Actually, that's not too far from the truth, Fergus. Your ears are huge.

FERGUS   I suppose you're right. I'd like to blame it on my age, but I'm afraid they've always been this size.

DOT   Are you a good listener?

FERGUS   I think so. I try to be.

DOT   It's your gift, Fergus—your ears! Your ears, my eyes!

FERGUS   My gift! I never considered that. They were always a target for the bullies on the block.

[*His concern returns to* DOT.]

Regardless, please continue. You lost your husband...

DOT   My folks took us sightseeing, shopping, to this farm and ranch auction way out in the middle of nowhere, and my mother was going on and on, questioning us about why we never had any children, and Bert, well, Bert just up and disappeared.

FERGUS   Disappeared?

DOT   Yeah. I lost him.

FERGUS   At the... auction?

DOT   Yeah. Somewhere between the bailers and the fertilizer.

FERGUS   I'm very sorry.

DOT   It was horrible—looking for him, frantically, thinking that we just separated from each other and I worried, horribly, about how he would get back to my parents. But then after a few days passed and the phone never rang and he never showed up... well, it became even more horrible because I realized that he pretty much just took off. You know? He just pretty much took off.

[*She turns away.*]

FERGUS   Between the bailers and the fertilizer?

DOT   Yeah.

FERGUS   I'm so sorry.

DOT   [*Painfully.*] Sometimes that happens, Fergus. Sometimes people just take off.

FERGUS   [*Reassuringly.*] Not me. I don't.

DOT   Well, that's a good quality, Fergus. Don't change. Don't ever change that about yourself.

FERGUS   [*He rises.*] I don't plan to. I'm very unchanging. I'm English.

DOT   I have an embarrassing confession to make here tonight and I'm surprised that I . . . Well, I'm just going to say it.

FERGUS   All right.

DOT   Men think that women are . . . excited by fly-by-night sort of things, you know? Running here and there, and it's just not true. Not an ounce of it is true, Fergus.

FERGUS   I'm not sure I understand . . .

DOT   [*She sits on the end of the bed.*] Men. They try to be something exciting when really that's not what does it for a woman.

FERGUS   [*Attempting to clarify.*] "Does it"? Are you insinuating an emotional sensation or a . . . physical one?

DOT   It's all the same. With a woman, it's all rolled up in the same bale of hay. Excitement like that—sightseeing, which I've run around trying to do all day, coming to New York, thinking this would help me finally let go of Bert.
[*She sits on the end of the bed.*]
It would have been best if the jerk had a massive coronary right there and fell over dead. It's *not knowing*, that's hard.
[*Referring to the newspaper column she had used earlier as a fan.*]
Eight years later and I'm still reading the daily obituary column, searching for some sort of an end to the nightmare.

FERGUS   Closure.

DOT   Yeah. Anyway, all of this . . . Well, it ain't *it*, Fergus. It's not what does it.

FERGUS   What is it then? Because you women seem to be as unique as . . . these quilts.

DOT   Comforters.

FERGUS   Yes, and that's what confuses me. What is it that does it for you?

DOT   For me specifically?

FERGUS   Oh! All right.

DOT   I'm not sure, Fergus. I've never to my knowledge actually had an . . .

[*She stops.*]

FERGUS   Oh, really?

DOT   Sad, I know.

FERGUS   Well, you would know *it* if you had.

DOT   I would?

FERGUS   Oh yes.

DOT   Then I haven't.
   [*Beat.*]
   I'm forty-eight. Forty-eight, Fergus.
   [*Vulnerable.*]
   I'm beginning to think there's something wrong with me.

[*She begins to cry.*]

FERGUS   [*He sits on the end of the bed.*] Oh, my Dot. There's nothing wrong with you. Nothing at all. To quote someone I'm growing quite fond of, "It's maybe not so much a change in you, but a change in your company."
   [*He stands.*]
   Let me ask you this—if you were to think you might know what would finally push you over that edge of tumultuous pleasure, what might that be?

[*Standing next to the headboard.*]

DOT   [*Sounding rather sure of herself.*] "Camp Town Ladies."

FERGUS   Pardon?

DOT   The song—"Camp Town Ladies." It's my favorite. I go hog wild. Bert would never sing it for me. Never. So I would sing it for myself, in my head as things . . .

FERGUS   Progressed.

DOT   Yes, progressed.

FERGUS   I see.

>   [*He's not going to sing.*]

>   Is there anything else?

DOT   "Camp Town Ladies" and . . . spending the night on this one-thousand-per-square-inch-thread-count comforter.

[*Pause.*]

FERGUS   Oh. Are you insinuating that we . . . the two of us . . . ? Here?

>   [*He begins to grow anxious.*]

>   I'm not sure about this, Dot. I've had this job for eighteen years now and I really enjoy it. Like you said, I think my gift might be listening and I get to utilize that gift at this job. I get to listen to customers . . . complain mostly, complain and drive me crazy mostly . . . but once in a great while, someone like you comes along and I would really, truly hate to lose my job because of it.

DOT   We can stay here and not lose your job.

FERGUS   How do you know? Are you certain?

DOT   Well, I guess there's no way to be truly certain about things like this.

FERGUS   [*Considering.*] It's a risk, Dot. A huge risk.

DOT   But that's why they call it a risk and not just another walk in Central Park.

FERGUS   I thought you said this sort of thing doesn't *do* it for you—dashing here and there . . .

DOT   Oh, we won't be dashing. . . .

FERGUS   Sightseeing . . . New York.

DOT   I've seen all I need to see.

FERGUS   Fly-by-night . . .

DOT Well, I'm hoping it won't be that, Fergus.

FERGUS Tell you what. How 'bout the two of us go down to the bagel shop on the corner and share a cup of coffee? That will surely get you up and vertical.

DOT Up and vertical?

FERGUS Espresso. Yes! We'll have ourselves an espresso and then we'll be all awake and we can hit the tall building with a single bound.

DOT What are you so scared of?

FERGUS [*Growing quite anxious and a bit angry.*] See? This is always what it comes down to—me not wanting to do something that someone else wants to do. And then it comes down to the ending of things—the ending of things like my job. My livelihood. Why does it always have to come down to my livelihood? My wife used to do this to me all the time.

DOT *Ex*-wife.

FERGUS She used to make it about me when really, all along, she just couldn't compromise. She had to have it her way. Why can't I be listened to as much as the one who wants to do the thing that I don't want to do?!

[*Pause.*]

DOT Yes. I see. You're right, Fergus—I'm not listening to you. I'm totally not listening to you and what *you're* wanting. I'm just making you wrong for not wanting to do the same thing I want. You're right.

[*She gets out of bed and picks up her purse.*]

Let's go. I'll buy you a cup of coffee and we'll head over to that . . . invisible building with the pigeons on it.

[*Beat.*]

But we'll have to see about doing it in a single bound.

[*She crosses to her shoes.*]

FERGUS Oh. We could take the lift.

DOT   Lift?

FERGUS   [*Dropping his accent.*] Elevator.

DOT   You betcha.

FERGUS   [*Totally relieved and surprised.*] Really?

DOT   Yes. I'm sorry. Of course, your job.
   [*Beat.*]
   Are you done with your closeout?

[*She crosses to the bed, sits, and puts on shoes.*]

FERGUS   Yes, I am, and the register is locked and tucked away, and I'm all ready to go.

DOT   Super. I might need a double, though.

FERGUS   Espresso?

DOT   Yeah, to keep me "up and vertical."

FERGUS   [*Nodding.*] Better you than me.

DOT   Yeah.

FERGUS   You really mean it? No more pressure?

DOT   That's right.

FERGUS   This is wonderful. Wonderful. Thank you, Dot.

DOT   I've been selfish.

[*She stands.*]

FERGUS   Oh, that's all right. I can understand you being tired and everything.

DOT   It's mostly my feet. They're killing me.

FERGUS   You have to wear nurse's shoes with high arches. All the women wear nurse's shoes.

DOT   I was wondering about that. I was starting to think that New York just had a lot of emergency-type help on hand, you know—ever since . . .

[*She stops.*]

FERGUS Yes, yes. No, no. Just comfortable shoes. "Quality of life."

> [*Growing romantic.*]
>
> You can stay at my place if you like.
>
> [*Explaining why.*]
>
> It's closer.

DOT Oh, I suppose once I get moving, I'll be fine.

> [*Responding to his romanticism.*]
>
> It's very nice of you to invite me out this evening, Fergus. I haven't had a worthwhile conversation since I've been here.

FERGUS [*Noticing just how beautiful she is.*] It's a difficult city, really.

DOT Yeah and it smells like pee.

FERGUS Well, it's August.

DOT I see.

FERGUS [*About to explode with romance.*] Dot, do you mind if I kiss you right now? You are so beautiful to me and I just have this overwhelming feeling...

> [DOT *takes hold of* FERGUS *and kisses him on the lips.*]
>
> Gosh, you're wonderful. I can't believe this. If I knew this was going to happen when I woke up this morning, I would have been in a much, much better mood.

[FERGUS *takes* DOT *into his arms and reciprocates with fervor, kissing her passionately. They fall back onto the display bed.* TINY, *the maintenance man, enters with a carpet sweeper.*]

TINY Oh, excuse me, folks. I thought everyone was gone for the night.

FERGUS [*Very nervously, he jumps out of bed and crosses behind the bed.*] Tiny! Hello! No. No, I was just closing up and this customer here... this woman... Dot. Well, she accidentally fell asleep on the display bed.

TINY Dot.

FERGUS Yes. Oh!

> [*He introduces them.*]
>
> Dot, Tiny. Tiny, Dot.

DOT That's funny—Dot, Tiny. Tiny dot.

[DOT *and* TINY *shake hands.*]

TINY Yeah, that *is* funny.

FERGUS Yes, yes. So you see? There's nothing really going on here out of the ordinary. Just the usual sort of everyday business that is to be expected in the luxury linen department of . . .

TINY You don't have to explain to me, Mr. Magilous. I heard something and just thought I'd check out this side of the store. But if you're going to be here, I'll make sure to *avoid this section* for the rest of the night.

[*He turns to go.*]

FERGUS [*Stopping* TINY.] *Avoid this section?* Oh no, Tiny. You don't have to do that. We weren't doing anything or anything. We were just heading out, actually. You go ahead and fix things or . . .

[*Taking* TINY*'s carpet sweeper, he begins to nervously sweep the carpet.*]

TINY [*Taking his carpet sweeper back from* FERGUS.] Mr. Magilous, could you step over here for just a sec?

FERGUS Oh. Yes. Certainly. Excuse me, Dot.

[DOT *crosses and sits on the downstage left corner of the bed.*]

TINY [*Taking* FERGUS *downstage right.*] How long have we worked here together?

FERGUS Oh, I'm not sure. Maybe . . .

TINY Ever since I started.

FERGUS Really?

TINY Yes. You were the very first sales consultant I met, and from that day on you have never disappointed me, Mr. Magilous. Never.

FERGUS Well, I'm happy to hear that, Tiny.

TINY Never. And I'm sick and tired of it.

FERGUS What?

TINY I'm not going to let you get away with this.

FERGUS [*His voice cracks.*] Get away with what?

TINY This. This thing you do.

FERGUS "This thing I do"? Listen, Tiny, I'm very sorry if I've appeared even a slight bit unpredictable this evening....

TINY Mr. Magilous, there's a time to be predictable and there's a time to be... well—not so predictable, if you know what I mean.

FERGUS I'm not following you...

TINY I might not have the fancy words you do, but I know a good thing when I see it.

FERGUS That could be your gift, Tiny.

TINY Gift?

FERGUS Yes, we all have them, you know.

TINY Well then, don't look a gift horse in the mouth and there...
[*He positions* FERGUS *so that* FERGUS *has a clear, straight view of* DOT.]
...there, Mr. Magilous, is your gift horse.

FERGUS Oh, I see. This is a bit of a *carpe diem* speech. Is that it?

TINY Carp, d-what?

FERGUS *Carpe diem*—seize the day.

TINY Oh no, sir. Seizing the day is not what I am talking about—seize the *woman*. Seize the *woman*.

FERGUS Yes, I see. Well, you might be right, ol' boy. You might just be right.

TINY So seize away.

[*He pushes* FERGUS *toward* DOT, *then calls out to them both as he leaves.*] Well, I've got some things to fix in the basement, so don't you worry about me! I'll make sure you two have the place to yourselves for the rest of the night!

[*He exits.*]

FERGUS   Well, what do you know about that?

DOT   What do you know?

FERGUS   Dot?

DOT   [*Quickly.*] I'm leaving it completely up to you, Fergus.

FERGUS   He "opened the door," didn't he?

DOT   Yes, he did.

FERGUS   [*Bursting with excitement.*] Dot, have you ever had a moment in your life when time stops getting in the way and suddenly everything opens up and all you can see is some kind of hope, some kind of possibility that the impossible could happen? Have you ever had a moment when a door was being presented to you and if you walked through it, you might just possibly discover what happiness really is?

DOT   I think so.

FERGUS   [*Being very still.*] Well, it's happening to me right now and . . . Well, I'm afraid to move, Dot. I'm afraid if I move one square inch, it will all go away.

DOT   One square inch?

FERGUS   Yes.

DOT   Tightly bound up against one another?

FERGUS   Yes.

DOT   You know, Fergus, they say that opportunity only knocks once. But I say hogwash. I say it keeps knocking until ya hear it.

FERGUS   Well, I hear it, Dot. I hear it loud and clear.

DOT   I'm not surprised, with those ears of yours.

FERGUS   Would you wait right here for me? Just for one brief moment?

DOT   Right here?

FERGUS   Yes.

DOT   I'm not going anywhere.

FERGUS   [*Backing out of the room.*] Right here.

DOT   That's right.
          [FERGUS *falls.*]
          Fergus Falls.

FERGUS   [*Rising and dusting himself off.*] Quite all right.

DOT   [*Romantically.*] But I'd rather be here with you.

FERGUS   [*Smiling.*] Lovely.

[*He exits.*]

DOT   Lovely.

[DOT *smiles. She thinks about sitting on the bed but doesn't. Instead she straightens out the comforter and waits, standing. Suddenly we hear* FERGUS *over the loud speaker, singing rather boldly.*]

FERGUS   [*Over the loud speaker.*] "De Camptown ladies sing this song. Doo-da, Doo-da. De Camptown racetrack's two miles long. Oh, de doo-da day. Gwine to run all night. Gwine to run all day. I bet my money on a bob-tailed nag, somebody bet on the gray."

[DOT *is delighted, absolutely delighted with his courage.* FERGUS *enters running and leaps onto the bed.*]

DOT   Fergus! The wrinkles!

[*She quickly sweeps the wrinkles from the comforter.*]

FERGUS   Yes, aren't they beautiful?! I did it, Dot. I sang. I sang in front of a person...

DOT   Me.

FERGUS ... and my voice did not compress!

DOT And over the loud speaker! What a voice. What courage! You surprise me.

FERGUS Good. I want to surprise you, Dot.

> [*He pulls her onto the bed.*]

> I want to surprise you and never leave. What do you think about that?

DOT Well, I think that's a heavenly idea, Fergus. Just ... heavenly.

[*They kiss softly, then pull away and try to move into the next stage of physical romance, but it's awkward. They try again but to no avail.*]

FERGUS How 'bout we wait on this?

DOT Okay.

[DOT *quickly gets out of the bed, as does* FERGUS. *Then together, working from opposite sides, they straighten out the bed as if they had been doing it together for years.*]

FERGUS My dear lady, might I suggest we step out the front door, walk just up the street, and have ourselves a view.

DOT Just up the street?!

FERGUS Yes. The Empire State Building is just up the street. Right out the front door and just up the street.

DOT Oh my God. I've been looking for that all day.

[*She picks up her purse and newspaper obituary column.*]

FERGUS Yes. Isn't that interesting how that works? And then suddenly one day, when you least expect it, what you've been looking for your entire life walks right into your department.

> [*He holds out his arm for her to join him.*]

> My lady?

DOT Fergus Magilous.

> [*She takes his arm.*]

> Oh, wait. Before we go, I would like to make myself a purchase.

FERGUS   A purchase? Why, we're closed.

DOT   I would like to buy myself this thousand-per-inch-thread-count comforter and take it back to my hotel with me this evening. I've decided it's time for me to start living this "quality of life" you've been talking about and I got me some catching up to do.

FERGUS   Oh, hogwash! Honestly, Dot, that's all just a silly sales pitch. You don't need thread count to have a quality life. You just need me.

DOT   [*Running her hand over the comforter.*] Still, though, it's awfully nice.

FERGUS   Well then, I've got one at home with sheets to match.

[*They kiss, then cross stage left to exit. Just before they do,* DOT *tosses her newspaper section into the garbage can. Lights fade out.*]

• • •

Dissonance

Craig Pospisil

For my father, Allan

Craig Pospisil

Craig Pospisil is the award-winning author of *Months on End*, *Somewhere in Between*, *The Dunes*, and the collections *Life Is Short* and *Choosing Sides*, all published by Dramatists Play Service. He wrote the book for the musicals *Drift* and *Dot Comet*, and is the author of more than fifty short plays, including *It's Not You* and *Tourist*, published by Playscripts in *theAtrainplays, vol 1*. His work has been published in numerous anthologies; seen at Ensemble Studio Theatre, Purple Rose Theatre, New World Stages, Bay Street Theater, and NYMF; performed on four continents; and translated into Chinese, Danish, Greek, and French.

···production credits···

Dissonance was commissioned by 3Graces Theater Company (Elizabeth Bunnell and Annie McGovern, co-artistic directors) and was given its world premiere by 3Graces as part of At the Corner of Faith and Reason at the Cherry Lane Studio Theater in New York City, opening May 24, 2011. It was directed by Jim Elliot; the lighting design was by Joshua Sherr; the sound design was by John D. Ivy; and the stage manager was Jennifer Marie Russo. The cast was as follows:

FITZ, William Peden

TRICIA, Deborah Jean Morgan

characters

FITZ, mid- to late 40s

TRICIA, early 30s

summary

TRICIA returns to the Berkshires to deal with her mother's death after a battle with Alzheimer's. At the funeral home she collides with FITZ, a prodigy and former piano student of her mother's, with secrets of his own, who challenges her loyalty and choices.

···

[*A room in a funeral home used for memorial services. There are a couple rows of chairs, although some are askew. The chairs face a narrow table at one end of the room. The top of the table is empty. At the other end of the room, by a set of doors, there is a tall side table.*

FITZ *opens the doors and leaves them open. He places an easel with a sign on it by the doorway, then disappears for a moment. He returns with two long, dark-colored runners, pens, and a condolence book. He carefully drapes one of the runners over the tall table near the door, and sets the book and pens on top. Then he crosses to the other table, where he lays the other runner across the top, making sure it is even and properly set before exiting.*

A few moments later he returns, carrying a framed photograph and a simple, metal box—a funeral urn. He crosses the room and places the urn gently on the table with the photo beside it. He carefully smoothes the runner on the table, starts to leave again, but stops in the doorway.

FITZ *turns and looks back at the urn, sadly taking it in. His eyes fall on the condolence book. He opens it, picks up a pen, and signs. The action seems to cause him some pain, however, and he winces slightly as he writes. When he finishes, he drops the pen and absently flexes his hand as he checks his watch. He looks over the room, silently counting the chairs, and leaves again.*

The room remains empty for a few moments. Then TRICIA *appears in the doorway. She glances at the sign by the door, then steps into the room. She sees the urn on the table and stares at it for a few moments before breaking free of its gaze. She sees the open memorial book and is surprised to see that it has already been signed. She puzzles over the signature, which she cannot quite read.*

Classical piano music begins to play, a little too loudly, and TRICIA *is startled, looking up at the speakers in the ceiling and then at the urn. She crosses slowly toward the urn, but cannot make it all the way across the room, stopping several feet short.*

FITZ *reappears in the doorway. He is surprised to find someone in the room and stops for a moment. He starts to turn away, then looks back at* TRICIA *and hesitates. Then he steps into the room.*]

FITZ   Good morning.

TRICIA   [*Startled.*] Oh. Hi. Morning.

FITZ   Are you here for the Roberts memorial?

TRICIA   Yes, I'm sorry. I know I'm early.

FITZ   That's all right. It's just—

TRICIA   [*Overlapping.*] I just wanted to—

FITZ   No, it's fine, but—

TRICIA   [*Continuing.*]—come in and see and ... see.

FITZ   I'm still setting up the room. Hold on, I was checking the volume of the music.

[FITZ *exits and the music soon stops. He returns.*]

TRICIA   That was very pretty.

FITZ   Thank you. I mean, it's a nice piece.

TRICIA   Sorry I interrupted.

FITZ   That's all right, but I'm still setting up for the service.

TRICIA   Oh, you can go ahead. I don't mind.

FITZ   Uh...well, usually we don't open the doors to guests until fifteen minutes before the service starts.

TRICIA   The doors were open.

FITZ   I'm bringing in chairs and things.

TRICIA   Oh.

[*Slight pause.*]

Well, that's all right. I won't get in your way. I promise.

FITZ   There's a waiting area with coffee and snacks by the entrance.

TRICIA   Thanks, but I'm not really hungry.

FITZ   No, I meant maybe you could wait there until the room was ready.

TRICIA   Oh. Of course. All right.

FITZ   Thank you.

[*She starts to go, but stops in the doorway.*]

TRICIA   How soon do you think I could come back in?

FITZ   Well, the service doesn't start for another hour, so—

TRICIA   [*Interrupting.*] But how much more do you have to do?

FITZ   Well, I need to set up the chairs, and—

TRICIA   That's not so much.

FITZ   We also like to give the family some time alone with the deceased before other guests come in.

TRICIA   I am the family. Helen was my mother.

FITZ   Oh! Oh, of course. I'm sorry, I didn't—I'm very sorry for your loss.

TRICIA   Thank you.

FITZ   I didn't realize. Usually the family meets with the director when they arrive. I'll get Mr. McKenzie for you.

TRICIA Oh, no, that...not right yet.

FITZ Okay, well...yeah, have a seat. Can I get you anything?

TRICIA No. Thank you.

> [*They stand there.* TRICIA *looks at the urn, but doesn't move any closer.* FITZ *is unsure what to do.*]

> Actually, could I have a moment alone?

FITZ Yes, of course.

[FITZ *instinctively gives a small nod, almost a bow, and then heads for the door.*]

TRICIA And a cup of coffee?

FITZ Ah...sure. Milk or sugar?

TRICIA Just black, thanks.

> [FITZ *exits.* TRICIA *looks at the urn for a few moments, then crosses to it. She opens her purse and pulls out a torn concert ticket. She reaches for the urn, pausing for a moment, then picks it up. She feels its weight in her hands, then looks for a lid or a way to open it, but can't find one.*]

> Had to make it hard for me, didn't you, Mom.

[TRICIA *sets the urn back on the table just as* FITZ *reappears in the doorway, holding a cup of coffee.*]

FITZ Here you go.

TRICIA Thank you.

FITZ Are you sure you wouldn't prefer to wait in the reception area? It just may not be very peaceful here with me coming in and out. I don't want to disturb you, and I'm sure the rest of your family will be arriving—

TRICIA Are you "Fizz?"

FITZ I'm sorry?

TRICIA Did you sign the book? I couldn't read what it said.

FITZ Oh. Yeah, I've got the penmanship of a four-year-old. Yeah...I knew your mother.

TRICIA   Really?

FITZ   She taught me piano for eight years, starting when I was nine or ten.

TRICIA   Wow. Long time.

FITZ   She was a wonderful teacher.

TRICIA   Thank you. She loved the piano.

FITZ   That she did.

[*Pause.* FITZ *sees that* TRICIA *has no plans to leave.*]

FITZ   Well, I'll be back.

> [FITZ *exits, and* TRICIA *sits with her coffee.* FITZ *soon returns with programs, placing them by the condolence book, then taking one over to* TRICIA.]
>
> Would you like one of the programs?

TRICIA   Yes, thanks.

> [*Slight pause.*]
>
> Do you still play?

FITZ   Piano? Not really, no.

TRICIA   Why not?

FITZ   I just... don't. I don't have a piano anymore.

TRICIA   Do you want one?

FITZ   What?

TRICIA   My mother's piano is in storage, and it's costing an arm and a leg. I don't play, and I couldn't take it back to New York with me even if I did. I'll give you a good deal.

FITZ   Ah... no. Thanks. I couldn't.

TRICIA   Know anyone who might be in the market for one?

FITZ   Not offhand. Excuse me.

[FITZ *turns away from her and begins arranging the chairs into neat, orderly rows.* TRICIA *digs into her purse for a business card.*]

TRICIA   Listen, if you happen to think of anyone who might want a piano, would you give them my number? It's been so long since I was back and—

[*She halts abruptly, then quickly changes gears.*]

I'm sorry. I'm being rude. I'm Tricia Roberts.

[*She holds out her hand. FITZ hesitates a moment and then reaches out to shake her hand. Perhaps he winces slightly or some pain is reflected in his face.*]

FITZ   Fitz. Miller.

TRICIA   Oh, "Fitz," not "Fizz." That makes—oh! You're *Fitzhugh*.

FITZ   It's just Fitz now. My folks called me "Hugh." Which I never really liked. Fitzhugh is this family name thing. No one ever called me that. Except your mother.

TRICIA   Fitzhugh Miller. You were Mom's favorite of all time.

FITZ   Oh, thanks.

TRICIA   Yeah, I remember you.

FITZ   Really? You couldn't have been more than seven or eight when I left for college.

TRICIA   She talked about you for years. Said you were gifted.

FITZ   We stayed in touch some. Can I get you more—

TRICIA   You got a big scholarship to Juilliard.

FITZ   . . . Yeah, I . . . was in New York for a while.

TRICIA   Mom went to Juilliard too.

FITZ   I know. Excuse me.

[FITZ *turns and leaves quickly.* TRICIA *checks her watch, then looks over the program.* FITZ *returns with two more chairs.*]

TRICIA   What are you doing here?

FITZ   Hmm?

TRICIA   Why aren't you playing anymore? You had a real career going.

FITZ   It's, ah, long story. Boring story.

TRICIA   I'm sorry. Was that a bad question to ask?

FITZ   No, no, it's fine. But Mr. McKenzie will want to greet you. I'll let him know you're here.

[FITZ *turns to leave.*]

TRICIA   Wait, can you tell me how this opens?

FITZ   What?

TRICIA   The urn. I want to put something in with her.

FITZ   Oh, there are screws in the bottom. Mr. McKenzie can help you with that.

TRICIA   Can't you do it?

FITZ   Well, he really likes to—

TRICIA   Because, actually, it involves you in a way.

FITZ   How's that?

TRICIA   It's a ticket from a concert my mother and I went to, like, ten or twelve years ago. It was a concert you were doing at Tanglewood.

FITZ   Really? You came? When? I played there a couple times.

TRICIA   Debussy. "Clair de Lune." It was lovely.

[*She holds out the ticket, which he takes and looks at.*]

FITZ   It was lovely to play. Yeah, this was the first time I was there. Why didn't you say hello afterward?

TRICIA   We tried, but they wouldn't let us backstage. They said you had a no-visitors policy or something.

FITZ   Oh. Yeah, I was a little full of myself for a couple years there.
        [*Slight pause.*]
        Sorry.

TRICIA   It's all right. Mom was disappointed, but she was very proud of you. Said she knew you'd be successful.

FITZ   I need to, ah . . . get some more chairs.

TRICIA   Could you get a screwdriver for the urn too?

FITZ   Sure. I'll take a look.

[FITZ *exits.* TRICIA *sits, suddenly exhausted. She looks over at the urn for several moments, before she breaks off and looks away determined not to cry. She composes herself, then checks her watch.* FITZ *returns with two more chairs, which he places in the last row that he started.*]

TRICIA   Do you know if anyone else has arrived?

FITZ   I didn't see, but I can check.

TRICIA   No, that's okay.

FITZ   I'm sure people will be arriving soon.

TRICIA   Did you find a screwdriver?

FITZ   Yeah.

> [*He picks up the urn.*]
> Why don't you follow me to the office, and—

TRICIA   Can't we do it here? I just want to slip it in. It doesn't have to be formal or anything.

FITZ   It's not very private.

[TRICIA *goes over to the doors to the room, peeks out, and then closes them.*]

TRICIA   Voila.

FITZ   All right.

> [FITZ *turns the urn on its head and sets it on the tabletop, then takes a screwdriver from his pocket.*]
> Why that ticket?

[*He works to loosen the screws holding the bottom plate in place as* TRICIA *talks. One or two of the screws are tight, forcing him to grip the screwdriver hard and bear down. This causes him some discomfort, and he gives a sharp intake of breath after one stab of pain, and nearly drops the screwdriver.* TRICIA *watches him as he struggles with the screws.*]

TRICIA   A good memory. Summer between junior and senior years at college. I was s'posed to go to Europe with my dad, but he cancelled. Seems he'd just met the very beautiful, young, and soon-to-be second Mrs. Roberts, so he decided to take her instead. You'd think I'd've been mad at *him* for being stuck in Pittsfield all summer—and I was—but he wasn't around, so I took it out on my mom instead.

[*Slight pause.*]

I think she knew why I was being such a jerk, though, because she took me everywhere that summer. Museums, theater at Williamstown, minor league baseball games. But my favorite was taking picnic dinners to Tanglewood for concerts like yours. And James Taylor.

FITZ Of course.

TRICIA By the time I went back to school we'd relapsed to our standard mother-daughter cat fights.

[*Pause.*]

By the next summer she'd been diagnosed. She thought she was being forgetful because she wasn't getting enough sleep.

FITZ I'm sorry I didn't see you after the concert.

TRICIA Oh, we had a good time. It was a beautiful night. Warm. Lying on a blanket and watching the stars overhead, while Debussy drifted through the air.

[*Pause.*]

Why don't you play anymore?

FITZ [*Overlapping.*] Okay, I think I got it.

[*He removes the bottom plate and steps back to allow* TRICIA *to come forward. She does so slowly, with the ticket in her hand. She looks down into the urn.*]

TRICIA What's that?

FITZ They put the remains in a plastic bag after cremation.

[*Slight pause.*]

One of the things you learn working here.

TRICIA Why *are* you here?

[FITZ *sees he can't escape her questions any longer.*]

FITZ It's...it's my hands.

TRICIA Yeah?

FITZ I have neuropathy.

TRICIA What's that?

FITZ Damage to the peripheral nervous system. It can happen if you get an inflammation that damages the sheath around your nerves. And that can cause a lot of different effects. For me, I have some loss of sensation in my fingers. Plus what doctors like to call "positive" phenomena. Which means I feel things that aren't there. Mostly pain. Although that feels pretty real.

TRICIA Oh my God.

FITZ All in all, it makes it pretty hard to play the piano. Or to play it very well at any rate.
[*Pause.*]
And there you are.

TRICIA How did it happen?

FITZ Don't know. There's a lot of possible causes. I had a bout of Lyme disease a few years ago. It could've been that.

TRICIA Is it always there?

FITZ Some days are better than others.

TRICIA I'm so sorry.

FITZ There are worse things, I guess.

TRICIA Yeah.

FITZ Do you want me to leave while you put that in with your mother?

TRICIA No, that's okay. I'm not a big one for ceremony.
[*She looks at the ticket, then into the urn, then she places the ticket carefully inside. Quietly.*]
Bye, Mom.

[*She looks into the urn for a moment longer, then turns to* FITZ.]
Well...that was anticlimactic.

FITZ   I don't think people ever feel the way they think they're supposed to. I see a lot of acting in here. People throw themselves on top of caskets and stuff. I don't know. Maybe they do really do feel that strongly, and I.... Maybe it's just something else I don't feel.

TRICIA   I just hoped it would be different.

FITZ   [*Indicating the urn.*] May I?

TRICIA   Sure.

[FITZ *replaces the plate on the bottom of the urn and screws it back together as they talk.* TRICIA *checks her watch and retrieves her purse. Once* FITZ *finishes the job, he turns the urn right side up again and places it in the center of the table again.*]
Well, thank you for that, and for all you've done.

FITZ   You're welcome.

TRICIA   I think I'll be going.

FITZ   Yeah, I'm sure some of your family's arrived by now. I'll walk you up.

TRICIA   No, I mean, I'm leaving.

FITZ   What?

TRICIA   Like I said, I'm not big on ceremony. And I did what I came to do.

FITZ   Wait, are you serious?

TRICIA   Yes, I just—

FITZ   It's your mother's memorial.

TRICIA   I'm aware of that. Thank you.

FITZ   You can't leave.

TRICIA   I can do what I want. Not that it's your business, but I don't feel like dealing with my family or answering all their questions.

FITZ   Really? 'Cuz you wouldn't stop asking me questions while I was trying to work in here.

TRICIA   Excuse me?

FITZ   "Why aren't you playing the piano?" "Why are you here?"

TRICIA   Look, I don't get along with my aunt or my cousins. None of them lifted a finger to help us when my dad left, so I don't have much to say to them, or feel like listening to anything they might have to say.

FITZ   Oh, you mean, like, where were you while your mother was slowly dying of Alzheimer's?

TRICIA   [*Long pause.*] Excuse me?

FITZ   Well, you didn't visit her.

TRICIA   I visited all the time.

FITZ   No, you didn't.

TRICIA   How would you know?

FITZ   Because I did.

TRICIA   What?

FITZ   I was there.

TRICIA   At the nursing home?

FITZ   With your mother. Someone had to be.

[*Silence.*]

TRICIA   Maybe I will see Mr. McKenzie. He might want to know how his staff deals with grieving clients.

FITZ   Oh, hey, if you wanna risk bumping into your aunt, be my guest.

[TRICIA *stalks over to the doors, but stops.*]

TRICIA   How often did you visit her?

FITZ   Two or three times.

TRICIA   That's it?

FITZ   A week.

TRICIA   Two or three times a week?!

[FITZ *nods. Pause.*]

For how long?

FITZ   The last five or six months.

TRICIA   Oh my God.

[*Pause.*]

Why?

FITZ   I "retired" from the concert circuit about two years ago. I tried playing through the pain. Just grit my teeth and hit the keys. And I could get through a concert, but...

[*He shrugs.*]

The bookings dried up, and the way it felt, I was relieved. So I came home. And did nothing. For a long time. Until my mother made me take this job.

[*Slight pause.*]

My dad was the one who heard your mom was at Stony Field. I knew she'd gone to Juilliard and done the concert thing too, so I thought she'd be the only one around who'd understand how I felt. I didn't know she had Alzheimer's.

TRICIA   Why did you keep going?

FITZ   I turned around to leave when I first saw her. But instead I got a chair and sat with her. Ended up babbling about what a nice day it was and stuff like that. Even wheeled her outside, but I got no response. So I'm bringing her back in, we pass the common room, and she sees the piano and points. So I push her over, and we play "Chop Sticks." Then she says, "Thank you, Fitzhugh."

[*Slight pause.*]

I wasn't sure I'd go back. But I did. For her.

TRICIA   "For her." I visited her. For years, while she got worse and worse, I was here every weekend. And it wasn't easy. I'm in

Manhattan. I don't have a car. I'd ride four hours on a bus, get into town late Friday night, stay in a dingy hotel, then Saturday get a cab to Stony Field. Sometimes she knew me, and we'd fight. Sometimes she didn't know me, and we'd fight. Sometimes she knew me, and she'd cry. Sometimes she didn't know me, and I'd cry. Then I got to turn around and spend another five or six hours getting back home.

[*Pause.*]

I left angry and upset, and she forgot I'd even been there as soon as I left the room. Then one trip home I found myself wishing she'd just die. Wanting her to die.

[*Pause.*]

So I just stopped going.

FITZ   [*Pause.*] You must've been relieved then.

TRICIA   You'd think. I was at LAX just about ready to board a plane when they called to tell me she died. I was too stunned to do anything but just get on the plane to come home.

[*Slight pause.*]

I got bumped up to first class. Isn't that something? I travel a lot for work, and I'd just gotten enough frequent flyer miles to make the Silver Medallion class of membership. And I got upgraded. It was like they knew. I sit down and they give me a hot towel, which I press to my face, let the warmth sink into my skin. Then they bring me a mimosa. And when I finish that one...they bring another. And a third. Then somewhere over Nebraska...I snap. And I get up in the aisle and start tearing my clothes off, telling everyone on the plane what a terrible daughter I am because my mother who I haven't seen in five months just died alone.

FITZ   [*Slight pause.*] You didn't take your clothes off.

TRICIA   Oh yes, I did, and I've got the court appearance ticket to prove it.

FITZ   Didn't the crew stop you?

TRICIA   They asked me to return to my seat. Does that count?

FITZ   And none of the passengers tried to help?

TRICIA   What, and miss the train wreck? I was almost totally naked before a flight attended wrapped one of those pathetic little blankets around me while I was trying to unhook my bra. They got me back to my seat, and then several passengers offered up Xanax... so the rest of the trip was pretty calm.

[*Silence.*]

FITZ   She used to ask for you a lot.

TRICIA   Oh, thanks. Yes, please. Pile it on.

FITZ   Some days I could distract her with the piano. But this one day, my hands hurt too much, and she just kept crying.

TRICIA   You're an asshole, you know that.

[*She heads for the door.*]

FITZ   So I told her you were coming.

TRICIA   What?

FITZ   I said you'd be there that afternoon. It just came out.

TRICIA   You lied to her?

FITZ   And she calmed down right away. I mean, really peaceful. We actually had a real conversation.

[FITZ *lapses into silence.* TRICIA *studies his face.*]

TRICIA   Oh. Tell me you didn't.

FITZ   Didn't what?

TRICIA   You kept telling her I was coming, didn't you?

FITZ   Yes. Every time I visited.

  [*Slight pause.*]

  And eventually that you'd been there.

TRICIA   What?

FITZ In the afternoon, she couldn't remember what'd happened in the morning. So I'd say, "Wasn't that a great visit with Tricia this morning? You two had so much fun talking." And she'd ask some questions... and I'd make up your conversation... and she'd smile and laugh.

TRICIA Great. Clearly you were a better daughter to her than me. Look, I'm sorry you're so disappointed in my behavior, but... get in line. Believe me, no one is more disappointed in me than me. Not even my mother.

FITZ She wasn't disappointed in you.

TRICIA Please. I was never interested in music, preferred politics, I never dated any guy for more than five or six months, I kept up a relationship with my dad.... The list goes on.

FITZ Everyone's got that list. She told me she was proud of you.

TRICIA Yeah, I don't believe you.

FITZ It's true.

TRICIA You lied to my mother. Why not lie to me? And even if she did say something like that... who's to know if she really thought it, or meant it, or felt it?

[*Slight pause.*]

Thank you for visiting my mother and being so kind to her. I wish I could've done it, but there was very little harmony in our relationship. Forgive the musical allusion.

FITZ People misuse the word *harmony*. They say it when they mean *consonance*, where all the notes complement each other and blend together smoothly. And consonance sounds great. But after a while, it's really boring. There's no tension in music like that. Nothing to be resolved. Dissonance may not sound pretty, but it's alive. I always like playing music that moves back and forth between consonance and dissonance. It means something's happening. That life is struggling to go on, to lift itself up.

[*Slight pause.*]

Harmony isn't angelic choirs or perfection. Some of the best harmony has an element of dissonance. It's there, lurking behind the other notes, grounding the piece in reality. I think that's why we like it. It's beautiful, but a little ragged too.

[*Slight pause.*]

Not everything goes. There were days she could still play the piano. And days she said she loved you.

[*There is a silence as* TRICIA *takes this in.*]

TRICIA   Would you like her piano?

FITZ   What?

TRICIA   I think you should have it.

FITZ   Why? No, I don't want it.

TRICIA   I think you do.

FITZ   I can't play it. Why would I take it?

TRICIA   You can play.

FITZ   No, I can't.

TRICIA   You played "Chop Sticks."

[*Off his glare.*]

Okay, you can't play as well as you used to. Or as you'd like to. But you can still play.

FITZ   What would be the point?

TRICIA   Just to be able to when you're having a good day. Just to be able to have that. Why did you ever play?

FITZ   I know what you want me to say. You want me to say I played the piano because I loved it and I loved music, and then you can say, "That's all you need, isn't it?" Well, no, it isn't. I need more. I need to be seen. I need to be recognized. I want my hands back. I want my nerves, my life. I don't want to be working in a fucking funeral home. But this is my life now, so why would I want a goddamn piano?! Like I need another reminder of what a failure I am? What possible use would I have for it?

TRICIA You could teach.

FITZ No, thanks.

TRICIA It was good enough for my mother. She didn't grow up wanting to teach piano to little snots in Pittsfield. She was ready to play concerts and tour. Until she had me.

[*FITZ is silent. TRICIA checks her watch.*]

Could you check and see if anyone else has arrived yet?

FITZ [*Slight pause.*] Sure.

[*FITZ exits. TRICIA crosses to her mother's urn. She kisses the tips of her fingers on one hand and then touches them to the top of the urn. FITZ returns a moment later.*]

Your aunts are in reception with Mr. McKenzie. But I'll show you out the back so you don't have to see them.

TRICIA No. I think it's time I said hello.

[*Slight pause.*]

That music you had playing when I came in . . . that was you, wasn't it?

FITZ I was just using it to check the volume.

TRICIA It's lovely. Would you play that for the service?

FITZ It's not what's listed in the program.

TRICIA My aunts won't have a clue.

FITZ [*Pause.*] Can I walk you over?

TRICIA Yes. Thank you, Fitzhugh.

[*They exit.*]

• • •

Creatures
a ten-minute play

Janet Allard

Janet Allard

Janet Allard is a playwright and book writer/lyricist. Her plays are published by Samuel French and Playscripts, Inc. Allard is the recipient of two Jerome fellowships at the Playwrights' Center. Her work has been seen at the Guthrie Lab, the Kennedy Center, Mixed Blood, Playwrights Horizons, Yale Rep, the Yale Cabaret, Barrington Stage, the Women's Project, Perseverance Theatre, Joe's Pub, with P73 Productions, NYMF, SPF, and internationally in Ireland, England, Greece, Australia, and New Zealand. She is a Fulbright fellow, a MacDowell Colony fellow, has an MFA in playwriting from the Yale School of Drama, and has studied at the NYU Graduate Musical Theatre Writing program. She currently teaches playwriting at UNCG in North Carolina.

··· production history ···

Creatures was produced by the Truffle Theatre Company in its 2011 Piglet Slaughter-house Festival. In addition, it was selected as a finalist for the Actor's Theater of Louisville National 10-Minute Play Contest and published in *Teaching Theatre*, Summer 2010, vol. 21, in an article by Bruce Miller.

characters

WOMAN

WEREWOLF

setting

In the woods. At a drive-in movie. A full moon.

• • •

[*A* WOMAN *and a* WEREWOLF *in a car at a drive-in movie. There is a full moon behind them. The* WOMAN *stares at the* WEREWOLF *in disbelief.*]

WOMAN So...anything else you'd like to tell me?

[*Pause. The* WEREWOLF *says nothing. He offers* WOMAN *popcorn.*]

No. You can't pretend this is normal, Tom. This is not a normal night at the drive-in anymore.

[*Screams come from the drive-in speakers. A horror film—a B movie.*]

So the monthly business trips to Vegas?

[*The* WEREWOLF *shakes his head.*]

Why didn't you tell me sooner?

[*The* WEREWOLF *is quiet.*]

Did you think I wouldn't find out?

[*Quiet. From the movie speakers:* "Run! Run for your lives! It's the creature!" *More screams.*]

When were you planning on telling me? At the altar?

[*Quiet. The* WEREWOLF *eats popcorn.*]

I already knew.

[*The* WEREWOLF *looks at her. Really?*]

   I found a strange hair in the bathroom.

[*The* WEREWOLF *goes back to eating popcorn.*]

   You are something else, you know that? I knew it. Somewhere in
   my heart I knew this was too good to be true. So . . . what now?
   What does this mean for us, Tom?

[*The* WEREWOLF *shrugs.*]

   YOU DON'T KNOW?! How can you be so nonchalant? It's not
   like this is going to blow over. Here's your ring. Here's your
   goddamn ring back!

[*The* WEREWOLF *stares at her. He offers her popcorn.*]

   I don't want popcorn!

[*The* WEREWOLF *howls.*]

   You don't scare me.

[*The* WEREWOLF *howls, the* WOMAN *howls. He grabs her. Movie: romantic
music . . . maybe a woman's voice—*"I'm not afraid of you . . . creature!"]

   No! I can't trust you, Tom! I mean . . . so what else? What next?
   Any other surprises you'd like to spring on me?

[*The* WEREWOLF *lights a cigarette.*]

   You smoke?

[*The* WEREWOLF *puts out the cigarette.*]

   What else? Bring it on.

[*The* WEREWOLF *shakes his head. This is everything.*]

   How am I supposed to believe that? You hide things—
   everything—the hair and the teeth . . . and I never would have
   known except then the moon—and then you just eat popcorn
   and—how can I trust you? It's BULLSHIT, Tom! I don't keep
   things from you! I don't have any secrets!

[*The* WEREWOLF *stares at her.*]

What? I don't.

[*The* WEREWOLF *looks at her.*]

Not like yours.

[*The* WEREWOLF *looks at her.*]

What?

[WOMAN *eats popcorn.*]

You know everything about me there is to know. I'm clear. Transparent.

[*The* WEREWOLF *stares at her.*]

What? What, what, what? What? Why are you looking at me like that? I'm not keeping anything from you.

[*The* WEREWOLF *sniffs her.*]

I am not hiding—

[*The* WEREWOLF *sniffs harder.*]

I am not hiding any—stop sniffing me!

[*The* WEREWOLF *sniffs her like crazy.*]

What are you?!—No!

[*The* WEREWOLF *pulls a chocolate bar out of her coat. Triumphant.*]

Chocolate! So what? I was going to share it with you.

[*The* WEREWOLF *goes to take a bite.* WOMAN *grabs it away.*]

Okay! I was hiding it. Hoarding it. I didn't say I was giving up chocolate forever, just for Lent. So what? I don't have to share!

[WOMAN *devours the entire chocolate bar. The* WEREWOLF *watches. Some sort of melodramatic music plays through the movie speakers.*]

It's not like I'm keeping something *huge* hidden—like the fact that I'm a *werewolf*. I am happy to eat chocolate out in the open! I love it! I don't care who knows it. And I will not share! And by the way, while we are coming clean—since this is "tell all night"!

[WOMAN *pulls a cigarette out of her purse and lights it.*]

I smoke too! I never quit. There. Those are my "shocking secrets." That's all I have to hide.

[*The* WEREWOLF *grabs* WOMAN*'s hair. It comes off.*]

All right. It's a wig. So what? I like how it looks.

[*The* WEREWOLF *tries to grab* WOMAN*'s purse.*]

Stay outta my purse!

[*The* WEREWOLF *gets a text message. They both freeze.*]

Is someone texting you?

[*The* WEREWOLF *shrugs.*]

Aren't you going to look?

[*The* WEREWOLF *shrugs.*]

You know, Tom, I think it's good that you revealed this werewolf business tonight. I think it's made us closer. With the nuptials fast approaching, we really need to be transparent, get it all out on the table now so it doesn't bite us in the ass, know what I mean? You're a werewolf, I hoard chocolate, we both still smoke. That's it. Is everything on the table now?

[*The* WEREWOLF *nods.*]

That's everything?

[*The* WEREWOLF *nods.*]

Good.

[*The* WEREWOLF *grabs* WOMAN*'s purse.*]

Give me back my purse!

[*The* WEREWOLF *holds the purse.*]

Go ahead. Go through it. I don't care.

[*The* WEREWOLF *starts to open the purse—gauging her reaction.*]

You know, Tom, I think trust is a choice. Maybe there are some little things we don't know about each other. We change. We choose. Every day. We choose to trust. I'm going to choose to trust you. I trust you. I love you.

[*The* WEREWOLF *smiles.*]

We're missing the movie. Put that down and we can cuddle.

[WOMAN *smiles.*]

Do you want more popcorn? I'm dying for some butter on this. Why don't you just run and—

[*The* WEREWOLF *opens the purse. Looks at* WOMAN *to see her reaction.* WOMAN *laughs.*]

Oh, Tom, you're so funny I told you I have nothing to—

[*The* WEREWOLF *sticks his paw into the purse.*]

NO!

[*The* WEREWOLF *rifles through the purse.*]

Hey, asshole—that's my passport! You have no right to look at my passport! Yes, I wear bright red lipstick sometimes. So? I have nothing to—yeah, a letter. So what. Go ahead. Open it. Yeah, pills. I had a—prescription—they're painkillers for my—give me my—

[*The* WEREWOLF *pulls out the ornate box. Stares at it.*]

Put that back—put that—

[*The* WEREWOLF *sniffs it.*]

Nothing's in that box. It's just an empty—you can open it—don't—

[*The* WEREWOLF *opens it. Screams from movie. Something in the box glows green. The* WEREWOLF *looks at* WOMAN *in disbelief. She sips her Diet Coke. She takes the box and puts it back in the purse. She takes the purse. Closes it. Puts it next to her. He looks at her. She takes off her wig.*]

Okay. There are some things you need to know about me. I—

[*The* WEREWOLF *shakes his head.*]

It's just that I—

[*The* WEREWOLF *puts his finger to* WOMAN*'s lips.*]

No, I do need to tell you. I—

[*The* WEREWOLF *puts his finger to* WOMAN*'s lips. He offers her popcorn. She eats popcorn. She starts to cry. He puts his paw on her leg. Romantic music plays. Maybe we hear something from the movie like: "I don't care to return to that world, creature. I'll live where you live. In outer space or at the bottom of the lake. As long as I'm with you." Passionate kissing on the movie screen. Love music. They watch.*]

I'm sorry, I just need to tell you I—

[WOMAN *leans over and whispers in the* WEREWOLF*'s ear. He looks at her.*]

And another thing…

[WOMAN *whispers in the* WEREWOLF*'s ear. He laughs. He whispers in her ear. Screams on the screen. He puts his arm around her. She puts her head on his chest. The sound of the movie overtakes them.*]

• • •

The Coyote Stratagem

a ten-minute play

G. Flores

G. Flores

Guadalupe Flores is the son of a career military man, and is a veteran himself, so he has called many places home, but uses Texas to store all of his stuff. He has worked in journalism and public relations, as well as a slew of other unremarkable jobs. He earned a bachelor's degree at the University of the Incarnate Word in English and theater arts, and is working on a master's in playwriting at Texas State University in San Marcos, where his full-length play, *Hurricane Season*, was produced in 2011. *The Coyote Stratagem* was written in his first semester at Texas State, and was a finalist in the Ten Minute Play category for the Kennedy Center American College Theatre Festival. It has since had productions at the Red Barn Theatre in Key West, Florida, and the ArtsCenter's 10 by 10 in the Triangle Ten Minute Festival in Carrboro, North Carolina, and will be part of the Northern Michigan New Works Festival in 2012. He was a recent participant in the prestigious playwriting intensive at the Kennedy Center, and his paper "Poetic Association: Shakespeare's Use of the Prologue in *Henry V* to Enhance Social Status" was presented at the Second Annual International Research Conference for Graduate Students at Texas State University. Flores has a sixteen-year-old son who is, fortunately, smarter and better-looking than he was at that age.

···production history···

Productions: The 2011 The Region 6 Kennedy Center American College Theatre Festival as a ten-minute play regional finalist, staged reading; the 2011 The Kennedy Center American College Theatre Festival as a ten-minute play national finalist, staged reading; World premiere production (2011) at the Red Barn Theatre in Key West, Florida. Second production (2011), Tenth Annual 10 by 10 Festival in the Triangle, ArtsCenter Stage, Carrboro, North Carolina. Northern Michigan University's Ten Minute Play Festival, Marquette, Michigan.

characters

AARON, a man in his late 30s, and very recent ex-boyfriend of Vicki

VICKI, a woman in her early 30s, and very recent ex-girlfriend of Aaron

time

Present, early morning.

setting

The garage of their shared home.

···

[AARON *enters the garage of his home, in shorts, T-shirt, and bathrobe, carrying a cup of coffee, a folding chair, and a tub of large colored chalk. He sets everything down at dead center, then draws a series of Xs around him in a large circle. He sits and waits.* VICKI *enters carrying suitcases.*]

VICKI   [*Sighing.*] Now what? Hey.

[*No reply from* AARON.]

I have to go. What are you doing in here?

[*She walks up to the marks.*]

What is this?

AARON   Barbed wire.

VICKI   Okay. What's it for?

AARON   To keep you out.

VICKI   I'm signing the lease at three.

> [*Silence from* AARON.]

> I know you're still hurt about everything, but I want to try to be something close to friends.

> [*Still no response.*]

> Please?

[*She steps closer.*]

AARON   [*Abruptly shouting.*] I told you it's fucking barbed wire! I'm not responsible if you get hurt!

VICKI   [*Pause, startled.*] It's chalk. You drew that. I get that you're a sensitive artistic type, fine, great. But sometimes you're just friggin' weird, and this is one of those times.

AARON   And what do you care? After five years together, you're walking away. If I want to wall myself off from the world, it's my choice. You can't say anything about it anymore. So go. Get the hell out of my life.

VICKI   [*Shouting.*] I don't want to get the hell out of your life! I love you, just not the way I need to so I can live with you.

[AARON *stands and grabs another stick of chalk. He steps between the Xs and begins to draw a new pattern.*]

AARON   You see this? This is lava. A whole ring of lava surrounding me. That's what I needed. Another layer of defense.

VICKI   This is crazy. Would you stop and talk to me?

AARON   [*Still drawing.*] Lava is molten rock. It's like thousands of degrees, and will burn the shit out of you. So if you know what's good for you, you'll go the hell away.

VICKI   [*Nearly screaming.*] It's stupid chalk, you stupid . . . ahhh! You're so damn infuriating! All right, fine. If this is how you want to do it!

[VICKI *starts toward the chalk.*]

AARON   NO! No, you fucking don't! This is my home, and if I say you can't do something, you damn well will not do it!

[VICKI *stops. She looks at him, then the marks around him. She begins to slowly walk around him, staring at the lines intently.*]

VICKI   There.

AARON   [*Confused.*] What?

> [VICKI *leaps and lands in a spot between the lava and the barbed wire. She leaps again and is in the middle of the circle. She grabs a stick of chalk and jumps out the way she came in.*]

> Damnit! That isn't fair! The barbed wire is at least six feet tall. You can't just jump over it.

VICKI   You didn't say anything about how tall it is. You set the rules, but you hafta say them first before I can follow them.

[*She begins to draw on the floor with the chalk.*]

AARON   What are you doing?

VICKI   Fighting back.

AARON   You can't fight back, because I'm not fighting. I refuse to.
[*Stressed.*]
Vicki…please. I can't—

VICKI   [*Angry.*] Oh, you will fight me. I don't care if I lose, but you will act and react to me. You mean too much to me to not have you talk to me before I go.

AARON   I can't. I can't do it. I just want to…

VICKI   No. You need to stop being stupid.

AARON   [*Shocked.*] I'm stupid!? Me, stupid! I'm not the one who's walking out on a perfectly fine relationship.

VICKI   It's not fine. Not at all. It's completely screwed up, but you won't see that, and the only way to save whatever is worth saving is to walk away. And since you won't do it, I will.

[*She finishes her drawing.*]

AARON   What is that?

VICKI   A grilled cheese sandwich.

AARON   Okay. Why?

VICKI   Do you remember how we met? My dad was getting another pointless award from his Knights of Columbus chapter.

AARON   Yeah, I remember. So what?

VICKI   I was at the snack bar, standing in line. My parents wanted beer, and I was hungry, so I volunteered to go get it. I was right there at the counter, looking at the menu, when you walked up and asked me, "Is there anything good here?"

AARON   Yeah. Yeah, I remember now.

VICKI   I said, "I dunno." And you said, "The grilled cheese sandwich looks good. At least hers does."

AARON   That old lady, the one with the walker! Yeah!

VICKI   So we both ordered the grilled cheese.

AARON   It was pretty awesome too.

VICKI   It was. Then we talked about how good it was. And we walked over to my parents and talked there for a while. Then we sat with your mom.

AARON   She was there to play bingo.

VICKI   And my folks stayed after the ceremony to play bingo. And we sat in the back and talked until they shut the place down for the night.

[*She steps closer.*]

AARON   Stop.

[*He bends down and draws, again around the periphery of the entire circle.*]
These are cannons, firing high explosive, depleted uranium warheads, capable of leveling a city block. Go the hell away.

VICKI   Damnit! I don't care what . . .

AARON   I said, GO THE HELL AWAY.

[*She stares at him for a moment, then walks to the other side of the circle, opposite the grilled cheese sandwich, and draws again. He watches her suspiciously. She finishes.*]

AARON Okay. What is it?

VICKI A turkey. It was the Thanksgiving after we met. You remember that?

AARON Yes.

VICKI What do you remember?

AARON Fuck off.

VICKI I'll tell you what I remember. We went downtown to watch the city turn on the Christmas lights. The whole center square downtown was lit up with all these colors, and it was cold so we were hugging tight to stay warm. I slid my hands under your jacket to warm them on your hips, and you yelled and laughed because they were cold. And then you wrapped your arms around me, then put your hands on the skin of my back, and I yelled and laughed because they were cold. And then you said…

AARON Shut up.

VICKI You said…

AARON I said SHUT UP.

VICKI …I love you.

AARON [*Snarling.*] Well, I guess it didn't matter, did it? Nothing I said matters because you're still leaving.

VICKI Of course it mattered. It still matters. Please. Just step outside the circle and talk to me, really talk before I go.

[AARON *bends down and draws several figures spaced around the edge of the circle.*]

AARON Do you see these? These are space-based unmanned weapons platforms, equipped with solar-powered lasers and rail guns. If the lasers don't fry you to a crisp, the rail guns will pound you into a bloody pulp.

VICKI Jesus. Let me point out again that these are just drawings and can't really hurt me. But even if they could, why would you *want* to hurt me?

AARON Because right now, I hate you more than anything. More than anything in the world.

VICKI You don't mean that.

AARON Yes, I do. But I don't want to go to jail for really hurting you. But if I could get away with it, I'd punch you square in the face.

[VICKI *struggles with this statement for a long moment, her emotions visible. She thinks, then walks to another side of the circle. She draws another figure. When she is finished, AARON stares at her, motionless. VICKI waits, then finally speaks.*]

VICKI When my mother died.

[AARON *turns away at this, refusing to look at her. She takes a step toward him.*]

AARON No.

VICKI When she died, it was the worst time of my life. But you were there, and you helped me get through it. You listened to me, all the stories about her, how she could make me angry and laugh at the same time. You listened while I worried about my father, and how he was going to deal with being alone. Held me when I cried. Brought me food and coffee in bed when I couldn't force myself to get out of it. You were the first one to make me laugh afterwards.

AARON You should leave.

VICKI You went with me the first time I visited her in the cemetery. And I loved how you talked to her there, as if she were still alive, with us right at that moment.

[AARON *takes off his robe and erases everything he has drawn, avoiding* VICKI's *drawings. He then makes two large circles around him.*]

What is this?

AARON An abyss. Endless. It goes on forever, and never stops. Neither one of us can cross it. So you should go, and leave me here. I'll be fine.

VICKI But I won't be. I can't leave and not have you connected to me somehow.

AARON   You don't need to be. And I don't want to be.

[VICKI *walks to the last empty side and makes her last drawing. She does not wait for* AARON's *response to explain it.*]

VICKI   This morning, while I was lying in bed, I heard you come into the room. I heard what you said.

AARON   I didn't say anything.

VICKI   You said, "I love you."

AARON   No, I didn't.

VICKI   I heard the door open, and then I felt you sitting on the side of the bed. I didn't move. I pretended to be asleep. Then you touched my hair.

AARON   Nope. Didn't happen.

VICKI   And I felt you bend down to kiss me. And then you said it.

AARON   No.

VICKI   "I love you. No matter what."

AARON   [*Angrily.*] Why didn't you say something when I did that?

VICKI   Because if I had, if I had turned around and said "I love you too," I wouldn't be leaving. We would drag this falling apart out for weeks, maybe months. I need to leave now. But I can't leave with us this way.

AARON   I don't want you to leave.

VICKI   And I don't want to leave. But I have to.

[AARON *looks at her for a long moment. He looks down at the drawing, then kneels down at the edge of the abyss.*]

AARON   Meet me halfway.

[VICKI *looks at him, confused, then understands. She kneels down, and they both make lines from each of their sides, creating a bridge. They stand, and meet in the middle. They embrace.*]

VICKI   [*Softly.*] I'm going to miss you.

AARON   I'm going to miss you too. Will I see you again?

VICKI   Of course. More than you expect. I'll be over here a lot, I think.

AARON   Good. Because I love you. I'm sorry I killed whatever we had.

VICKI   Baby, you didn't kill it. Love doesn't die. It just changes. Sometimes into hate, but that didn't happen with us. And I'm glad about that.

AARON   [*Pulling away but still holding hands.*] Can I help you out with your bags?

VICKI   [*Grinning.*] Dressed like that? We've given our neighbors enough to talk about as it is. Stay here. Get used to the place without me.

   [*She pulls away from him, and gathers her things. She looks around one last time, then turns to* AARON *and smiles.*]

   Have any plans for dinner?

AARON   [*Smiling.*] As a matter of fact, no. I just broke up with my girlfriend, so I'm free as a bird. But . . .

VICKI   But?

AARON   I think . . . I think I need a few days.

VICKI   Okay. I get that. But soon, all right?

AARON   Soon. I promise.

VICKI   Okay. Love you.

[*Exits.*]

AARON   [*Long pause.*] I love you too. No matter what.

[AARON *looks at the door for a long time. He then looks at the floor. He exits.*]

• • •

Chocolates on the Pillow

Arlene Hutton

Arlene Hutton

Arlene Hutton is a three-time winner of the Samuel French Short Play Festival and a six-time Heideman Award finalist. Her first one-act, *I Dream Before I Take the Stand*, premiered at the Edinburgh Festival Fringe, was presented at the first New York Fringe Festival, and appears in several anthologies. She is best known for *The Nibroc Trilogy*, which includes *Last Train to Nibroc* (Drama League nomination for Best Play), *See Rock City* (In the Spirit of America Award), and *Gulf View Drive* (*LA Weekly* Theatre Award nomination and Ovation Award nomination). An alumna of New Dramatists, Hutton is a member of the Dramatists Guild and Ensemble Studio Theatre. Her plays have been presented Off- and Off-Off-Broadway, regionally, in London, and around the world.

···production history···

Chocolates on the Pillow was presented by Artistic New Directions, Janice L. Goldberg and Kristine Niven, artistic co-directors, in March 2010. It was directed by Lori Wolter Hudson and stage-managed by Jacob Moore. Costume design was by Beth Lincks. Cast:

> **DEBBIE**, Amanda Sykes
>
> **BILL**, Raife Baker
>
> **MARYANN**, herself

An earlier version of *Chocolates on the Pillow* was developed at New Dramatists for *Nude Dramatists*, directed by Thomas Edward West. Cast:

> **DEBBIE**, Alana West
>
> **BILL**, Jack L. Davis
>
> **MARYANN**, herself

characters

> **DEBBIE**, a nice, average young woman in her twenties or early thirties
>
> **BILL**, her nice, average boyfriend, around the same age
>
> **MARYANN**, a very old and worn stuffed animal, probably a monkey, about three or four years younger than Debbie

···

[*A bedroom suite in a "Victorian" bed and breakfast. Suitcases. BILL, in khakis and a sweatshirt, enters, carrying car keys, a handful of tourist brochures, and two glasses of sherry, which he places carefully on the bureau.*]

BILL   [*Calling toward the bathroom.*] The car is now parked.

DEBBIE   [*From offstage.*] Thanks!

BILL   [*Going through the brochures.*] There is so much to do here. Hiking. Rafting. Tubing. Hiking. Horseback riding. Hiking. Museum.

> [*He tosses that one in the trash.*]

> Rock climbing. Antique stores.

> [*Balls that one up and throws it in the trash.*]

Tubing. Ballooning. Ballooning? Hiking. Hey! We're only twenty miles from the Appalachian Trail!

[*He is still looking at the brochures as* DEBBIE *enters. She wears a pretty nightgown and robe set, soft and romantic.*]

DEBBIE   What did you say?

BILL   [*Still engrossed in his flyers.*] The Appalachian Trail. It's only about twenty miles from here. We're gonna have a great weekend.

DEBBIE   They've got the cutest little soaps. Crabtree and Evelyn.

BILL   There's no light in here.

DEBBIE   I turned it down.

BILL   I can't read the brochures.

DEBBIE   Do you really want to read the brochures?

[BILL *looks at her for the first time and notices her outfit.*]

BILL   Hel-lo.

DEBBIE   Hi.

[BILL *lamely holds out some brochures.*]

BILL   There's lots to do here.

DEBBIE   We can look at them in the morning.

[DEBBIE *takes the brochures out of his hand and puts them down.*]

BILL   Don't you want to decide what we're gonna do tomorrow?

DEBBIE   We might want to sleep in.

BILL   Oh. Right. Yeah. Good idea.

DEBBIE   Or not sleep in.

BILL   Just stay in?

DEBBIE   Whatever you want.

BILL   Hel-lo.

DEBBIE   I went ahead and showered. While you were parking.

BILL   I got to talking with Ron and Shirley. I should've—

DEBBIE   That's okay.

BILL   They make French toast on Saturdays, serve it—

DEBBIE   Don't you just love a bed and breakfast?

BILL   —in the garden.

DEBBIE   Yay.

BILL   Oh! And they gave us sherry. Since we got in too late for dinner.

DEBBIE   That's so nice. What is sherry, anyway?

BILL   We're gonna find out.

DEBBIE   Don't people cook with sherry?

BILL   We're gonna cook with sherry tonight.
[*Perhaps he holds an imaginary microphone and he sings.*]
"Sherry, Sherry baby Sher-ry, Sherry baby."

DEBBIE   Hello, Tiger!

BILL   [*He can't stop looking at her.*] Hel-lo. You're way ahead of me here.

DEBBIE   The shower's great. Big fluffy towels.

BILL   I'm there.
[*He looks at her, grins boyishly.*]
Wanna join me?

[BILL *starts taking off his shoes.*]

DEBBIE   I'm gonna finish unpacking.

BILL   Oh, come on.

DEBBIE   Tomorrow. We can take a long bath together tomorrow. After the hike.

BILL   [*Pulling his arms down in victory.*] Hike. Yes!

[BILL *sings as he pulls hiking boots from his suitcase.*]

DEBBIE   [*Smiling at him.*] Oh! Look! There's chocolates.

BILL   Where?

DEBBIE   On the pillow.

BILL   Nice.

[BILL *starts singing again as he takes off his sweater.* DEBBIE *picks up a chocolate.*]

DEBBIE   Really nice.

> [DEBBIE *takes the chocolate out of its little paper cup or wrapping.*]
> Godiva.
> [*DEBBIE eats the chocolate, slowly, sensuously. It's really good.*]
> Mmmm. Oh. Mmmm.
> [DEBBIE *licks her finger, innocently.*]
> Yum.

BILL   [*Watching her.*] Hel-lo!

> [*Singing.*]
> "Come, come, come, come on tonight."

DEBBIE   [*Laughing.*] Stop it.

> [BILL *kisses her and continues undressing.*]
> What a great place.

BILL   Mike brought Marlene here the weekend before the Super Bowl. Takes her on a trip every year. The weekend before the Super Bowl. Genius.

DEBBIE   Genius. Thank you for this weekend.

BILL   Thank Mike. He suggested this place. Gave me the extra day off.

DEBBIE   Thank you, Mike.

BILL   Happy Valentine's Day a week early.

DEBBIE   Happy Valentine's Day a week early. Mike's idea?

BILL   Genius. The ole romantic bed and breakfast getaway. Here's the bed. And here's your breakfast.

[*He hands her a glass of sherry and maybe sings a bit of the "Sherry" song.*]

DEBBIE   Here's to Mike.

BILL   Here's to you, beautiful.

DEBBIE   [*He's so sweet.*] Ooooh . . .

BILL   Cheers.

[*He downs his sherry like a shot.*]

DEBBIE   [*Sipping her sherry to taste it.*] So that's sherry.

BILL   [*Singing.*] "Sherry. . . ."

[BILL *sings bits of various songs from the sixties as he undresses down to boxers and a T-shirt.* DEBBIE *unpacks a small stuffed toy monkey, once made of brown plush cloth, now threadbare and gray.* DEBBIE *puts the monkey on a table.* BILL *picks it up and looks at it.*]

What's this?

DEBBIE   MaryAnn. You've seen her before.

BILL   Well, in your bedroom.

DEBBIE   Well, yeah.

[DEBBIE *smiles at* BILL. *She takes* MARYANN *from* BILL *and sits her on a love seat, facing out, and unpacks some* MARYANN-*sized clothes from her suitcase, neatly placing them in a stack on the bureau. A pause.*]

BILL   What's it doing here?

DEBBIE   She. She always travels with me.

BILL   That? You always—

DEBBIE   MaryAnn. Yeah.

BILL   But it's sad.

DEBBIE   She's just old. I've had her since I was five.

[DEBBIE *takes one of the articles of clothing from the stack on the bureau. It is a small nightgown. She starts to take off the outfit that* MARYANN *is wearing.*]

BILL   What are you doing?

DEBBIE   I thought we were going to bed.

BILL   No, with that.

DEBBIE   Her name is MaryAnn. Turn around.

BILL   What?

DEBBIE   Turn around.

BILL   [*He turns around.*] Why?

DEBBIE   She's shy.

BILL   What?

DEBBIE   I'm changing her clothes.

BILL   Why do you have to change her clothes?

DEBBIE   I'm getting her ready for bed.

BILL   [*He turns back to face her.*] What?

DEBBIE   Turn around.

>   [*He does.*]

>   I'm getting her dressed for bed.

BILL   That's not sleeping with us.

DEBBIE   Don't be silly. Of course she isn't sleeping with us.

BILL   Okay.

DEBBIE   Silly. She'll just sit—

BILL   Can I—

DEBBIE   —right here.

BILL   Can I turn around now?

DEBBIE   Yes.

[DEBBIE *has placed* MARYANN *on the bureau, sitting up and looking out.* BILL *takes this in.*]

BILL   [*After a pause, still looking at* MARYANN.] That's, like, weird.

DEBBIE   Bill, you've seen her in my bedroom.

BILL   That's different. Why'd you bring it?

DEBBIE   I always take her with me.

BILL   You never brought it to my place.

DEBBIE   That's different. I don't take a suitcase to your place. I just stay over.

BILL   [*After a beat.*] Okay.

DEBBIE   You wanna shower in the morning instead?

BILL   Don't I need to shave?

DEBBIE   I'll manage.

BILL   Aren't I stinky?

DEBBIE   [*She sniffs him.*] Stinky good, not stinky bad.

[*They stand there, awkwardly staring at each other.*]

BILL   You look beautiful.

DEBBIE   You look pretty good yourself.

BILL   [*He sniffs her.*] You smell nice too.

DEBBIE   It's the soap. Sandalwood. From Crabtree and Evelyn.

BILL   [*He nuzzles and sniffs her.*] Thank you, Crabtree. And thank you, Evelyn. Whoever you are.

DEBBIE   [*Breathless.*] Did you put the do-not-disturb sign on the door?

BILL   [*Groping her.*] Yes.

DEBBIE   Good.

[*They are in an embrace, rubbing bodies together. Suddenly BILL sees MARYANN and stops the foreplay.*]

BILL   Ummm.

DEBBIE   What?

BILL   She's looking at us.

DEBBIE   What do you mean?

BILL   She's like, watching. I can't—

DEBBIE   You've seen her sitting in my room.

BILL   That was different.

DEBBIE   Different how?

BILL   I don't know. Just different.

DEBBIE   Bill.

BILL   I can't...um...put her in the suitcase.

DEBBIE   What?

BILL   I can't...just put her in the suitcase.

DEBBIE   Why?

BILL   I can't...

   [*There is a very long pause as they look at each other.*]
   Let's go to bed.

DEBBIE   Okay.

[*She starts kissing him again. He doesn't respond.*]

BILL   I mean, let's go to sleep.

DEBBIE   It's our first weekend away together.

BILL   Yeah. Um.

DEBBIE   What's wrong?

BILL   Nothing.

DEBBIE   Should I brush my teeth again?

BILL   Um. No need.

DEBBIE   What?

BILL   I have to pee.

DEBBIE   Oh.

BILL   You want the bathroom?

DEBBIE   No. Go ahead. Are you tired?

BILL   No.

DEBBIE   You did all the driving. I would've—

BILL   Yeah. I'm tired.

DEBBIE   That traffic was terrible.

BILL   Yeah.

DEBBIE   Do you want something to eat?

BILL   No.

DEBBIE   I have some peanuts in my bag.

BILL   I just need some sleep. Get some sleep.

DEBBIE   Well, sunrise sex is—

BILL   I'm just going to—

[*Points to the bathroom.*]

DEBBIE   [*Nodding.*] Yeah, go on.

BILL   Okay.

DEBBIE   D'you want your chocolate?

BILL   Give it to MaryAnn.

[BILL *exits into the bathroom.*]

[*Lights slowly fade to a pin spot on* MARYANN. *Then blackout.*]

• • •

And Yet . . .
a short play inspired by Shakespeare's "Sonnet 130"

Steve Feffer

For my wife, Laura, who sent me this sonnet

Steve Feffer

Steve Feffer's plays have been produced or developed by theaters that include the O'Neill National Playwrights Conference, Ensemble Studio Theatre, Stages Repertory Theatre, Ruckus Theatre, and Untitled Theatre #61. His play *Little Airplanes of the Heart* was published in *Best American Short Plays 1997–98* and in *Plays from the Ensemble Studio Theatre 2000* (Faber and Faber), and has been produced at regional, university, high school, and community theaters around the country. Other publications include *The Wizards of Quiz* (Dramatists Play Service); Heinemann Books and New Issues Press have published additional plays and performance pieces. Feffer has won a number of national playwriting awards, including the New Jewish Theatre Project Award from the Foundation for Jewish Culture for *Ain't Got No Home* and the Southwest Plays Award for a Play for Young Audiences for *The House I Call Love*. Feffer is a professor in the Creative Writing Program at Western Michigan University (in Kalamazoo), where he directs the graduate and undergraduate playwriting programs. He has served as a regional chair for the National Playwriting Program of the Kennedy Center American College Theatre Festival.

···production history···

And Yet... was presented in February 2011 as part of the Gwen Frostic Series at Western Michigan University in Kalamazoo. This version of the play was first developed and staged in the Cafe Ypsilon Theatre in Prague, Czech Republic, as part of WMU's Prague Summer Program at Charles University. An earlier version of *And Yet...* was commissioned and premiered as part of *Burning Love, Short Plays Inspired by Shakespeare's Sonnets* at the Whole Art Theatre, Kalamazoo, Michigan (Tucker Rafferty, producing artistic director) and featured Steve Feffer, Max Hardy, Eli Rix, and Sarah MacClean, directed by Martie Philpot.

characters

SAM, late 30s

SHAYNA, early 20s, played by a television set, where the images of a
   female actor are projected

DAVE, Sam's friend

SHAYNA'S MANAGER, manages a coffee shop

time and place

A small upper-Midwestern city. The present.

author's note

When *And Yet...* was first performed, a female actor played the role of SHAYNA live backstage, where a video camera broadcast the images of her live onto the television that was onstage. This worked very well in performance. The play has also been done with the images pre-recorded and then broadcast on the television.

   This play should be performed on a unit set, with each location suggested by perhaps one set piece or object. There should be no blackouts or scene changes during the play. SAM moves the television as SHAYNA through the space, as if he is escorting her around the stage.

Shakespeare's "Sonnet 130"

My mistress' eyes are nothing like the sun;
Coral is far more red, than her lips red:
If snow be white, why then her breasts are dun;
If hairs be wires, black wires grow on her head.
I have seen roses damasked, red and white,
But no such roses see I in her cheeks;
And in some perfumes is there more delight
Than in the breath that from my mistress reeks.
I love to hear her speak, yet well I know
That music hath a far more pleasing sound:
I grant I never saw a goddess go,
My mistress, when she walks, treads on the ground:
And yet by heaven, I think my love as rare,
As any she belied with false compare.

• • •

[*In the dark: A harp plays versions of some of today's popular songs or current hits, especially those that seem particularly ill-suited for the harp (such as hip-hop or dance music). The harp music continues, as at rise: A hotel Sunday brunch buffet. A television on a wheeled stand is stationed behind a harp. This is* SHAYNA, *and whenever the script refers to* SHAYNA, *it is referring to the television set. On the television screen is the image of a female eye. It should not be a still image, and the eye should be blinking, looking around, etc. The stand should be as unobtrusive as possible—though there should be no effort to hide that this is a television on a television stand.*]

[SAM *is eating Sunday brunch with* DAVE *at a hotel.* SAM *is staring at* SHAYNA.]

SAM   I think my love as rare, as any she belied with false compare. I really do.

    [SAM *listens to the music for a beat.*]

    Good, huh, Dave?

DAVE   Delicious. Nobody does Sunday brunch like the Radisson. I'm gonna get more shrimp.

SAM   No, her playing.

DAVE Oh, yeah . . . Great.
[*They listen for a beat.*]
What song is this?

SAM How do I know? It's the harp. She's good—that's what matters.

DAVE How do you know? I mean, I've never heard you listen to anything but the Wu-Tang Clan.

SAM You don't have to know shit about the harp to know she's good. And besides: It doesn't make a difference whether I think she's good. She's gotta have confidence in herself. She's a damned good harp player and she spends all her time working at that coffee shop.

DAVE She doesn't have any gigs?

SAM She's a harp player. Of course she doesn't have any gigs. She does the occasional wedding. And she plays this brunch buffet. But that's it.

DAVE There's an orchestra in town.

SAM They got a harp player. Some woman who's fucking ninety years old. Goddamn harp is the only thing keeping her alive. They're going to bury her in her harp case.

DAVE Harp's a tough gig, man. You gotta know that going into it.

SAM She's playing your wedding.

DAVE I know.

SAM Well, I appreciate that.

DAVE We love Shayna.
[*Beat.*]
What's the weather gonna be like on the wedding day?

SAM Hey, do I ask you about my heating and air-conditioning when you're not working?

DAVE I just wanna know what I should tell the outta town guests. It looks like there's a snowstorm coming.

SAM   Watch my show tonight.

[*Beat.*]

I just wish I could give her the confidence to stick with it. I should be able to do that. I mean, look at her behind that harp.

[*Beat.*]

Hmmm. Her eyes are nothing like the sun.

[*Beat.*]

Does she look tired to you?

DAVE   Not really.

SAM   It's like the blues edict: Slinging espresso on Saturday night. And playing harp at a brunch on Sunday morning.

[*The lights change. The harp playing continues, as the image on the television screen changes to an image of a female cheek. SAM addresses the audience. A weather map appears behind him. It's a local map. It has a cartoonish picture of an impending snowstorm bearing down on its center. There is a place on the map marked "The Radisson."*]

We met at a reception for the town's annual meteorological awards. She was playing the reception. I thought she looked familiar. She had served me my latte every morning and then there she was playing harp in the Radisson.

[SAM *points to the weather map.*]

I had won the award for our town's best new meteorologist. And I guess I was drunk and a little full of myself, but I got up the courage to talk to her. And I asked if she remembered me, and she said, oh yes, I get dressed to you every morning. And we laughed. And then at one point Robert Daley sat in her harp chair and wouldn't get up. I mean, Daley has been the big meteorologist in this town since... I don't know... there first was weather on TV. And I told him to get out of her chair. Actually, I said, this is the harpist's chair, motherfucker. And he got up. I asked what she was doing after work, and if she needed help pushing her harp home. And we slept together that night.

[*Beat.*]

Today there is a massive winter low approaching.

[SAM *points to the weather map.*]

It will either be what I am calling a "Winter Wallop" or a "Winter Whimper." But I can't decide. I can't seem to call it, and I go on the air any moment now.

[SAM *puts his pointer down and takes a picture out of his wallet. The picture then appears where the weather map was. It is the same idealized image of a female cheek we see on the television.*]

We really have the most wonderful time. And I have been without someone for so long. We are getting married in June. I'm very excited. I'm thrilled. Today she is with her mother trying on wedding dresses. I know she is going to look so beautiful.

[SAM *looks at the picture in his wallet for a moment. He uses his pointer to point to the female cheek that has replaced the weather map.*]

Hmm. I have seen damask'd roses, red and white, but no such roses do I see in her cheeks.

[SAM *looks again at the picture and returns it to his wallet. The weather map returns. The cartoonish snowstorm is closer. The lights change.* SAM *escorts* SHAYNA *across the stage. The image on the television screen changes to that of an image of female lips. Again, as with the previous image, the lips are active and moving, though they are silent.* SHAYNA *is behind an espresso machine.* SAM *is distracted, staring at* SHAYNA. SAM *stands with* SHAYNA'S MANAGER *at the coffee shop.* SHAYNA'S MANAGER *wears a green apron.*]

SHAYNA'S MANAGER So what do you think, Sam? A "Winter Wallop" or a "Winter Whimper?"

SAM Huh?

SHAYNA'S MANAGER Your weather report this evening was…kind of inconclusive. You said we were in "a zone of uncertainty." What does that mean?

SAM Look, man, do I ask you to make me coffee when you're not here? I'm just dropping off Shayna.

SHAYNA'S MANAGER Well, you sure got a winner there. We just love Shayna. And the costumers do too. She makes a mean latte.

SAM You know she plays the harp?

SHAYNA'S MANAGER Oh, yeah? . . . Like the blues harp? The harmonica?

SAM The harp, man. The big-ass mother-fuckin'-you-gotta-roll-it-down-the-street-on-it's-own-wheels harp.

SHAYNA'S MANAGER I didn't know that.

SAM You ever think of having a harp night here? On a weekend or something. Maybe entertain the folks.

SHAYNA'S MANAGER That's a great idea.

SAM So whattaya say?

SHAYNA'S MANAGER Unfortunately, corporate is real strict about the music we play here. I mean, for example, we can only play corporate-endorsed CDs. Like this one: *Norah Jones Sings Songs About Coffee.*

SAM Well, maybe Shayna could play some coffee songs on the harp. I mean, you gotta hear her. She shreds at the Radisson brunch out by the airport.

SHAYNA'S MANAGER Well, I'll run it by corporate and see what they say. . . .

SAM [*Watching her.*] Coral is far more red than her lips are red.

SHAYNA'S MANAGER Hmmm?

SAM There's a lot of steam from those machines. I think it's chapping her lips.

SHAYNA'S MANAGER I hadn't heard of that.

SAM You should look into that. And the harp thing.

> [SAM *crosses to* SHAYNA *and then walks her over to a table as the lights change.* SAM *and* SHAYNA *have pasta in front of them. The image on the television screen changes to an image of female hair. Again, the hair is moving and lively. But all we see is hair. The television screen is across from him.* SAM *raises his glass to her.*]

Mmmm. You are such a great cook. This pasta is delicious.
These mushrooms. How?

[*Beat.*]

You make great espresso drinks. You play awesome harp. And
this fungi. Ridiculous.

[SAM *stops eating for a moment. There is a hair in his pasta.*]

What? It's nothing. Just a hair. No. It happens. What do I care if
I have one of your hairs in my pasta. Like I've never had one of
your hairs in my mouth before.

[SAM *examines the hair.*]

If hairs be wires, black wires grow on her head.

[SAM *stares at the hair.*]

Actually, I'm full. I don't want a new bowl. Fine, if you'd feel
better. But it really doesn't matter to me. I'll just have some more
wine...lotsa wine.

[SAM *crosses with* SHAYNA *to the bed as the lights change. The image on
the screen changes to an image of a female breast.* SAM *sits on the corner of
a bed.* SHAYNA *is next to the bed.*]

I just want you to be satisfied. That's my whole thing. If you got
off, then I'm okay with that. I have been under a great deal of
stress at work lately. One doesn't think of being a meteorologist
as stressful, but it is. It's a lot of blame. And this particular storm
is very confusing to me. I actually called it a "zone of
uncertainty" on the air today. I mean, what the hell does that
mean? It means: I don't know. It means: I don't have a pithy
phrase for it like "Winter Wallop" or "Winter Whimper" or
some fucking thing. I come home from the meteorological
center and I drink myself into oblivion. And all night long my
weather radio is waking me up with advisories and warnings—
and I'm haunted by them because I couldn't see them coming.
Your body is still very exciting to me. I love your body.

[*Beat as* SAM *looks* SHAYNA *over.*]

I mean, granted, if snow be white, then your breasts are dun.
Dun. No, not "finished" dun. Dun. Dunnish. It's a color. A

brownish gray color. Bad? Why would that be bad? White is
sickly. White breasts are like so sixteenth century.

[SAM *walks with* SHAYNA *as the lights change. Winter. An image of*
SHAYNA's *breath is on the television screen. We see the lips from the earlier*
scene. We see her breath turn into steam as she breathes on a frigid winter
day. SAM *and* SHAYNA *are "walking" together. He pushes the television*
along next to him. Snow falls throughout the scene.]

It's a "Winter Wallop." Oh, it's a "wallop" all right. I said
"whimper" and it's a "wallop." I shoulda just stuck with "zone of
uncertainty" and let people look out their goddamn windows.
Shit. We're going to be late to Dave's wedding. Oh my God,
you're freezing. You're dressed for a "whimper." I let you down.
Again. It's you I think of when I'm forecasting and I let you
down. Here . . . Let me hold you.

[SAM *turns his back to the audience and reaches for her, but does not touch*
her. He steps back for a moment.]

In some perfumes is there more delight than in the breath that
from my mistress reeks.

[*Beat.*]

Have you started smoking again? No? Lotsa coffee at the store?
Interesting. Well, we better get you inside. You're freezing.
Here. Put my scarf around your mouth. It will keep you warm.

[*The lights change. Again the image is of lips. The steaming breath is gone. For the*
first time SHAYNA's *voice is heard. The voice comes through the television speakers.*
SAM *is staring at the weather map.*]

SHAYNA   I do charitable works. I'm on the board of the synagogue. And
yet . . . I want you to think I'm attractive. That's important to me.
I have my problems with you. You're exhausting. You're no good
with money. You drink way too much. You're vain.

SAM   I love to hear her speak—yet I well know that music hath a far
more pleasing sound.

SHAYNA   Are you listening to me?

SAM   Of course.

SHAYNA What did I just say?

SAM You do charitable works.

SHAYNA After that?

SAM Something about Carly Simon.

SHAYNA Carly Simon?

SAM "You're So Vain."

SHAYNA I said, *you're* so vain.

SAM That's what I said.

SHAYNA Please hurry up and get dressed.

SAM I don't understand why we have to devote a whole weekend to this wedding.

SHAYNA Because Hannah is my good friend. And I am playing harp for her as she walks down the aisle.

SAM I don't like that Dave, I really don't.

SHAYNA Well, he doesn't like you.

SAM He's blaming me for ruining his wedding weekend. The outta town guests are snowed out of town. I don't make the weather. I just overreact, interrupt prime-time television, and misreport it.

SHAYNA I can't believe what you did last night at the prenuptial dinner. When she asked if we want to sit with them . . .

SAM She scares me.

SHAYNA You had better be on your best behavior tonight. After all, that's going to be us in a few months.

SAM I give that wedding six months. Don't give a gift.

SHAYNA I wonder what people say about us.
[*Beat.*]
Will you dance with me?

SAM Slow dances.

SHAYNA Slow dances are what I like.

> [*The lights change. At a wedding. On the video screen we see images of female legs. The legs are seen dancing on a wooden dance floor at a wedding. An unseen Jewish wedding band plays the "Hora." We hear the voice from the television, but we see only the legs dancing on the wooden dance floor on the television set.*]
>
> Dance with me.

SAM Not the "Hora."

SHAYNA I'm going up.

SAM Go.

SHAYNA You're dancing the "Hora" at our wedding.

SAM Too Jewish.

SHAYNA You're Jewish.

SAM Shhh. It's the best-kept secret in the meteorological community.

[*The song ends. Beat.*]

SHAYNA You see, I spend the whole song arguing with you and it's over. If this is a slow one, you are dancing.

SAM I said, I would.

[*A wedding band cover version of Elvis's "Can't Help Falling in Love" is heard.*]

SHAYNA Well?

SAM Sure.

> [SAM *begins to dance* SHAYNA *around the stage. He and the television twirl and move to the music. As he does, the images on the screen begin to change rapidly among those that we have previously seen during the play. The music reaches a crescendo, as the images cycle through quicker and quicker. A beat.*]
>
> And yet, by heaven, I think my love as rare as any she belied with false compare.

[*The lights blackout. In the dark, we see the television images for a few more beats. The television blacks out.*]

• • •

A Song for Me, or Getting the Oscar

John Bolen

John Bolen

John Bolen is a novelist/playwright/actor living in Southern California. He has been published by Indigo Rising, Scars Publications, The Write Place at the Write Time, OC180news, Eunoia Review, and YouthPLAYS. Bolen is the producing artistic director of the New Voices Playwrights Theatre and Workshop. His plays have been produced throughout the U.S. His play for a young audience, *Aurelia's Magic* (under its original title *Dancing on a Grave*), was produced by the Vanguard Theatre and Garden Grove Playhouse. Readers Theater Television produced *Dancing on a Grave*; a radio play adaptation was produced by Shoestring Radio Theatre and was broadcast on 111 other stations across the United States through the National Public Radio system. Bolen has just completed a novel adapted from the story of *Aurelia's Magic*. As an actor, Bolen has worked extensively in theaters throughout Southern California, although he is probably best remembered for his roles in the cult films *Mega Shark vs. Giant Octopus* and *The Call of Cthulhu*. He has appeared in numerous feature films and TV shows. As a voice actor, Bolen has recorded forty audiobooks.

···production history···

The play was first produced August 21–September 5, 2010, as part of a production of one-acts titled EIGHTudes at the Empire Theatre in Santa Ana, California. Produced by the New Voices Playwrights Theatre, it was directed by Paul Millet and starred John T. Cogan and Gwendolyn Edwards.

characters

JAKE, male, late 20s to mid-30s, a singer/songwriter

EMMY, female, late 20s to mid-30s, a singer

setting

The den of a small house in Venice, California.

• • •

[*It is late night.* EMMY *is in her robe, playing a sweet, haunting melody at the piano.* JAKE *enters, dressed in his robe, and listens off to one side before he interrupts.*]

JAKE You disappeared.

EMMY I had to come up for air.

JAKE That was very intense.

EMMY It was nice.

JAKE I checked in on Sam. He slept through it all. I was afraid I was making too much noise.

EMMY When you're four, you can sleep through anything.

JAKE That's true. You remember that song?

EMMY Of course, I remember the song. How many women have a song written for them by the immortal Jake Legend? I remember, it was the first time we got together, and you played it for me and swept me off my feet. I felt like that again tonight. It's been a while, and it's nice to feel that way again. Thanks, Jake.

JAKE For what?

EMMY For going with me to marriage counseling.

JAKE   I'm not going *with you*. We go together, Emmy.

EMMY   I really think Madeleine has helped us a lot. Getting us to be honest with one another and really listening to each other, it's made a lot of difference. Every time you went out on tour, I was going nuts with jealousy, but I feel like that is all in the past. Do you feel the same?

JAKE   Yeah, I do.

EMMY   I think we've reached the point where we don't need to go to counseling anymore. What do you think?

JAKE   We just have to be honest. And listen too. Yes, I think we are to that point.

EMMY   Being really honest with one another is something we really hadn't been doing for a long time.

JAKE   That is so true.

EMMY   And I think we're really at that point where we can be open and truthful and not jump to anger but listen to each other.

JAKE   Yeah, well...

EMMY   Don't you agree?

JAKE   Yes, well...

EMMY   I love you, Jake.

JAKE   Yeah, well...uh...this is hard, but...but I should be honest... Well, I guess I should tell you.

EMMY   Tell me what?

JAKE   If we are going to be open and honest with one another, I should be truthful, even about stuff in the past, right?

EMMY   I think that is what Madeleine wants us to do.

JAKE   Then I guess I should come right out and tell you.

EMMY   Just say it, Jake. Tell me what?

JAKE   I didn't really write that song for you.

EMMY   [*Hurt.*] My song? You didn't write my song for me?

JAKE   Emmy, you need to understand. It was the first time we were together, and I really, really wanted to seduce you in the worst way. And I'm sitting down at the piano and playing the song, and you asked me what it was . . . so I lied. I said I had written it for you, and I thought it might help me get you in bed, and it did.

EMMY   My song is not my song.

JAKE   It is your song now. But if we are going to be honest with one another, I thought I should tell you the truth.

EMMY   [*Hurt and starting to anger.*] But that was my song. How could you not have told me? All of this time, and you never bothered to tell me?

JAKE   I know it was wrong. I'm sorry. But it's best that I'm finally honest now, isn't it? Isn't that what Madeleine wants us to do?

EMMY   [*Hurt and really angry.*] Yes, you're right. You're right. But that was my song, Jake. It was special, really special to have.

JAKE   Look at it this way. I seduced you and we got together and now we've been married five years. We have a beautiful four-year-old son. Something great came from all of it.

EMMY   You're right. I guess I should be honest myself and tell you.

JAKE   Tell me what?

EMMY   About Oscar.

JAKE   What about Oscar?

EMMY   I should be honest and tell you about him?

JAKE   What do you mean him?

EMMY   Oscar was my lover before I met you.

JAKE   [*Shocked.*] You're telling me that the pet name you use for my cock is the name of the guy you were screwing before you met me?

EMMY   Well, it all happened rather innocently.

JAKE   [*Getting angry.*] What could be innocent about calling my pecker by the name of your previous lover?

EMMY   Now don't get angry.

JAKE   [*Exasperated.*] Don't get angry?

EMMY   Don't you remember, we were pretty drunk when we got together that first time, and we were making love and when I first saw your erection I accidentally blurted out, "Oh my, Oscar, look at you!" You asked me what I was saying, and I just quickly covered by saying I was referring to your penis as Oscar. I think I mumbled something like it was a little golden statuette. Well, after that, it was you that kept referring to it as Oscar, saying things like "Oscar wants attention." And "Oscar's feeling lonely tonight." And "Emmy's going to get the Oscar tonight." I couldn't stop you, you just kept on going on about Oscar this and Oscar that.

JAKE   [*Really angry.*] And every time I was saying the name of your lover before me.

EMMY   Yes.

JAKE   That is like so wrong in so many ways.

EMMY   It just happened, Jake. But look at it this way. We spent that night together and every night after. And we've been married for five years and have a beautiful son together. It really worked out for the best, didn't it?

JAKE   Yeah, you're right. I mean, really, what's in a name. A rose by any other name would smell as sweet.

EMMY   Well, it doesn't really smell that sweet.

JAKE   You know what I'm saying.
          [*Pause.*]
          Jessica was her name.

EMMY   Whose name?

JAKE   The girl I wrote the song for.

EMMY   You not only didn't write the song for me, but you wrote it for another girlfriend?

JAKE   She wasn't a girlfriend.

EMMY   You wrote a song for a girl that wasn't even a girlfriend?

JAKE   She was just this groupie who would ride on the bus with us when we were on tour before I knew you, and she would go from one guy to the next, giving us head.

EMMY   You wrote the song for a whore.

JAKE   She wasn't a whore. We never paid her. She just wanted to blow any guy that had the slightest chance of becoming a famous rock and roller.

EMMY   Oh, great. The song I thought you wrote for me wasn't written for a whore, but a giant slut instead. That is so much better. I'm supposed to trust you whenever you are on tour and you're dragging along the world's greatest slut.

JAKE   That was back then, Emmy. It's not like that now.

EMMY   You don't have any sluts riding around with you now?

JAKE   Well, there are groupies, but I don't have anything to do with them.

EMMY   Like I'm supposed to believe that.

JAKE   Yes, you're supposed to believe that. But what about you? I'm supposed to believe you're living the life of a nun while I'm gone. I'm sure there are guys lined up for the chance to be with the great Emmy B. Sweet. You think I don't read the tabloids?

EMMY   You know the tabloids are full of shit.

JAKE   Do I?

EMMY   You know damn well they are.

JAKE   Well, maybe sometimes they hit upon some truth.

EMMY   Well, then I'd better be perfectly honest and tell you about Sam before the tabloids spill the beans.

JAKE Tell me about Sam? Oh no. Oh no! You sick, sick.... You're telling me that... that... Sam isn't my son.

EMMY Jake...

JAKE Do you know who the real father is?

EMMY Jake...

JAKE Or has there been such a long procession of guys you've screwed when I'm out of town that you don't even know for sure.

EMMY Jake, listen...

JAKE Well, isn't this great. You've ruined our lives you hateful, hateful...

EMMY Damnit, Jake, listen. You're Sam's father.

JAKE I am.

EMMY Of course you are. I was just going to say that I know you have this rule about refined sugar, but when you're out of town, I let Sam have candy. That's what I was going to say. Candy!

JAKE Candy?

EMMY Yes, candy. And you go off on this weird paranoia trip, thinking you're not Sam's father. Is that all you think of me?

JAKE Well, candy's not good either. So all this time when Sam kept asking if I was going out on tour, it wasn't because he was going to miss me. Instead he wanted me to leave so he could have candy. Something is really wrong.

EMMY I don't know, Jake. Maybe we're not meant to be together.

JAKE No, that's not it. Maybe we're just doing it wrong.

EMMY Doing what wrong?

JAKE What Madeleine asked us to do. If we were doing it right, we wouldn't feel this bad, right?

EMMY Right! Definitely right! We must be doing it wrong, that's all.

JAKE   I'll go call and leave a message for her. Maybe we could get an appointment to see her tomorrow.

EMMY   Yes! Yes! We're just doing it wrong. That's all.

[JAKE *exits to make a call.* EMMY *absentmindedly starts to play the song again, realizes what she is doing, and slams her arms down on the piano.*]

• • •

Scar Tissue

Gabriel Rivas Gomez

Gabriel Rivas Gomez

Gabriel Rivas Gomez received his MFA in dramatic writing from the University of Southern California in 2007, where he was mentored by Oliver Mayer, Velina Hasu Houston, and Luis Alfaro. His plays *Chasing Monsters* and *Scar Tissue* were produced at Company of Angels in downtown Los Angeles. His play *Circus Ugly* was showcased in 2007 as part of USC's Under Construction series and in 2006 as part of Cypress College's New Play Festival, and is set to be produced in the summer of 2012. He teaches writing and theater classes at the University of La Verne. When he is not busy writing or teaching, he can often be found playing with Play-Doh with his daughters, who, along with his wife, Elsie, are the source of his drive and strength.

···production history···

Scar Tissue received its world premiere at Company of Angels (Armando Molina, artistic director) in Los Angeles, California, on January 7, 2011, as part of *Fatigued* (Amelia Worfolk, Daniel Muñoz, Juanita Chase, and Joshua R. Lamont, producers). It was directed by Nathan Singh; the set and light design was by Ivan Acosta; the sound design was by Howard Ho; the costume design was by Laura Quiroz; the projection design was by Tamika Simpkins; fight choreography was done by Gwendolyn Druyor; and the stage managers were Jenefer Perez and Raquel Muniz. The cast was as follows:

> **CLAUDIA**, Monica Sanchez
>
> **ALMA**, Carolyn Zeller
>
> **LEE**, Chris Hampton

characters

> **CLAUDIA**, heart surgeon. 50s. Attractive. Cold.
>
> **LEE**, her patient. Mid-20s. A veteran. He is a ball of nervous energy. He always knows where any exits to any building are. Tall buildings make him uncomfortable. He avoids bright colors as they make him a target.
>
> **ALMA**, a ghost. Claudia's daughter. Early to mid-20s, but needs to be able to "be" everything, from an infant to a teen to a young adult…

the time/the place

The then and there, the here and now. USC Medical Center, Afghanistan, and inside the depressed mind of Dr. Claudia Torres.

author's note

This play should focus more on pace and theatricality than "reality" and fact. A projector is needed. Live drumming (perhaps a *cajón* or *tumba* drum) is preferable for many of the beats or effects in the play. If this is not available, drumming should be scrapped and sounds should be replaced with engineered, surreal sounds. Timing of projections should be altered to best fit the production and staging.

• • •

[*Rhythmic drumming in the darkness. The drumming produces projected images: a ragged doll, an opened envelope, a game of Operation, Clifford the Big Red Dog, an American flag, toy soldiers, a little girl. These images repeat a few times in different orders at different speeds. The drumming becomes a heartbeat. The images stop circling and settle on a heart.* DR. CLAUDIA TORRES *sits with her patient,* LEE GARDNER, *in her office.* DR. TORRES *uses a laser to point to different areas of the projected heart.* ALMA *is dressed like a research assistant. She sits across the room taking notes. She seems unnoticed.*]

CLAUDIA Mr. Gardner... this really—

[LEE *scans the room.*]

Are you listening?

LEE Call me Lee.

CLAUDIA Lee. This really seems like the best option to me, given your age and prior health problems.

LEE What about medication?

ALMA Carvedilol? Quinapril? Zoloft?

CLAUDIA You haven't responded to the medications prescribed, and if we don't act soon—

LEE My neighbor, he had this thing where they used a balloon, and he was fine in a couple days.

CLAUDIA Mr. Gardner, You're referring to a balloon angioplasty. With some patients, we can insert a catheter into the blocked artery (she demonstrates) and inflate a small balloon—here—in order to compress blockage and allow for better blood flow.

LEE Why not try that?

CLAUDIA It's like stepping on top of the trash instead of taking out the garbage. It's a quick fix. That procedure wouldn't help you long-term, and it wouldn't address the second problem.

ALMA [*Writing.*] Taking out the trash....

LEE What second problem?

CLAUDIA Atrial fibrillation.

ALMA Uh-oh.

LEE What's that?

CLAUDIA You have an irregular heartbeat. See, your brain sends electrical impulses to your heart in such a manner that your heart's rhythm is disrupted, further reducing blood flow.

LEE And that problem's not related to the other?

CLAUDIA They are two separate problems; however, I think we can address both in the same surgery.

LEE You're going to operate on my brain?

CLAUDIA No, Mr. Gardener—

LEE Lee.

CLAUDIA Lee. I operate on hearts. We'll start with the coronary artery bypass—here.
[*The heart on screen becomes a game of Operation.*]
We will take small portions of veins or arteries from other parts of your body and transplant them—here. While we have you opened up, I can also address the irregular heartbeat, via the Maze procedure.

ALMA Mazes are always tricky.

LEE I don't understand.

CLAUDIA Do you work on cars?

LEE Yeah.

CLAUDIA If my pressure plate went out, and you were fixing my car, what would you suggest?

ALMA Xanax?

LEE Well, I'd take a look at the clutch, because it's probably about to go too, and if I'm taking everything apart anyway—

CLAUDIA   Exactly my point.

ALMA   Splendid metaphor.

LEE   You said it was in my brain.

CLAUDIA   I'll make small incisions here and here, which will create scar tissue.

LEE   Why?

CLAUDIA   Scar tissue doesn't conduct electricity. It's like electrical tape. It prevents unwanted surges, thereby regulating your heartbeat.

ALMA   Electrical tape. Nice.

LEE   You mean to tell me that you plan to fix my heart by fucking it up?

ALMA   Such is life.

CLAUDIA   I don't know if I'd call it "fucking up"—

ALMA   You don't need those parts anyway.

LEE   What would you call it? Because where I'm from, if someone's cutting up your heart, it's called fucking it up. And it sounds like you want to fuck it up for the sake of fucking it up.

CLAUDIA   I'd call it your best chance. Sometimes your body needs to handle a little damage before it can properly fix itself.

ALMA   ACE!

LEE   So with one surgery—

CLAUDIA   With one surgery, we could fix two problems.

LEE   Is it risky?

CLAUDIA   Any procedure of this magnitude is risky, Mr. Gardner.

[LEE *bangs on the desk, then composes himself.*]

LEE   Dr. Torres, it's a small thing I'm asking for. I been overseas for two stints. And I'd be there again if I wasn't defective. Over there, I'm Gardner. Here I'm … call me by the name my mother gave me. I've *earned* it.

CLAUDIA   Lee. I think you should think about it. Talk to your family. I wouldn't consider your case urgent, but it should be taken care of sooner rather than later.

LEE   While I was in Afghanistan, I got my divorce papers. That's the closest to family I got.

CLAUDIA   Oh. I'm sorry.

LEE   It happens.

CLAUDIA   We can get you a second opinion.

LEE   This is my heart we are talking about.

CLAUDIA   I understand that.

LEE   What's the long-term prognosis?

CLAUDIA   ...Not great.

LEE   So you're saying I'm fucked. Funny, because when I brought up the balloon—

CLAUDIA   I SAID that this is a better option than the angioplasty and I stand by that. This is your best option. Period. But if you want a second opinion—

LEE   Wait...

[*He scans the room.*]

I'll do it.

CLAUDIA   Okay. If you're not sure—

LEE   I'm not one of those who comes home ready to die, understand?

CLAUDIA   I didn't say you were.

LEE   I want to *live*. And if I don't have a ton of time left, I need to get on with it. I looked you up. They say you're the best.

CLAUDIA   I am.

LEE   So if you say this is what I need...you're probably right.

CLAUDIA   Okay. We'll get you scheduled.

[LEE *shakes* CLAUDIA's *hand and gets up to leave.*]

Lee?

[LEE *turns to face her.*]

You'd really go back?

LEE   You're damn right I would.

[LEE *exits.* CLAUDIA *sits for a bit. The drumming returns. Softly at first.* ALMA *whistles a Marine Corps cadence.* CLAUDIA *grows more and more uncomfortable. A series of pictures of a little girl decorate the screen. None of these pictures feature* CLAUDIA. ALMA *stops and watches. The drum creates a "knock" at an imaginary door.* ALMA *clears her throat.*]

ALMA   January 17, 2010—

[CLAUDIA *opens a bottle of pills. She pops a few.* ALMA *sits and looks stoned.* ALMA *"transforms" into a one-year-old little girl. She props herself up, wobbles, and starts to walk, perhaps for the first time. She staggers to an invisible person as* CLAUDIA's *pager goes off.*]

I WALKING!

[CLAUDIA *turns off her beeper and watches* ALMA.]

CLAUDIA   Yes, you are!

[ALMA *ages. She is now ten. She is a contestant in a spelling bee.*]

ALMA   A-N-T-I-D-I-S-E-S-T-A-B-L-I-S-H-M-E-N-T-A-R-I-A-N-I-S-M. Antidisestablishmentarianism.

[ALMA *smiles. A bell rings. Applause. She produces a medal from her pocket and puts it around her neck. She looks over at* CLAUDIA. CLAUDIA's *pager goes off.*]

I won. I won. I WON!

CLAUDIA   I knew you would.

ALMA   Let's celebrate.

CLAUDIA   I've got surgery.

ALMA   You've always got surgery.

[ALMA *ages. She is now thirteen.*]

Oh my God. Ohmygod ohmygod ohmygodohmygodohmygod—

[CLAUDIA's *pager goes off again.*]

CLAUDIA I'm working!

ALMA I'm bleeding.

CLAUDIA Did you disinfect it? There are alcohol swabs in the cabinet. Peroxide might be better. Get some cotton—

ALMA No. I'm *bleeding*.

[*She turns to reveal that she has started her period.*]

CLAUDIA Oh. Check under the sink.

[ALMA *pulls a tampon from her pocket.*]

ALMA But how…

CLAUDIA Alma, I'm working. This is not an emergency.

ALMA You're… right. I guess… it's… not.

> [CLAUDIA *and* ALMA *both sit in a trance.* ALMA *eventually moves to* CLAUDIA. ALMA *studies* CLAUDIA, *waives her hand in front of* CLAUDIA's *face, and prods her.* CLAUDIA *is asleep with her eyes open.*]
>
> You're working?… You're working…. You're *working*?!

[CLAUDIA *snaps out of her trance as* ALMA *(an assistant again) escorts* LEE *onstage in a hospital gown. He is sheepish.* CLAUDIA *approaches* LEE, *rarely taking her eyes off her clipboard.*]

CLAUDIA Okay, Mr.—

LEE Lee.

CLAUDIA Sorry. Lee. We're going to run a heart cath. I'm assuming the results will support what we found in the preliminary tests, but we need to be sure.

[ALMA *produces a long, pointed tube.* LEE *looks at her strangely and offers her his arm.*]

ALMA Huh-uh.

> [LEE *opens his mouth.*]
>
> Nope.

[CLAUDIA *puts on rubber gloves.*]

CLAUDIA   We go in through the groin, Lee.

[LEE *grabs his balls.*]

LEE   You're shitting me.

CLAUDIA   What's the matter, soldier? You'd go back to war but you're afraid of a little tube?

LEE   You're a bitch.

CLAUDIA   We will sedate you.

[ALMA *gets LEE to a gurney and injects him. She straps him down as* CLAUDIA *lubes the catheter up and runs it up his gown.*]

LEE   What the fuck?

CLAUDIA   Lee, relax. I've seen it before.

LEE   You said—

CLAUDIA   Sedated, Lee. But I need you awake. You won't feel anything.

[ALMA *checks* LEE's *pupils.* CLAUDIA *straps on an X-ray vest.* LEE *can only stare at it.*]

I'm going to inject you with what you might call a series of markers, which will show up on an X-ray. That way we can monitor blood flow and get a firm grasp of the sorts of blockages we're dealing with.

ALMA   This will take a while. Try to relax.

[LEE *is sweating.*]

LEE   I'm ... this is fucked.

CLAUDIA   Lee, I can't cut blind. Be brave.

ALMA   Ready?

[ALMA *slides* LEE *into the "machine." As she does, we see his face on the screen.*]

CLAUDIA   You are going to hear a clicking sound. It's normal.

ALMA Here we go.

> [ALMA *turns the machine on. A drum beat becomes the "clicking" of the machine.*]

> Hold still, Lee.

CLAUDIA Lee, I need you to slow your breathing a bit.

[*LEE closes his eyes. On the screen we get flashes of pictures in his mind: a Hummer, a desert sunset, a child's drawing, a soldier's boots.*]

LEE I think there's something wrong with the machine.

CLAUDIA Try not to talk.

[*On the screen we are back to* LEE's *face. He's sweating.*]

ALMA Lee, I can't get a read unless you hold still.

> [*To* CLAUDIA.]

> Do something!

[CLAUDIA *eyes* ALMA, *then reluctantly takes* LEE's *hand.*]

CLAUDIA Lee, I want you to take a deep breath and hold it.

> [*He does. She snaps a three count.*]

> One. Two. Three. Exhale.

> [*He does.*]

> Again.

> [*He does. She snaps again.*]

> One. Two. Three. Let it out.

[LEE *calms.* CLAUDIA *adjusts his catheter. As she does, we see different pictures of hearts on the screen. These should vary from medical pictures to valentines to children's drawings. They should be interspersed with shots of* LEE's *face and pictures of soldiers, dolls, and sunsets. The drumming settles into the beating of a heart.* ALMA *becomes a student who reads a comic book.* CLAUDIA *watches the screen but is also very aware of* ALMA. CLAUDIA's *pager goes off.*]

ALMA The heart doesn't feel pain. At least, not directly. Its fibers are wired in such a manner so that pain is routed differently. Right?

CLAUDIA It's not so simple.

[ALMA *seems impressed that she's got a piece of* CLAUDIA's *attention.*]

ALMA   When something's wrong with your heart, it goes a little haywire and it becomes electrically unstable. So you feel pain in other places: fingers, back...jaw....Sometimes, there's no pain at all. If the nerve fibers never cross, people might not have a clue until it's too late.

CLAUDIA   Hold still, Lee. Don't be so reductive. That's usually limited to diabetics or elderly. It's not as simple as—

ALMA   Ironically, when your heart is in pain, it's the rest of your body that feels it. Right?

CLAUDIA   There it is.

[ALMA *approaches* CLAUDIA.]

ALMA   Sometimes a person with 90 percent blockage is better off than someone with 50 percent. Your body learns to expect it and finds new routes. Like if you're living in Los Angeles, and every day the 405's a parking lot. And you know it's a mess, so you plan new routes. You know all the side streets, and you're always on time. But if you're new to the area and, say, there's an accident. You're fucked.

[*The image on the screen stops on a little girl.* CLAUDIA *looks at* ALMA.]
If you work at it enough, if you plan, you might forget the 405 exists at all.

[*As if on cue,* CLAUDIA *pops a couple pills.* ALMA *wilts.*]
Mommy...why do you work so hard to forget me?

[CLAUDIA *just stares at* ALMA. LEE *fights his constraints.* CLAUDIA's *attention is torn between* LEE *and* ALMA. *The screen is racing with dolls, drawings, Hummers, boots, vests.*]

CLAUDIA   It's not you I'm trying to forget.

[ALMA *becomes the assistant.*]

ALMA   Dr. Torres?!

CLAUDIA   I saw what I needed to see.

[*A few days later. LEE dresses himself in a hospital room. He has an open textbook near him. CLAUDIA walks in on him. ALMA follows as her assistant.*]

Physical therapy?

LEE I'm going to work with disabled vets.

CLAUDIA Medicine-lite. Good for you.

LEE Excuse me?

CLAUDIA The tests confirmed what I had thought. We can schedule the surgery in a few weeks. Give your kidneys a chance to rest. In fact, I think you are an ideal candidate for the da Vinci.

LEE I'm lost.

CLAUDIA A machine. We can reduce your recovery time, so you can get to your studies.

LEE I don't think it would kill you to start with, "Hey, Lee. How you feeling?" or "I know running a tube up *through* your groin isn't comfortable. Can I get you anything?"

CLAUDIA You think I should kiss it and make it better?

LEE Like prostitution-lite?

ALMA Damn . . . his was funnier than yours.

LEE I heard about your bedside manner.

CLAUDIA You didn't come to me for bedside manner. I cut. That's what I do. You want stickers and a pat on the head, pediatrics is on the fourth floor. I have a job to do.

LEE That doesn't mean you have to be an asshole.

CLAUDIA Yes. It does. You of all people should understand, soldier.

LEE You can kiss my ass, Claudia.

CLAUDIA It's Dr. Torres. I didn't go through medical school—

LEE You wouldn't have gone to school at *all* if it wasn't for people like me. I'm Lee. You're Claudia. Get over yourself.

[*Before* CLAUDIA *can respond,* ALMA *rhythmically snaps her fingers.*]

CLAUDIA You're right, Lee. I shouldn't... you know. It's not professional. I'm trying to understand some things.

LEE Understand what?

ALMA What's it like to fire a gun? Do you know you're a puppet of the government? Do you support the war on terror? Did you *kill* anybody?

CLAUDIA Why would you go back?

LEE You *can't* understand that.

CLAUDIA You think I'm stupid?

LEE No. I think you've got a nice car to park in a nice house where you eat nice food. You've never needed anybody else unless they are washing your nice car or cleaning your nice house.... I think you don't notice that half the nurses on this damn floor wear bright-ass colors that make them targets. And they *insist* on opening the shades no matter how many times I close them. You don't see that the parking garage would be an excellent fucking place for a sniper. You don't notice these things because you've never *had* to notice these things. Wars are started by people like you, but they are fought by people like me.

CLAUDIA So that's it? Money?

LEE No. Like I said, you wouldn't understand. Your robot surgery. You want to do it because it's best for me, or best for you?

CLAUDIA Both.

LEE At least you're honest.

CLAUDIA As your doctor, I'm saying it's what's best for you. As head of this department, I'm saying it's what's best for the hospital.

[LEE *splits.* ALMA *shakes her head in disbelief.*]

ALMA You don't listen.

CLAUDIA Will you stop?

[ALMA *pretends to read a letter.* CLAUDIA *faces her and doesn't see* LEE *come back for his jacket.*]

ALMA We regret to inform you—

CLAUDIA ENOUGH! I can't do this right now.

[*She pops a couple pills.*]

ALMA Then when *can* you do this? You don't see—

CLAUDIA I see you *everywhere*, Alma.

ALMA You went *years* without seeing me.

> [ALMA *points to* LEE. *He and* CLAUDIA *just look at each other for a moment before he grabs his jacket and leaves. On the screen, a picture of Leonardo da Vinci.* CLAUDIA *checks her watch.*]
>
> You've got work.
>
> [CLAUDIA *gathers herself and moves downstage for her presentation.*]
>
> Unbelievable.

[ALMA *preps* CLAUDIA. *She takes off* CLAUDIA's *coat, places goggles on her face, and places handles in her hands.* ALMA *then moves behind* CLAUDIA. ALMA *becomes an extra pair of robotic hands. She hums.*]

CLAUDIA The da Vinci robot can allow us to perform complicated procedures.

[*As she "operates,"* ALMA *begins to march in place.* ALMA *goes into cadence at different times in* CLAUDIA's *speech. She should repeat each line (like call and response) as needed.*]

CLAUDIA As you can see, this procedure is dramatically less invasive than CABG, and as a result requires far less recovery time. The da Vinci surgical system allows a surgeon to get a closer view of the heart and mimics the surgeon's movements. In addition, it compensates for minor, involuntary motions, which would otherwise

ALMA I wanna be an airborne ranger.
Saving lives of perfect strangers.
Keep me out of the drop zone.
I just wanna go back home . . .

[ALMA *demonstrates.*]

make the procedure impractical. In addition to controlling the arms, the surgeon can also control the scope of his or her view. "Zoom."

[ALMA *moves beside* CLAUDIA.]

The most difficult part of the procedure is the attachment of the blood vessel to the aorta. While the standard procedure allows the surgeon to use her hands to sew the tissue together, the da Vinci model uses a different method.

[*Louder, faster*]

My girl's a pretty girl.
She's a LA city girl.
I'd buy her anything.
To keep her in style.

[*She demonstrates.*]

It punctures a small hole, here, and anchors the vessel similar to how a small rivet would work.

[ALMA *steps back behind* CLAUDIA, *then to her other side.*]

You'll notice the heart is still beating. This procedure, in most cases, is performed off pump, which is ultimately safer for the patient. What's more, the surgeon doesn't even need to be in the same room as the surgery. He can perform the procedure from his office with other attendees in the OR.

[*Frantic.*]

She's got black wavy hair.
Just like a grizzly bear.
I'd give most anything.
To watch her smile.

[ALMA *moves back behind* CLAUDIA.]

This is the future, ladies and gentlemen.

This is the future, ladies and gentlemen.

CLAUDIA   In ten years, standard coronary bypass will be obsolete.

[CLAUDIA *sets her instruments down.* ALMA *moves to the crowd and poses as different doctors with questions. She moves about the crowd with each question.*]

ALMA   Dr. Torres, the cost for such a machine, as you've listed in your notes, is dramatic. In your opinion, is it worth it?

CLAUDIA   While the da Vinci machine is not cheap, we can expect to recover costs in twelve to fifteen months. At which point, it actually becomes a very cost-effective procedure.

ALMA   Doctor, you mention a reduced recovery time for patients based on smaller incisions. Are there any other benefits to the patients with this procedure?

CLAUDIA   The recovery time with this procedure is cut by 25 percent. What's more, since it is performed on a beating heart, the patient does not need to rely on a heart and lung bypass machine. As you know, the use of these machines has been called into question as some studies have shown a correlation between them and long-term depression.

ALMA   Dr. Torres, while the da Vinci machine seems to enhance precision and recovery time, it also creates an even greater distance between doctor and patient. You mentioned being able to perform the procedure from your office. Do you really think it is wise for a doctor to be that far from his patient when something could so easily go awry? It seems to make the patient a video game instead of a person.

CLAUDIA   We are in a result-oriented profession, doctor. If the patient lives, we have succeeded. If not, we've failed. So far, nineteen surgeries have been performed with the da Vinci machine. Zero have died. In fact, all of them have recovered at an extraordinary rate. We are not motivational speakers or therapists. We are not kindergarten teachers or priests. We are not paid to be people's friends. We are paid to do what most other people can't do: save lives. And this robot does that incredibly efficiently. I've selected the twentieth Da Vinci patient. You are welcome to observe. Once you do, I think you will agree that this machine should be a fixture at USC medical.

[ALMA *marches in place.*]

ALMA   You never even told them.

CLAUDIA   This meeting is finished.

> [CLAUDIA's *pager goes off.* ALMA, *now a teen, bursts into her office.* ALMA *is a mess.*]
>
> What's wrong?

ALMA   I used to sing him to sleep, you know that?

CLAUDIA   Who? Wha—

ALMA   He had trouble sleeping and I'd sing him songs till he fell asleep, you know? Even if it was over the phone.

CLAUDIA   It damn well *better* be over the phone—

ALMA   He's going to Florida. And he says he will meet so many new "people." And that it "isn't fair to me."

> [*She starts to hyperventilate.*]
>
> He just wants to set himself up to get as much ass as he can get. It's not about what's fair—he said he *loved* me!

[CLAUDIA *slaps her on the cheek.*]

CLAUDIA   ALMA!

ALMA   What? Are you seriously—

CLAUDIA   Take a breath and hold it.

> [*She does.* CLAUDIA *snaps her fingers with each count.*]
>
> One. Two. Three. Exhale. Again. . . . One. Two. Three. Exhale— give it three seconds, then you let it go. Let whatshisname go to Florida. You stay here and focus.

ALMA   You don't even know his name? He broke my heart.

[CLAUDIA *wipes* ALMA's *face and cleans her up.*]

CLAUDIA   Here's what I understand. People break your heart because you let them. Because you think you need them around to be complete. So then you start to give up pieces of yourself to keep them around. It's bullshit. Sometimes you need to know that all you've got is *you*. And if you know that, you don't *let* anybody break you. Don't *let* people see you cry. Don't be *that* woman. A weepy woman will never make it in a man's world.

[ALMA *just looks at* CLAUDIA *like a kid who knows she's been ripped off.*]

Be brave, Alma. Be brave.

[ALMA *leaves.* CLAUDIA's *pager goes off again.* ALMA *appears with a graduation cap. She looks around the crowd for* CLAUDIA. CLAUDIA *watches from her desk.*]

I'm so proud of you, baby.

ALMA   You're working. . . .

CLAUDIA   I do this for you. Do you know the opportunity…

ALMA   Heidi Fleiss's dad is a doctor. Did you know that?

CLAUDIA   You're a smart ass.

ALMA   I've made a decision. I'm a woman who is going to make it in a man's world.

[CLAUDIA *is beaming.*]

I joined the army.

[ALMA *reveals her fatigues. (Note:* ALMA *should be in her fatigues for the rest of the play).* CLAUDIA *stands stupefied.* ALMA *splits.* LEE *walks into* CLAUDIA's *office.*]

LEE   Excuse me?

CLAUDIA   What are you doing here?

LEE   My therapist says a lot of soldiers lash out at people. Not because they deserve it, but because we have trouble…verbalizing. So the other day, even though you were being an asshole, I shouldn't've said it.

CLAUDIA   …I don't know if that is what your therapist meant. Is that an apology?

LEE   I used to be afraid to go home too.

CLAUDIA   I'm not af—

LEE   Fine. Let's not get in another pissing contest. I know what it's like. We'll leave it at that.

[*He looks around the room as if he sees something/someone we don't.*]

CLAUDIA You really notice all those details daily?

LEE You have no idea.

CLAUDIA What's it like?

LEE You know when you were little and you wound a jack-in-the-box and you cringed when you thought he was about to pop out? It's like that. Always.

[ALMA *appears with blood on her hands.* CLAUDIA *just watches her.*]

Hello? Torres? Are you listening to me? Look, I'll give you some time.

[*He gets up to leave.*]

CLAUDIA When I was a resident, I had a man wake up on the operating table. He *woke up.* His chest is open, he's got catheters running in from different directions. . . . He's trying to scream, but there's a tube down his throat.

[ALMA *screams silently.*]

And I'm frozen. Terrified. Pissing myself. Literally. Because I'm feeling so bad for this sonofabitch. I should have been *doing* something, but I was too busy *feeling bad.*

LEE What happened?

CLAUDIA They medicated him somewhere into next week so he wouldn't remember. But I couldn't forget.

LEE You shouldn't be telling this to someone you are going to cut open.

CLAUDIA Emotion gets in the way of the job I do. *Feelings* are mistakes. *Mistakes* can be fatal.

[LEE *nods in understanding.*]

LEE Who were you talking to?

CLAUDIA I wasn't talking to anybody.

LEE She looks like you.

CLAUDIA   You can *see* her?

LEE   She's why you want to know why I'd go back?

CLAUDIA   Maybe.

[ALMA *looks over at* LEE. *He sees her.*]

ALMA   Tell her.

LEE   No.

ALMA   Please.

LEE   No.

[ALMA *leans in to tell* LEE *a secret.*]

ALMA   Help.

[*She salutes him. He waits for a while before reluctantly returning her salute.* ALMA *grabs a helmet and an imaginary gun.*]

LEE   Whenever we'd caravan through villages in Afghanistan, we'd get crowds. Little kids especially. Why the hell parents would let their kids near... I don't know. But we were a show. And everything is a mess, understand? You've never seen a mess like this. And *everything* is a threat. A speeding car... threat. Open window... threat. An abandoned car on the side of the road: big fucking threat. But one day we get word from our CO That—

ALMA   The haji have started putting IEDs in dolls.

CLAUDIA   Dolls?

LEE   Dolls!

[*The screen transitions to show a child's drawing: a stick-figure family.*]

CLAUDIA   Oh God.

LEE   What kind of fucked-up shit is that? And he's cold when he says—

ALMA   Eliminate. Threats.

LEE   And I'm not like him. I lay awake at night and my stomach hurts. My back hurts. Because I'm afraid I might have to obey an order I have no business obeying.

ALMA   There's no such thing as a warning shot around here. Either there is a reason to shoot, or there isn't. Warning shots only serve to warn haji of your position.

LEE   But my *brothers*, they got children too. I was there when one of them got baptized. And they've got dolls. . . . And no way can I let them see their daddy in a box.

CLAUDIA   Did you—

LEE   So we roll up, and sure enough here come the kids. And we start waving our arms for them to get the hell away—

[LEE *and* ALMA *wave their arms in unison. The picture on the screen transitions to a little girl.*]

—but the haji, when you wave your arms, they think it's an invitation to come closer. And right about then I see it. A girl. Her doll. And a mangy-ass dog that won't shut up.

[*Clifford the Big Red Dog lights up the screen.* ALMA *growls.*]

You know how they get? When they got their tail tucked between their legs trying to look brave?

[*The drumming intensifies as the pictures on the screen move from a doll to a drawing to toy soldiers to a dog.*]

He won't shut up. He won't—SHUT UP!

[ALMA *stops. She raises her rifle.*]

I can't tell you if it was an accident. I can't tell if it matters. . . . I squeeze.

[*The drum bangs as* ALMA *fires. The screen goes blank.*]

I shot his bottom jaw clean off.

[ALMA *holds her jaw.*]

CLAUDIA   You did what?

LEE   He makes these noises.

[ALMA *lets out a high-pitched, low-volume squeal.*]

The girl drops the doll. And it's just a fucking doll. And all I can see is this girl trying to put pieces of his mouth back on. And I freeze.

[ALMA *freezes.*]

My CO pulls a pistol and puts the dog out of his misery.

[ALMA *pulls an imaginary pistol and fires quietly.*]

I told you, he's a bigger man than me. And the girl's come undone. He takes off his watch and gives it to her.

CLAUDIA Why?

LEE Because what the hell else are you gonna do? And that's that. We move on.

[ALMA *turns and marches away.*]

CLAUDIA That's why you want to go *back*?

LEE I'm the son of an alcoholic.

CLAUDIA What does that have to do with anything?

LEE I always made friends with other sons of alcoholics. Because I'd have to pick him up from bars when I was thirteen. And they knew what that was like. Back there . . . they understand what it's like. Problem is, they're there, and I'm here. . . .

CLAUDIA Defective.

LEE Yep. Out here, people aren't accountable. They don't understand the—

CLAUDIA Cost of living. To do your job—

LEE To heal—

CLAUDIA Or to hurt.

LEE Means you have to be a little—

CLAUDIA Less human. People don't get it.

LEE We're not that different, me and you.

CLAUDIA I *save* lives!

LEE What the *hell* do you think I was doing?!

CLAUDIA You're . . . right.

LEE   You think *you've* got ghosts?

[LEE *motions around the room.*]

CLAUDIA   Lee, crazy people see ghosts.

LEE   The pills don't help.

CLAUDIA   Excuse me?

LEE   Or the booze. Or the drugs.... When I got back, I had a *lot* of time on my hands and a fair amount of money. It didn't work. If they have something to say to you, they're gonna say it. And they're gonna say it and say it and say it.

CLAUDIA   So now you're here to fix me?

LEE   You aren't crazy, Claudia.

CLAUDIA   Of course I'm not.

LEE   And you are going to have to forgive yourself.

CLAUDIA   For what?

LEE   For her.

CLAUDIA   How *dare* you.

LEE   We're like alcoholics' kids, me and you.

[*She backs him down.*]

CLAUDIA   *We* are not anything.

LEE   Weird thing is, I *get* you.

[*She starts to shove him.*]

CLAUDIA   You don't get shit.

LEE   You pushed her away, didn't you. That's why you're scared to go home?

[*She tries to slap him. He catches her wrist. She tries with the other hand. He catches that one too. He pulls her arms to her sides. She fights. They wrestle.*]

CLAUDIA   Let go of me. Let *go* of me!

[CLAUDIA *is frantic. She fights.* LEE *restrains her.* ALMA *returns to the stage.* ALMA *plops down to the floor and opens a letter. Some photos fall out.*]

ALMA   Alma, I hope this finds you.

> [*The photos from the box appear on the screen. Most are of a stoic* CLAUDIA.]

I watch the news and hunt the Internet to find stories about your unit and have found nothing. I guess that's a good thing.

> [CLAUDIA *fights. She is ferocious. Feral.* LEE *holds her strongly. Gently. He turns her to watch* ALMA.]

Not much on this end to update. Just me. We had a Marfan patient the other day. Tall, lanky kid. He saw his doctor complaining of joint pain. Luckily his doctor was bright. I cut. We prevented aortic rupture. He's now pretty upset that he won't be playing football anymore, but he's alive. Anyway, I'm sure I'm boring you. Like I said, it's just me.

> [*Finally,* CLAUDIA *submits. The struggle transforms into a hug. One of the photos shows* CLAUDIA *in the background smiling.*]

They had a little birthday party for me at the hospital and that was okay, I guess. They took pictures, so I sent them to you.

CLAUDIA   That's not what I said.

> [*The screen zooms on* CLAUDIA.]

That's not what I . . . meant.

ALMA   Be brave. Come home! Mommy.

[*The screen zooms again, showing only* CLAUDIA'*s smile.* ALMA *smiles and kisses the picture.* LEE *holds* CLAUDIA *for a moment.*]

LEE   I should get a second opinion.

CLAUDIA   Because I'm—

LEE   You're *not* crazy . . . but you're not right.

[CLAUDIA *looks like she might challenge him, but thinks better of it.*]

CLAUDIA   That's logical.

[*They sit quietly. Eventually* CLAUDIA *pulls out her pills.*]

LEE   They are not going to help.

CLAUDIA   I'm the doctor, remember?

LEE   What happened to her, if you don't mind me asking?

CLAUDIA   I mind you asking.

ALMA   You didn't tell anybody. You didn't even take off work.

LEE   You didn't?

CLAUDIA   This is *none* of his business.

ALMA   You want *me* to tell him?

CLAUDIA   Alma! Some things are private.

ALMA   And some things aren't. Be. Brave.

CLAUDIA   Parents of soldiers know they're fucked when three strangers knock on their door. One to deliver the news.

ALMA   Two. In case you faint.

LEE   Three. In the car. In case you get violent.

CLAUDIA   They have it down to a science.

[CLAUDIA *hands* LEE *a letter. He opens it and reads silently.* ALMA *opens an identical letter. She opens it and reads aloud.*]

ALMA   January 17, 2010. We regret to inform you that late last night Sergeant Alma Torres was involved in an ambush attack just outside of Kandahar. She was fatally wounded. The details of this conflict are sensitive and cannot be given at this point. Please know that her actions were heroic. Her ultimate sacrifice is acknowledged by your government, and it is with our deepest sympathies that we send you this notification of her death. You will be put in contact with a grieving coordinator who will help you with funeral arrangements and grief counseling. Please contact him with further questions.

[LEE *folds the letter and gives it back to* CLAUDIA.]

CLAUDIA   [*To* ALMA.] You happy now?

[CLAUDIA *is about to take a few pills. She considers, then puts them back.*]
I can refer you to Dr. Kwong. He's good. Thorough. You'll be in good hands.

[LEE *grimaces and grabs his jaw.* CLAUDIA *has turned away from him and can't see him.*]

Not *as* good, of course, but more than competent. He hasn't been trained on the da Vinci, so—

ALMA Mommy—

CLAUDIA Also . . . I hope you will use some . . . discretion.

[LEE *has fallen to the ground.*]

ALMA CLAUDIA!

[CLAUDIA *sees* LEE *on the ground.*]

CLAUDIA Goddamnit.

[ALMA *helps* LEE *offstage, then pushes him onstage prepped for surgery as* CLAUDIA *"scrubs in." The sounds of an operating room (heart monitor, etc.).* CLAUDIA *walks over to him, ready to operate. Drumming returns as a heartbeat.*]

Lee, you went into arrest. We almost lost you. We revived you, but we need to do the surgery now, or we risk significant damage.

ALMA Mr. Gardner, I need you to count backwards from ten.

LEE Ten. Nine. Eight. Sev . . .

[*He's out. The drumming heartbeat is replaced with the beeping of a heart monitor.*]

CLAUDIA Scalpel.

ALMA Scalpel.

[ALMA *and* CLAUDIA *stand on opposite sides of the gurney. They spin in circles. The spinning accelerates with each revolution.*]

I arrived in a C-130. Combat landing. Meaning we got up high and corkscrewed to the ground to avoid AAM's. I felt sick when we landed and the world was orange. Someone next to me said, "Welcome to Mars."

CLAUDIA   I'm working, Alma.

ALMA   The sand gets in your teeth. The water stinks. And you can't open your eyes in the shower.... Mars.... And I was thinking, as a medic, I'd never see battle. But that's the way it is on Mars. One minute, you are "safe" and the next you are in the middle of shit.

[*An explosion.* ALMA *falls to the floor beneath the gurney.*]

CLAUDIA   GODDAMNIT!

[CLAUDIA *assesses the damage and tries to fix the bleed.* ALMA *uses the gurney like a bunker.*]

ALMA   Oh my God. Ohmygod ohmygod ohmygodohmygodohmygod —I'm *bleeding.*

CLAUDIA   Alma, please...

[CLAUDIA *manages to stay focused on* LEE *even with* ALMA *at her feet. The screen shifts to show toy soldiers.* ALMA *talks on her radio.*]

ALMA   Raptor Six, this is Three-Two. Requesting backup. Over. *Raptor Six*, this is *Three-Two.* Requesting backup. Over.

[ALMA *looks up at* CLAUDIA. CLAUDIA *finally plays along.*]

CLAUDIA   *Three-Two*, what is your situation?

ALMA   Caravan lead has been blown up. Then the rear. Haji are coming out of the street like roaches.

CLAUDIA   What is your grid?
[*Another explosion.* LEE *flat-lines.*]
I need the paddles.

ALMA   Send help!

[CLAUDIA *mimes defibrillation paddles.*]

CLAUDIA   CLEAR.
[LEE*'s body bounces. So does* ALMA*'s. Still no pulse.*]
CLEAR.

[LEE *and* ALMA *bounce again. Nothing.* CLAUDIA *tosses the "paddles" aside and reaches in to pump* LEE's *heart with her hands.*]

Lee, please . . .

ALMA   There's someone out there. He's wounded worse than me. . . . Mommy, I can help.

CLAUDIA   Take care of yourself.

ALMA   Breathe, Alma. . . . Breathe.

[ALMA *takes a deep breath and snaps three times.*]

One. Two. Three.

CLAUDIA   Beat, you bastard. Alma, stay here.

ALMA   Again.

[*She takes a deep breath and snaps three times. She seems calm.*]

Be brave.

CLAUDIA   Goddamnit, do *not* be brave. Be a fucking coward and—

[*But it's too late.* ALMA *has scampered off.*]

Come home to me.

[*The drum bangs.* ALMA *falls to the floor.*]

COME HOME TO ME!

[CLAUDIA *re-gathers herself and pumps* LEE's *heart.*]

Beat, you motherfucker. BEAT.

[ALMA *rolls over.*]

ALMA   You should call it.

CLAUDIA   I'm not done fighting.

[ALMA *understands and moves to the side.*]

ALMA   Fight. Five minutes.

[*Waiting.*]

Ten minutes.

[*Waiting.*]

Fifteen.

[*Waiting.*]

Twenty-two minutes before you hit the ground.

[*Exhausted,* CLAUDIA *stops pumping the heart and slumps.*]

CLAUDIA Time of death...

[*She can't finish.*]

Did you know?

[ALMA *shrugs.*]

You bitch.

ALMA I did this for you. Sometimes you need to handle a little damage before you can properly fix yourself.

[CLAUDIA *pulls her pills out of her pocket.*]

Be brave, Mommy.

CLAUDIA It hurts. So. Bad.

ALMA Be brave.

[CLAUDIA *drops the pills.*]

Be. Brave.

[ALMA *watches* CLAUDIA, *though* CLAUDIA *can no longer see her.* CLAUDIA *gasps like a patient waking up in the middle of surgery. The drums pick up with a heartbeat. On the screen we see pictures of toy soldiers, boots, a game of Operation, a doll, a sunset, an envelope. Clifford the Big Red Dog, a drawing, and a girl. A girl. A girl.* CLAUDIA *takes a deep breath and snaps her fingers three times. With each snap, we zoom on the face of the girl.* CLAUDIA *exhales as lights begin to fall, and she starts to cry. Softly at first. But the tears build. Lights go out as her cries turn to sobs.*]

• • •

Snowbound
a play in one act

Brent Englar

Brent Englar

Brent Englar is an aspiring playwright from Baltimore, Maryland, where he works as an editor for an educational content provider. Prior to that, he taught high school English for several years; he has also lived in New York City and Los Angeles. His plays have been produced throughout Maryland, including Baltimore, as well as New York, Chicago, and Austin. A member of the Dramatists Guild, he is also the director of the Mobtown Playwrights Group, an offshoot of Baltimore's Mobtown Players; its season consists of public readings of three new plays by local writers, culminating in a full production of one of the selected plays.

···production history···

Snowbound was given a public reading by the Baltimore Playwrights Festival at the Fells Point Corner Theatre in December 2010. Director: Miriam Bazensky; Cast: Hillary Mazer as SHERRI; Rodney Bonds as ANDY; David Kellam as CLIFF. *Snowbound* was also given a reading in April 2011 as part of Dezart Performs's Third Annual Play Reading Series. And it was produced by the Old Opera House Theatre Company (Charles Town, West Virginia) in June 2011 as part of the 2011 New Voice Play Festival. Director: Shannon Potter; Cast: Lorraine Bouchard as SHERRI; Dan Rice as ANDY; Alecia Schulz as CLAIRE (i.e., CLIFF: the role is gender neutral).

characters

SHERRI BLOUNT, mid-50s

CLIFF, late 20s, her boarder (CLIFF may be played by a woman by changing the character's name to CHRIS [CHRISTINE when SHERRI says CLIFFORD]. Feel free to leave SHERRI's line, "Lord, if I had a dollar for every new girl I've seen at breakfast," as is.)

ANDY BOWDEN, 50

time

The present; late January. During a blizzard.

place

Baltimore. A row house owned by SHERRI BLOUNT. The power has been out since dawn. A fire burns in the fireplace. Windows in the stage-right wall flank the front door and vestibule and reveal a narrow street blanketed with snow. Through the vestibule—the sides of which mask actors from the audience—a small parlor opens into the dining room, which connects to an offstage kitchen by a door in the stage-left wall. Upstage of the parlor, the stairway to the second floor winds out of sight. Furnishings, modest yet tasteful, include a well-polished table in the dining room and four or five chairs. A mirror with an ornate frame hangs on the upstage wall, alongside pictures of SHERRI at various stages of her life; in most, including the large portrait directly behind the table, she is embracing a heavyset man with a boyish grin. Above this portrait is a framed needle-point quoting chapter 19, verse 5, from the Book of Matthew: "And they twain shall be one flesh."

• • •

[*Lights up on* SHERRI, *wrapped in a shawl and seated at the dining room table. She holds a cup of tea in both hands and close to her face for warmth. Her accent is unmistakably but not comically Baltimore, and when she speaks, her voice is full of easy laughter. For a long moment she sits, the picture of contentment, softly humming old ballads and taking an occasional sip of tea. At last* CLIFF *knocks open the front door and shuffles into the vestibule. We hear him stomping his boots and brushing snow from his coat; then he crosses into the parlor.*]

CLIFF   Hey, Sherri—

SHERRI   Clifford, I swear, you don't take off them boots—

CLIFF   I stomped them. You swear what?

SHERRI   And wipe up, while you're at it.

[*She sets the tea on a coaster and throws* CLIFF *a towel draped over a nearby chair. He catches it, grinning, and returns to the vestibule. We hear him struggling to pull off his boots, followed by a crash.*]

What on earth was that?

CLIFF   [*Calling from the vestibule.*] Snow shovel. I'm fine.

[*His boots and coat removed,* CLIFF *strolls back into the parlor. He pauses to wipe the floor clean of slush, then tosses the towel into the vestibule and joins* SHERRI *at the table.*]

It's a real mess out there.

SHERRI   Still coming down?

CLIFF   I've never seen anything like it.

SHERRI   Then what are you doing shoveling the walk for? Just have to go back out and shovel again.

CLIFF   So I'll shovel again.

SHERRI   Only person I know looks for an excuse to shovel the walk.

CLIFF   Did you know if somebody slips and falls on account of your icy walk, they could sue you?

SHERRI   Nobody's suing me. Who's even outside?

CLIFF   I didn't see anyone.

SHERRI   You should be working on your dissertation.

CLIFF   The power fixed?

SHERRI   What do you need power for? Pick up a pen and some paper and finish the thing.

CLIFF   My notes are on my computer.

SHERRI   Clifford, you're obviously stalling.

CLIFF   I have till June.

SHERRI   You've had six years.

CLIFF   I'll tell you what—you give me back those six years, I'd select an entirely different field of study.

SHERRI   What's the matter with your current field of study?

CLIFF   Nobody ever told me there were so many books written on it. I'd have found something original.

SHERRI   Original like what?

CLIFF   Seriously?
    [*Standing.*]
    Hold that thought. . . .

SHERRI   Where—

CLIFF   To get a book.

[CLIFF *crosses to the stairs.* SHERRI *stands.*]

SHERRI   Just a minute, Cliff, while you're up there—

CLIFF   Yep?

SHERRI   Check in on Mr. Bowden for me.

CLIFF   Who?

SHERRI   My new boarder.

CLIFF   The man from last night? How long is he staying?

SHERRI   [*Shrugging.*] He's been in his room all morning—didn't even come down for breakfast. Just give his door a knock and see that he's all right.

CLIFF   What if he's not?

SHERRI   You know CPR, don't you?

CLIFF   No.

SHERRI   For what little I charge you each month, you don't know CPR?

CLIFF   Was I supposed to?

SHERRI   Just make sure he's all right, Cliff.

[CLIFF *nods, slightly confused, and bounds upstairs.* SHERRI *takes a long sip of tea. From the street comes the groan of shifting gears and squealing brakes.* SHERRI *crosses to the window and peers outside. Calling upstairs.*]

CLIFF, IT'S THE SNOWPLOW!

[*Watching for a moment.*]

WHY'S HE NOT TURNING DOWN THIRTIETH?

CLIFF   [*Offstage.*] WHAT?

SHERRI   HE'S IGNORING THIRTIETH!

CLIFF   [*Offstage.*] SIDE STREET!

SHERRI   WHAT?

CLIFF   [*Offstage.*] WE'RE A SIDE STREET!

[ANDY *enters from the second floor. He is trimly dressed in suspenders, a jacket, and a tie; liberal amounts of gel fix in place his thinning hair.*]

SHERRI   [*Still peering outside.*] CLIFF, YOU SEE THEM POWER LINES?

CLIFF   [*Offstage.*] WHAT?

SHERRI   THEY LOOK LIKE WHITE TOOTSIE ROLLS!

[ANDY *crosses to the window and stands behind* SHERRI, *who does not sense his presence. The sound of the snowplow fades away.*]

ANDY [*Finally.*] It's very pretty.

[SHERRI *gasps and turns.* ANDY *steps back, equally startled.*]

SHERRI Mr. Bowden—

ANDY Andy—

SHERRI *Please* don't do that again.

ANDY I'm sorry.

SHERRI How'd you sleep?

ANDY I didn't.

SHERRI Something wrong with the room?

ANDY Room's fine.

SHERRI [*Crossing to the stairs.*] Let me get you an extra blanket.

ANDY You asked to see me?

SHERRI Pardon?

ANDY Young man said—

SHERRI I asked Clifford—

ANDY Didn't even knock first.

SHERRI I'm sorry, Mr. Bowden, let's start over. Would you care to sit down?

ANDY Not particularly.

SHERRI You know, with age, they say, comes wisdom, but for every year that passes I'd trade some of that wisdom for the strength I had back when I was young and dumb. Seems like every time I stand up, I need to sit down again. If you'll excuse me...

[SHERRI *crosses to the table and sits facing* ANDY, *who remains standing in the parlor. A long moment passes as each waits for the other to speak. Finally.*]

Your first time in Baltimore?

[ANDY *nods.*]

It's not usually this bad.

ANDY   Snows in Cleveland too.

SHERRI   That where you're from?

ANDY   Yep.

SHERRI   Be some time yet before they clear the roads. Baltimore never could handle a snowstorm. I swear, you put a little snow on the ground, something slips inside us. Some of the sweetest people I know, I've seen go at it like pit bulls, and all for a parking spot.

ANDY   It's like that most places, in my experience.

SHERRI   Well, I'm sorry for your experience.

ANDY   Just human nature. Hey, you know something?

[*Crossing to the mirror.*]

I believe I've got this same mirror in my bedroom. Where'd you get it?

SHERRI   Lou bought that for me...must be fifteen years ago. On the boardwalk in Ocean City.

ANDY   Lou your husband?

SHERRI   [*Nodding.*] Used to spend every summer down the ocean. Not so much the past few years.

ANDY   Since he died, you mean?

SHERRI   That's right.

[ANDY *crosses to the large portrait behind the table; he leans forward to study the grinning man.*]

ANDY   That him?

SHERRI   Yes.

ANDY   You look very happy together. I bet Lou made you very happy.

SHERRI   Mr. Bowden...

ANDY   Yep?

SHERRI   I'm not sure this is a conversation we should be having.

ANDY   I'm sorry.

SHERRI   I don't mean to sound unpleasant—

ANDY   No, you're right, I overstepped.

SHERRI   What about you?

ANDY   Me?

SHERRI   Got a picture of your wife?

ANDY   I say I was married?

SHERRI   Aren't you?

ANDY   Don't recall saying I was.

SHERRI   Isn't that a wedding band you're wearing?

[ANDY *glances at his ring finger and smiles, conceding the point. He sits at the table.*]

ANDY   Understand, this isn't me pressing . . . not trying to press. I was just asking last night to know who else was living here—just making conversation, really, while you were checking me in— and you mentioned your husband had died. You said it kind of casual, if that makes sense—at least, you sounded so to me . . . but maybe you've had more time to come to terms. My wife, Karen—my *deceased* wife.

SHERRI   I'm sorry.

ANDY   Diagnosis was a lifetime ago, but she lingered, and weakened, and regained strength, and weakened some more. . . . When did it happen for your husband?

SHERRI   Three years ago November. It was a heart attack.

ANDY   I can't help thinking that suddenness would have been better.

SHERRI   Better for you?

ANDY   For us both. She died in March. . . . I'm still not sure how to feel about it.

SHERRI   Mr. Bowden…Andy. There's no one way to feel.

ANDY   For a long time I left everything just as it had been. Even now… haven't thrown anything out. But with the new year—seemed I should at least get moving in that direction. I found a packet of old letters, back of one of her drawers, letters I hadn't written her…from another man. See, I traveled a lot. I was a reporter— no longer—laid off. I was on the road a lot, and during one of my trips, it seems, about fifteen years back, she took a lover. That sounds tawdry. I don't know why I'm telling you.

[*He stands and wanders back upstage.* SHERRI *watches him but says nothing.*]

Technically I'm not laid off. They call it a voluntary buyout. If you say no, then they lay you off.

SHERRI   That must have been—

ANDY   Awful. Shocking. Got his address from his letters. That's why I'm in Baltimore. I'm here to confront him.

SHERRI   What do you mean?

ANDY   Knock on his door. Look him in the eye. Say, "That was my wife you were fucking all these years."

SHERRI   Why?

ANDY   I can't confront her.

SHERRI   I don't think—

ANDY   Anyway, doesn't matter. Can't do it now.

SHERRI   The snow's going to stop, Mr. Bowden. And when it does, if you take my advice, you'll get back in your car and drive home to Cleveland.

ANDY   Why is that your advice?

SHERRI   What do you think this man will say to you? I'm sorry? What if he's not? What will you do then?

ANDY   Punch him.

SHERRI   You ever punch a man?

ANDY   No.

SHERRI   What if he's sorry? What do you gain?

ANDY   Nothing much to lose.

SHERRI   Lou and me—we were together thirty-three years, and in that time we learned things about each other neither of us wanted to know. You accept that as a part of what it means to be married. You learned a terrible thing about your wife, but what's worse is you don't know if your marriage would have survived the learning. Confronting this man won't change that.

ANDY   Neither will driving home.

[CLIFF *enters from the second floor, carrying an armful of books.*]

CLIFF   Sorry—couldn't find it.

SHERRI   What?

CLIFF   The book.

SHERRI   Looks to me you found plenty.

CLIFF   You wouldn't like these.

[CLIFF *dumps the books on the table, pulls a pen from his pocket, and sits down to read. For a long moment there is silence. Finally he looks up.*]

Am I interrupting?

ANDY   I was just explaining to your mother why I'm here.

CLIFF   Mother?

SHERRI   He's not my son.

CLIFF   Just another boarder, man.

SHERRI   Going on four years.

CLIFF   No shit? Sorry.

SHERRI   I'm not your mother.

CLIFF   Be strange when I finally move out.

SHERRI Clifford is studying to be a doctor of philosophy.

CLIFF I also do home repairs.

SHERRI He's very handy.

ANDY What are you studying?

CLIFF Philosophy.

SHERRI Boy, he's asking about your thesis.

CLIFF It's not very interesting.
[*Standing.*]
I can go back upstairs if I'm interrupting.

SHERRI We were just having a conversation. Reason the Lord made snowy days. You just sit back down and tell us what you're studying.

CLIFF You've heard it a million times.

SHERRI Well, Mr. Bowden hasn't heard it once.

ANDY Really, it's fine—

SHERRI He's modest too. Tell you what—I'm going to make tea. So nobody needs concern themselves with what I've heard a million times.
[*Crossing to the kitchen door.*]
Anyone else for tea?

ANDY The power's out.

SHERRI Gas range. What kind of unsophisticate do you take me for?

CLIFF I'll have a coffee.

SHERRI Your coffee's disgusting. Mr. Bowden?

ANDY No. Thank you.

[SHERRI *exits into the kitchen.* CLIFF *sits and continues to read, glancing occasionally at his cell phone as he works.* ANDY *paces, then crosses into the vestibule. We hear him open the door.*]

CLIFF Can you shut that?

ANDY [*From the vestibule.*] Can't even see the street.

CLIFF It's cold.

ANDY Goddamnit!

[*He slams the door and re-enters the parlor.*]

Isn't there someplace I could walk to?

CLIFF Not dressed like that.

ANDY I'm sorry—wasn't expecting a blizzard when I packed.

CLIFF There's probably spare boots and a coat somewhere upstairs.

ANDY I'll manage. Look, I can't sit here all day.

CLIFF You could check out the avenue. They got restaurants, bars, funky shops—

ANDY They open?

CLIFF Probably not.

ANDY Then why bother telling me?

[CLIFF *shrugs and returns to his book.* ANDY *joins him at the table.*]

I'm sorry. I hate rude people. What are you reading?

CLIFF Nothing that's interesting.

ANDY You make it a habit to read and write about what you don't find interesting?

CLIFF Don't have much choice. I want to get my degree.

ANDY Must have been interested at the start.

CLIFF Sure. You know that song "Buffalo Gals"?

ANDY I guess.

CLIFF Sure you do. What's it about?

ANDY Prostitutes?

CLIFF You see?

ANDY No.

CLIFF How do you know that?

ANDY Buffalo gals are prostitutes from Buffalo.... They're not?

CLIFF Not to my mother singing it to me every night at bedtime—it's cute and it's harmless and it's about dancing women who look like buffaloes.

ANDY I think you're being too literal.

CLIFF But where in the song is the evidence they're whores?
[*Singing tunelessly.*]
"Buffalo gals won't you come out tonight
Come out tonight
Come out tonight
Buffalo gals won't you come out tonight
And dance by the light of the moon"

ANDY There's other verses. You're the one brought it up.

CLIFF My point is, I went my whole life thinking that song was about what it says it's about—why can't there be buffalo gals without someone having to turn it into something dirty?

ANDY Who's turning it into anything? Didn't anyone just ask the guy who wrote the song?

CLIFF Suppose they did. And suppose he said, actually, I was writing about Bigfoot. Or space aliens? Or prairie dogs? Are we obligated to interpret the song as an ode to prairie dogs just because that's what the writer intended?

ANDY He intended to write about prairie dogs?

CLIFF I'm just thinking aloud. Anyway, lots of smart people have already exhausted the question of author's intent. I decided to tackle the more fundamental question of how to verify interpretation itself.

ANDY I don't know what that means.

CLIFF Is there anything we can point to in a work of art that proves conclusively that my interpretation is true and yours is false? Or at least that mine is *more* true than yours is? Or is every interpretation in fact equally good? Or bad? Or neither?

ANDY   This is what you're studying?

CLIFF   More or less. Only it didn't take me long to realize that lots of smart people have already considered that question too.

ANDY   In my line of work, what's on the page should match what you're trying to say, and what you're trying to say better match what's on the page.

CLIFF   [*Nodding toward the kitchen.*] You sound just like her.

ANDY   Sherri?

CLIFF   She takes everything so literally. You can't do that with poetry or literature. You can't take a *symphony* literally. You religious?

ANDY   What?

CLIFF   Word to the wise, don't get her started on the Bible.

ANDY   She one of those?

CLIFF   Crazies?

ANDY   Doesn't seem it.

CLIFF   She's not crazy. She's a sweet old woman.

ANDY   How old is old?

CLIFF   She just has no imagination when it comes to religion. You said you're a writer?

ANDY   I wrote for a newspaper.

CLIFF   Oh. Well, that makes sense.

ANDY   What?

CLIFF   Newspapers you should take literally.

ANDY   For a time I tried writing fiction. Don't quite know what happened. Most things, it seems, the learning curve rises quickly at first, and it sucks you in—you imagine it'll rise like that forever; instead it plateaus. You have to be honest with yourself— are you content being a hobbyist?

CLIFF   What's the problem with being a hobbyist?

ANDY   It's not what I imagined for myself.

CLIFF   There's what you do for a living, and there's what you do to live. This philosophy of art stuff—I can teach it, but I'm finding my true interests lie elsewhere. Which is only to be expected.

ANDY   Why is that?

CLIFF   [*Gesturing toward his books.*] I've put something like six years into this. Eventually you run out of questions to ask. You want to know the best thing about living here?

ANDY   The weather?

CLIFF   With Sherri, I mean? She's genuinely interested in what you're doing.

ANDY   What *I'm* doing?

CLIFF   Anyone! Half the reason I can't finish this damn thing is I keep explaining to her what it's about. It's a mystery to me how someone that's so interested in some things can be so set in her ways for others.

ANDY   Meaning religion?

CLIFF   I should probably shut up before I offend someone.

ANDY   I don't offend easily.

CLIFF   Neither does Sherri!

   [*Gesturing toward the portrait behind him.*]

   Now that guy right there—I bet there wasn't a day went by he didn't tell me to shut it. Amazing they got along. Course, to be fair, he was pretty sick at the end.

ANDY   You knew the husband?

CLIFF   Not well. Only reason they got a boarder was to help cover the medical bills. Then when he died, I guess she didn't want to be lonely.

ANDY   Thought it was a heart attack.

CLIFF   There were a couple smaller ones before the big one. Actually, it was Mr. Blount's death that got me thinking about God.

ANDY   Pretty common, I hear.

CLIFF   She's convinced they're going to meet again in heaven. You believe in heaven?

ANDY   No idea.

CLIFF   Well, she's positive. Not that it's unusual . . . and it really does seem to help. Which is also not unusual. Doesn't make it true, but it got me thinking. . . .

[*Looking hard at* ANDY.]

I didn't ask if there *is* a heaven—I asked what you *believe*.

ANDY   Honestly haven't given it much thought.

CLIFF   It's not something we're encouraged to do, you know? Heaven, God—we hear the words constantly, and we absorb them or we don't. But not being a believer, anymore than I was a disbeliever, left me free just to think. Until eventually I concluded I *do* believe in heaven. And God. Within the proper context, of course.

ANDY   What context?

CLIFF   Love.

ANDY   What?

CLIFF   I think the key is love.

ANDY   You met a girl?

CLIFF   No. That's my whole point.

ANDY   You met a guy?

CLIFF   I can think about this *rationally*. I have no allegiance to any side but the truth.

[SHERRI *enters from the kitchen, carrying three cups of tea on a serving tray. She sets the tray on the table and distributes cups to* CLIFF *and* ANDY.]

SHERRI   Forewarned is forearmed—I'm not one to add milk and sugar.

ANDY   Why not?

SHERRI   It's excessive. Like mixing chocolate and peanut butter.

CLIFF   I wanted coffee.

SHERRI   I don't know how to work that thing.
[*To* ANDY.]
This blend is perfect as is.

CLIFF   He didn't want anything.

SHERRI   He was just being polite.
[ANDY *brings the cup to his lips.* SHERRI *stays his hand.*]
Mr. Bowden, you'll burn yourself.

ANDY   Oh...

SHERRI   You should blow on it first.

CLIFF   This isn't the man's first cup of tea.

SHERRI   Hush.

ANDY   Really wasn't thinking either way....

[ANDY *moves to put down the cup.* SHERRI *stays his hand again.*]

SHERRI   Mr. Bowden!

ANDY   What?

SHERRI   Please use a coaster.

ANDY   You didn't give me a coaster.

SHERRI   Lord, you're right! Clifford, I believe there's another in the kitchen.

CLIFF   You want I should...?

SHERRI   Grab one for yourself while you're in there. Thank you, Cliff.
[CLIFF *shrugs and exits into the kitchen.* SHERRI *sits beside* ANDY.]
You give any more thought to my advice?

ANDY   Not really. Too busy learning about Buffalo gals.

SHERRI   I never knew they were prostitutes either.

ANDY   I have a dirty mind, apparently.

SHERRI   I'm sure your mind is fine. So Clifford told you his thesis?

ANDY   A bit. Seems he's more interested in love.

SHERRI   If only that were true.

ANDY   Sounded that way to me.

[CLIFF *re-enters with two coasters. He hands one to* ANDY *and keeps the other for himself.*]

CLIFF   Where do you buy coasters, anyway? I'm only asking out of curiosity.

ANDY   You tell her God is love?

CLIFF   I didn't say God is love—the *key* is love.
[*Sitting.*]
Ain't that right, Sherri?

SHERRI   Is this your theory of soul mates?

CLIFF   I would never speak of something as trite as "soul mates."

SHERRI   I don't understand how you believe in souls without God.

CLIFF   If God is love, when people love each other, we can say they're in the presence of God.

SHERRI   Now there's no ifs about it.

CLIFF   [*To* ANDY.] You see?

SHERRI   Don't talk to him—talk to me.

CLIFF   All right. The Bible says that a man and his wife shall be one flesh.

SHERRI   Matthew 19:5.

ANDY   You know the verse?

SHERRI   [*Pointing to the needlepoint on the wall.*] It was a wedding gift.

CLIFF   But what does it *mean*? It's obviously not literal—husbands and wives maintain distinct bodies.

SHERRI   Not in death they don't.

CLIFF   Exactly. What if in death your soul is reunited with the souls of those you love—not merely reunited, but joined. So that by loving another person, and being loved in return, your spirit— your *consciousness*—is enlarged. By loving, you become a more complete person—and now I'm speaking literally—two souls become one, and the resulting person, when this soul is reborn—

SHERRI   The Bible doesn't say anything about reincarnation—

CLIFF   The resulting person carries the accumulated wisdom of *two* people. And when *this* person loves and is loved in return, the souls join again, they're reborn—

SHERRI   Clifford—

CLIFF   And the resulting person carries the accumulated wisdom of three people, or four, or sixteen, or however many lovers joined in death to create life. So that our purpose in living is to love, and in a perfect world, as we achieve our purpose, we move inexorably toward that moment when every soul that has ever existed is joined together in perfect love. And this is heaven. And this universal soul, bound by love, encompassing all creation, is God.

[ANDY *takes a sip of tea—his first.* SHERRI *turns to him.*]

SHERRI   Mr. Bowden, I hope he's not offending you.

ANDY   I'm not offended—why would I be offended?

SHERRI   Now there's no need to get defensive.

ANDY   I have a question. You mind if I ask a question?

CLIFF   Go for it.

ANDY   My question is, what kind of a world you're living in to call it perfect. Because the world where the rest of us live is anything but.

CLIFF   You're right. And it follows that if love brings souls together, hatred must tear them apart.

ANDY   Hatred?

CLIFF   Enforced pain, suffering—call it what you will. When we hurt another person—whether intentional or no, I haven't decided— we lose a piece of our soul. When we die, if on the whole we have hated more than we've loved, we return a *less* complete person—our soul is less capable of love.

ANDY   What if the other person deserved it?

CLIFF   What if, what if—the end result is the same. In an imperfect world we move inexorably *away* from other people until finally each soul is cut off behind an insurmountable barrier. Love is impossible. And this we call hell.

ANDY   And Satan?

CLIFF   What about him?

ANDY   Where does he enter the picture?

CLIFF   This isn't about good versus evil.

SHERRI   You can't talk about God in His heaven and leave out good and evil.

CLIFF   No, that's the problem. There's enough jerks already setting down rules for how to live. Loving other people isn't even a commandment.

SHERRI   If by jerks you mean preachers—

CLIFF   I don't mean anyone in particular. Look, you want to hate somebody—

SHERRI   Nobody wants to hate anybody.

CLIFF   Plenty of people want to hate somebody. Be my guest! All I'm saying is the consequence of hatred is you end up alone.

ANDY   And the consequence of love is you don't?

CLIFF   The consequence of love is the union of souls.

ANDY   That's a mouthful of bull. I know plenty of people that fell in love and got married—

CLIFF   I didn't say anything about marriage.

ANDY   They end up just as alone as if they'd never loved at all.

CLIFF   Because of death?

ANDY   Because of life! Because of white lies and everyday stress. Because of absent children and adultery.

SHERRI   Mr. Bowden—

ANDY   Because to love until death do you part requires a greater miracle than what brought you together in the first place.

SHERRI   Mr. Bowden, he doesn't know what you're talking about.

CLIFF   Sherri, I've been in love.

ANDY   She love you back?

CLIFF   Yes.

ANDY   How do you know?

CLIFF   Because she told me.

ANDY   How do you *know*?

CLIFF   Because I loved her.

ANDY   No more?

CLIFF   That's a good question.

ANDY   What's the answer?

CLIFF   It's kind of beside the point. She lives in Albuquerque now, and I live here.

[CLIFF *takes a sip of tea and grins at* SHERRI.]

Soon as the power's fixed, I'm teaching you to make coffee.

[CLIFF *glances at his cell phone. He presses several buttons, as though scrolling through a text message.*]

Sweet!

[CLIFF *leaps to his feet and hurries into the vestibule. We hear him pulling on boots and a jacket.*]

ANDY   Where are you going?

[CLIFF *pokes his head—now covered in a stocking cap—into the parlor.*]

CLIFF   Snowball fight in the park.

SHERRI   I think I'll pass.

CLIFF   I'll shovel the walk when I get back.

[CLIFF *disappears into the vestibule. The front door opens and slams shut.* SHERRI *calls after him.*]

SHERRI   AND FINISH YOUR THESIS!

       [*To* ANDY.]

       Did you want to go with him?

ANDY   No.

SHERRI   Mr. Bowden, I apologize if Clifford seems tactless. To hear that talk about love, you'd expect to find a wedding band on his finger. Lord, if I had a dollar for every new girl I've seen at breakfast—

ANDY   He was right about me and Karen.

SHERRI   Pardon?

ANDY   Looking back, I can't say we were ever much in love.

SHERRI   I'm sure that's not true.

ANDY   You don't know anything about it. I'm not begging for pity, I'm stating a fact. We stayed together out of duty to each other, not love.

SHERRI   Duty's nothing to take lightly.

ANDY   These letters say you're wrong.

       [*He pulls a bundle of opened letters from his jacket pocket.*]

       Duty's a bigger sham than love, Mrs. Blount. Love makes fewer promises.

SHERRI   There were times I'd have agreed with you. When Lou and
          me were fighting over what, I can't recall. Duty kept us together
          till the love could find its way back. Love that was all the more
          sweeter for having been so nearly lost.

ANDY   You have no idea how near.

SHERRI   I've got a better idea than you, I think.

ANDY   Mrs. Blount, it was your husband she was having the affair with!
          [*Tossing the letters on the table.*]
          That's his name on the envelopes. That's his signature inside.
          You still want to tell me about duty?

SHERRI   I want you to leave my home.

ANDY   Where should I go?

SHERRI   Anywhere but my home!

ANDY   Mrs. Blount—

SHERRI   Don't you dare come any closer!

ANDY   You had a right to know.

SHERRI   You smug little—I already knew.

ANDY   What?

SHERRI   My husband was a salesman. He traveled to places all over the
          Midwest. On one of those travels, Mr. Bowden, he met your
          wife. They started an affair, lasted thirteen months. They ended
          it, and he told me. That was over sixteen years ago.

ANDY   They didn't end it.

SHERRI   They ended it. Didn't you read the dates of those letters?

ANDY   They were still writing each other when he died! That letter on
          top—read it for yourself. Not sixteen years ago. Three!
          [ANDY *holds up a letter for* SHERRI *to see. She takes it from him, removes
          it from the envelope, and begins to read.*]
          Mrs. Blount, I—

[SHERRI *cuts him off with a gesture. She finishes reading, returns the letter to its envelope, and hands it back to* ANDY.]

I shouldn't have come here. I've hurt you . . . I'm sorry.

[SHERRI *stands. Without a word, she crosses into the parlor and exits up the stairs.* ANDY *looks at the letter for a long moment. Then he tears it in half, followed by the other letters. Outside, the snowplow groans its return. The front door opens and closes, and* CLIFF *enters from the vestibule; his pants are soaked with melted snow.*]

CLIFF   Plow's coming through.

ANDY   What?

CLIFF   Case you need to get somewhere.

[*Calling upstairs.*]

HEY, SHERRI, WE'RE PLOWED!

ANDY   No.

CLIFF   GIVE ME AN HOUR—I'LL CLEAR THE STOOP!

[CLIFF *hurries through the dining room and exits into the kitchen.* ANDY *stands and crosses to the window. He watches the snowplow move slowly down the street.* CLIFF *re-enters, carrying a metal trash can lid.*]

ANDY   What's that?

CLIFF   Shield.

ANDY   What?

CLIFF   It's brutal out there, man.

[CLIFF *crosses to the vestibule.* ANDY *stops him.*]

ANDY   Tell me about the husband.

CLIFF   Who?

ANDY   Her *husband*. You knew him, right?

CLIFF   Sure.

ANDY   And?

CLIFF   Really great guy.

[CLIFF *pounds on the lid as though preparing for battle and exits into the street.* ANDY *continues to watch from the window; when the world is quiet once more, he turns to go back to his room. As he reaches the stairs,* SHERRI *re-enters from the second floor, carrying a small box. She crosses slowly to the dining room table and sits.* ANDY *follows, lost.*]

SHERRI   Mr. Bowden, please have a seat.

ANDY   Mrs. Blount—

SHERRI   Please sit down.

[ANDY *sits.* SHERRI *watches him closely. She drums her fingers on the box.*]

ANDY   What's that?

SHERRI   Do you carry pictures of your wife?

ANDY   Why?

SHERRI   I want to know what she looked like.

ANDY   Before or after the chemo?

SHERRI   The moment he first laid eyes on her.

ANDY   I can't help you there.

SHERRI   No. I didn't think you could.

[*She passes him the box. He grabs at the lid, then hesitates.*]

ANDY   Should I—

SHERRI   You opened everything else. Might as well.

[ANDY *opens the box. He removes a bundle of letters, also opened.*]

ANDY   From Karen...
      [SHERRI *nods.*]
      What do they say?

SHERRI   I never read them.

ANDY   Why not?

SHERRI   They're not addressed to me.

ANDY   You giving them to me?

SHERRI   Do you want them?

>   [ANDY *nods.*]

>   Then they're yours.

ANDY   Mrs. Blount, I can't—

SHERRI   Suit yourself.

[SHERRI *takes back the letters, stands, and crosses to the fireplace. She opens the gate.*]

ANDY   What are you—

SHERRI   Mr. Bowden, I don't intend to re-think over thirty years of marriage just because you walk into my home with a pile of letters. I have letters of my own. And if nobody wants them, I'm going to burn them.

[SHERRI *holds out the letters, as though to give* ANDY *one last chance to take them. He stares, greatly tempted, and finally snatches them from her hand.*]

ANDY   Fair's fair. . . .

[ANDY *removes his wallet from a pocket and pulls from it a small photograph. He hands the photograph to* SHERRI. *For a long moment she looks, her face expressionless. Then she tosses it into the fire.*]

SHERRI   How long will you be needing a room for, Mr. Bowden?

ANDY   Till the snow melts, I guess.

SHERRI   They're already talking another storm this weekend.

[SHERRI *closes the fireplace. She glances at herself in the mirror, instinctively brushes a few stray hairs, then crosses into the parlor.*]

ANDY   Where are you going?

SHERRI   A walk.

>   [SHERRI *exits into the vestibule.* ANDY *flips through the letters. A moment passes, then* SHERRI *re-enters, wearing a winter coat, boots, and a scarf.*]

>   Care to join me?

ANDY   No. Thank you.

SHERRI You ever live in the country?

ANDY What do you mean?

SHERRI Just someplace where the snow stays fresh for days after a storm. Sometimes weeks. Instead of turning to slush. You got people already racing to shovel themselves out—take a look outside, you don't believe me.

ANDY Can't really blame them.

SHERRI City never looks so lovely as just after it snows. You almost forget where you are.

[ANDY *nods, only half listening.*]

If you do go out, Mr. Bowden—

ANDY What?

SHERRI Please remember to lock the door.

ANDY Yep.

[SHERRI *exits into the vestibule. The front door opens and closes, and a key turns in the lock. Then all is still.* ANDY *opens a letter. He falls to reading as the lights fade to black.*]

• • •

Eleanor's
Passing

John Patrick Bray

John Patrick Bray

John Patrick Bray is a lecturer in the Department of Theatre and Film Studies at the University of Georgia. He earned his PhD in theater at Louisiana State University, and his MFA in playwriting from the New School (Actors Studio Drama School). He has written under grants from the National Endowment for the Arts and the Acadiana Center for the Arts in Lafayette, Louisiana, and has earned commissions from organizations in Louisiana and Off-Off Broadway. His work has been published by Next Stage Press, Smith and Kraus, JACPublishing, Heartland Plays, Inc., and the Riant Theatre. Bray is a member of the Dramatists Guild of America, Inc., and he is an Equity membership candidate.

···production history···

Eleanor's Passing was one of eight winners of the Heartland Theatre Company's 2011 Annual Ten-Minute Play Festival in Normal, Illinois. It opened on Thursday, June 9, 2011, with the following cast:

MOE, Larry Eggan

GUS, Dave Lemmon

TALL GLASS, Kevin Woodard

The production was directed by Christopher Gray.

setting

Present day, MOE's back porch in Southeast Louisiana.

characters

MOE, in his 70s

GUS, in his 70s

TALL GLASS, in his 70s

synopsis

Now that MOE's wife, Eleanor, has passed away, his old friends GUS and TALL GLASS stop by to cheer him up. Share a beer. Help him out with his house. And his garden. Move in. With a dog. Friends gotta stick together, y'know?

• • •

[*Lights up. A back porch. Two rocking chairs with a table in between. It is late evening in the late autumn in Southwest Louisiana. The lighting is dim.* MOE *enters with a small electric lantern. He is dressed mostly in black. He walks with a little bit of a limp. He sets it down between the chairs. He turns and looks at the chairs. A moment. He sits in one. He looks over at the other one.* GUS *enters.* GUS, *also an old-timer, is carrying a hunting magazine. He is holding a Bud Light. He looks at* MOE *and at the other rocking chair.* MOE *looks up at him. Then away.* GUS *continues to look at him, drinking his beer.*]

MOE   You going to keep on staring at me, or are you fixin' to take her chair?

GUS   I wouldn't ask it of you.

MOE   Go ahead.

GUS   I'd say yes, but I don't want you to get the wrong idea. I like to think we're close, but not that close.

[MOE *chuckles*.]

Bud Light?

MOE   If I start at this point, I doubt I'd stop. Ever.

GUS   Right.

MOE   How long we know each other, Gus?

GUS   Too long.

MOE   Thought so.

GUS   You want me to ... I don't know ... do something?

MOE   Like what?

GUS   It's what I keep asking myself. You know. What can I do? I want to do something. All I got is beer.

[*Pause*.]

I got a dog too.

[MOE *gives him a severe look*.]

Now you think of how I regard Wallace before you start looking at me like that.

MOE   [*Chuckles*.] I'm sure Eleanor wouldn't approve.

GUS   Why not?

MOE   The dog has a prettier name than me. She wouldn't abide that.

GUS   Sure she would.

MOE   It might tear through her garden. How could I have something that would dig up her garden? That's all I ...

[*Slight pause*.]

GUS   What do you think is going to happen?

MOE   I don't know. Do something, I guess.

GUS   Guess so.

MOE   Wait for my turn.

GUS   Yes, sir. You could do that.

> [*Beat.*]

> While waiting for God, I enjoy a Bud Light. You sure you don't want one? I know the kids these days drink Purple Haze. Named after a sixties rock-and-roll song.

MOE   I know the song.

GUS   Tourist shit, you ask me. Come down here. Show off their boobies if you throw them beads. Me? I like Bud Light. It's unpretentious. The common denominator, you know? You can go into any store from here to Santa Fe, and you'll find Bud Light.

MOE   Any store in America.

GUS   That's right. Any store in America.

> [*Beat.*]

> I'm going to miss Eleanor, Moe.

[*Pause.*]

MOE   She didn't look that old. You know? I look like hell. She still skipped. She had an actual skip in her step. Her cheeks were like . . . big plums, you know? Just ripe. And that smile. Lord . . . that smile.

GUS   Yessir. She really looked good. Kept the house looking good too. And that garden. Gorgeous.

> [*Pause.*]

> The thing is, I . . . well, what I mean is . . . what are you going to do with the house?

MOE   What do you mean?

GUS   The house, Moe. What are you going to do with it?

MOE   I don't know. Nothing, I suppose.

GUS Nothing?

MOE Why? What you want me to do with it?

GUS I was just thinking. With the two rooms upstairs. The divide between the kitchen and the backroom. You could really fix it up.

MOE And what? Sell it?

GUS Sell it? What you want to sell it for?

MOE Well, you're getting all these ideas about my house.

GUS It's a beautiful house!

> [*Beat.*]

> Moe, you're broke.

> [MOE *turns away.*]

> Been broke for years. Me and Tall Glass. Well, we've been thinking.

MOE That'd be a first for you two.

GUS Hell, he's better at saying it than me anyway.

[TALL GLASS *enters.*]

TALL GLASS Hey, young-timers.

[TALL GLASS *sits in the other rocking chair without a thought.* MOE *and* GUS *look at him.*]

GUS That's my chair.

TALL GLASS I didn't see the brass plaque.

GUS That's *my* chair!

TALL GLASS Were you sitting in it?

GUS I was fixin' to!

TALL GLASS You shouldn't take so much time fixin' to.

GUS It's still my chair.

TALL GLASS Moe, what does he mean this is his chair?

MOE Last time I checked it was my chair. I'm sitting in Eleanor's.

GUS   You're sitting in Eleanor's?

MOE   Yes, sir.

GUS   And you let me just stand here!

MOE   You were having some kind of crisis. I figured I should just leave you alone.

GUS   [*To* MOE.] Look here, I'm his *best friend. Best friends* sit together!

[TALL GLASS *reaches over and puts his hand on* MOE'*s.* GUS *looks annoyed.*]

MOE   [*Wryly.*] Thanks for coming over and making me feel better, boys.

GUS   Oh, wait—

TALL GLASS   We shouldn't be behaving this way, it's just . . .

MOE   It's just what?

TALL GLASS   Well, we've both been eyeing this spot.

MOE   Eyeing this spot?

[*The moment is tense.*]

TALL GLASS   Sure. For the, for the plan. When we all move in with you.

MOE   Who all is moving where?

TALL GLASS   We all is . . . moving . . . that is, we are . . . us. That's why . . . [*To* GUS.]

. . . you never got around to talking to him about it?

GUS   I was fixin' to.

TALL GLASS   That's you, Gus. Always fixin' to, never doing. A true Texan.

GUS   Now, you take it easy on that Texas stuff! You might have the Tigers, but we have the Longhorns, you hear? Let your Tigers go pro and see what happens!

MOE   You want to move in? With me?

TALL GLASS   No, no.

GUS [*Beat.*] Yes.

MOE Why?

GUS It's just that...well...

TALL GLASS We ain't getting any younger.

GUS That's the truth.

TALL GLASS And between your gout and my back pain, and Gus's chronic "fixin' to" condition...

GUS We thought that three heads would be better than one.

MOE Three heads?

TALL GLASS That is, we all need a little looking after.
[*Beat.*]
When's the last time the kids come down?

MOE They're here enough. Too much.

TALL GLASS Christmas.

MOE Yeah. Christmas.

TALL GLASS And they'll be here again?

MOE They were just here.

GUS And they'll be here again *when*?
[*Beat.*]
They're like what we call the C and E's over at the church. The Christmas and Easter Christians. Show up on the two big holidays, and forget about the big guy the rest of the year.

[*Pause.*]

TALL GLASS I could take the upstairs guest room.

MOE That's Millie's room.

TALL GLASS On Christmas, I can duck out.

MOE What's wrong with your place?

TALL GLASS   Not sure how much longer I'm going to keep it. The pawn shop is doing terrible. And all those stairs.

MOE   How are my stairs different?

GUS   When he hollers, he'll have a couple of fools to laugh at him.

TALL GLASS   It's true. The sound of hollering to yourself. It's not the way I want to go.

GUS   Me neither.

> [*Pause.*]

> Eleanor wouldn't want you to be alone either, Moe.

[*Pause.* MOE *stands up and exits.*]

TALL GLASS   [*To* GUS.] You were supposed to *talk* to him!

GUS   I was—

TALL GLASS   Fixin' to, fixin' to. We sound like damn fools!

GUS   Maybe I should tell him.

TALL GLASS   Tell him what?

GUS   I'm losing my house. The kids want to ship me off in an old folk's home.

TALL GLASS   How'd you find out?

GUS   Just speculating.

> [*Beat.*]

> It's what I wanted to do with my folks!

[MOE *enters. He is holding a third rocking chair with a small cooler on it. He sets it down, opens the cooler, revealing more Bud Light.*]

MOE   Just one rule. I want three years of peace.

TALL GLASS   [*Beat.*] Where you plan on going in three years?

MOE   Nowhere. Three years of peace just sound nice, doesn't it?

[*The men chuckle.* MOE *takes a Bud Light; hands a fresh one to* GUS *and one to* TALL GLASS. *They pop them open.*]

TALL GLASS   Eleanor started a garden.

MOE   She did.

GUS   You know, I'm good with my hands. I'm fixin' to ...

[*Beat. The men look at him.*]

Drink my beer.

[*They all sit on their chairs. It gets later. Stage goes dark.*]

• • •

A Marriage Proposal

Kimberly La Force

Kimberly La Force

Kimberly La Force was born on the island of St. Lucia and moved to New York in her early twenties. She has written several poems, plays, and fiction pieces and has been published by the *New Tech Times*, *City Tech Writer*, and *Pulse*. Her feature screenplay, *A Marriage Proposal*, was a finalist for the Lou Rivers Drama Writing Award and was performed at the Literary Arts Festival. She lives and works in Brooklyn.

···production history···

Venue: Klitgord Auditorium, 285 Jay Street, Brooklyn, April 12, 2011

characters

MONA, a thirty-six-year-old mother of two

MATT

NARRATOR

TYLER

···

···scene one···

[*The auditorium goes dark.* MONA *has just put her sons in bed for the night and sits in her cramped bedroom deep in thought. On the mike from one of the aisles of the auditorium* MONA's *phone rings. She picks up.*]

MONA   Hello.

MATT   Hello, Mona, I want you to be my wife.

MONA   Excuse me? You must have the wrong number!

MATT   No, I am sure I have the right person. You are Mona James, recently unemployed secretary from Lewis and Lewis Chambers, mother of two boys named Tyler and Perry, ages three and seven. You experienced a bitter divorce two years ago, where all you received from the settlement were monthly child support payments for your boys. Your house is in foreclosure, and you found yourself in mounds of debt and recently started attending the First Baptist Church on the corner of Seventh avenue. You...

MONA   *Who...are...you,* and how *dare* you talk about my life in that manner! Tell me, were you hired by my ex-husband to interrogate me? Now listen, I don't know how you found out this information, but don't you *ever* call me again.

MATT   Wait, wait, Mona, please do not hang up. I heard your story from your testimony in church last Sunday. My intention was not to scare you. I am here to make you an offer. Please, will you listen?

MONA   Is that how you propose an offer? By introducing yourself, a total stranger to me, with the question of marriage?

MATT   I assure you, Mona, that I mean nothing bad, just give me a chance to clearly explain myself from the very beginning. Let me start by telling you that my name is Mathew Joseph, but everyone calls me Matt. I also attend the First Baptist Church service.

MONA   [*Sighs.*] Ohhh, so you got to know me from my testimony. You know something, I did not even know that I said so much about myself during that testimony, but tell me, how did you get my number?

MATT   That is the beauty of Google, it gives you *everything*.

MONA   I guess I can praise God for technology then.

MATT   Trust me, Mona, I have a story to tell and it ties in to why I am calling you. Just give me your attention for a while.

MONA   I'm listening, go on.

MATT   Well, let me start from the beginning. I have been a farmer for years; never too smart but always good with my hands. At first I was a banana farmer in St. Lucia. I had a wife and two young boys and we made good money back then, but the banana industry collapsed when free trade was introduced.

MONA   [*Sarcastically.*] Awww, Matt, that sounds like a wonderful story, but you are wasting my time here.

MATT   Imagine if someone had said that during your testimony, imagine how you would feel. It's okay to listen in church, but then the message goes right out when you leave the church doors. Please, Mona, I am simply asking that you listen.

MONA   [*Hesitantly.*] I . . . I apologize, I'm listening.

MATT   So the demand for our bananas dropped and we were put out of business. Funny thing is that when my money was gone, so was my wife, and I was left with nothing but a field of weeds. I traveled to Texas in 2000 and got small jobs farming there. It was very peaceful, and I harvested for a small canola seed farmer. One day a major company threatened to tell the authorities that my boss was housing illegal immigrants. I was fired and hitchhiked all the way to Florida.

MONA   Wow…life just has a way of changing on you and challenging you to catch up.

MATT   Yes, that's definitely true. So I became invisible, always looking over my shoulder and avoiding the law. I no longer wanted to live life in that way, constantly suspicious of others and always on the move, so I started exploring options. I looked for any loopholes in the law.

MONA   I had a friend who went through the same thing. So I know how difficult it must be for you. Ever tried the visa lottery program?

MATT   Every year for the last ten years. I tried it all, the temporary visa program, community colleges, lawyers, army recruitments, and churches. They all told me they could help and took my money, but gave no results. I even went under an assumed name, and worked under the Social Security number of a dead man. For three years I was known as Michael Jones, until I was suspected by authorities. I did so much but to no avail, and now I see that the only option for me is to find a wife, and her only qualification is that she is a U.S. citizen.

MONA   Hold on a second—what makes you think that I would marry a man that I do not know, much less love? Do you think that because you heard my story, you could pick some vulnerable woman to marry you?

MATT   I did not think so at all. I came to you only because after hearing your story, I sensed that you had the maturity to see that marriage is an economic arrangement, not an emotional one. I don't need love from you and I did not come empty-handed. In Texas, the asking price for marriage is about $15,000. I came to you because your problem is financial, and mine is legal. Together we can help each other.

MONA   Well, Mathew, sorry to disappoint you, but I believe in love, and I believe that the bond created through love is extraordinary. This love you are trying to deny is the basis of my belief in marriage. What good would it do for me to compromise my beliefs? My philosophy is to never doubt the verdict of my mind. Do you know why people go crazy in this country? It's because they contradict their beliefs. I may be poor, but at least I'm sane.

MATT   [*Chuckles.*] You had that love, Mona, and it ended in abuse and heartache. Yes, you believe in love, but at the cost of what? You are not compromising your morals in any way, just altering them. You will only go insane if you cannot justify your actions to yourself. People go insane for many reasons, but mainly because they act irrationally and cannot justify their actions. Why don't you try a practical approach for once? And what about survival? There is no right or wrong in the eyes of survival. Do you believe in the survival of your next generation? You can barely afford to feed your kids. Please tell me how love would help you do that.

MONA   I have *never* been worried about money. And worse yet, to accept money and enter into a fraudulent marriage. The money will only last for a few months, maybe a year. Then what? I would be legally stuck to a stranger. Who knows, you could have a criminal record and my sons could be targeted because you may be involved in drugs and bring nothing but horror to my family.

MATT   True, but I may also be a hardworking man who can be an added support for you. Marriage is always a chance. I can tell that your moral judgment must have foreseen your divorce.
[*Pause.*]
Look, Mona, you tried the love route and it did not work. Why not try a different approach?
[*Pause.*]

And to think that your sons will be targeted because of me—no, think again, prisons are full of young men who failed the fifth grade reading test in school and then kept going down, down, down from there. So with you not working and your kids barely surviving, you are already preparing them for a targeted life. If you are so concerned about your sanity, I have a suggestion: think of the money as . . .

[*Pause.*]

. . . a dowry and our marriage as arranged.

MONA   I don't believe in arranged marriages. And what would I say to my family and my friends?

MATT   We will think of something, but how many of them have offered to help you through this ordeal? At church you said that the people who you expected to be your support were never around when it mattered. What difference is it what they think? I may not be smart, but I know that people tend to look out for their own benefit. We never suspected that free trade meant us losing one of our sustainable industries. I am coming to you with a direct offer. My interests are exposed to you. You may gain or lose, as with any option.

MONA   You said that you considered all your options, but why be invisible here? Why not just go back home?

MATT   Going back is *never* an option for me. It's like saying that I sacrificed ten years of my life for no reason. My only option is to get married. I have offered you my entire savings—$15,000 cash.

MONA   How would you know what the cost of marriage is anyway?

MATT   Craigslist.

MONA   [*Smile.*] I see that you spend a lot of time on the computer.

MATT   Just enough to get around.

MONA   Listen, Matt, this is all so sudden. I do need the money, but I also believe in love. This is not the way to marry, and I refuse to waste any more time on this argument.

MATT Well, just give it some thought. My offer still stands.

[*Pause.*]

I guess I will see you at church on Sunday.

MONA Yeah, sure. Good night.

MATT Good night.

[MONA *hangs up the phone.*]

MONA Marriage, an economic arrangement. That guy had some nerve!

NARRATOR Mona's son Tyler rushes into the room.

TYLER Mom, it's Perry, come quick.

NARRATOR Mona rushes out the room.

···scene two···

NARRATOR Mona stands greeting some people after church service on Sunday. She is about to leave when a man walks up to her.

MATT Hey, Mona, good morning. I'm Mathew Joseph. We spoke a couple nights ago.

MONA [*Shaking hands.*] Oh, right. Hi, nice to meet you. I remember you. You take care of the church gardens. You did a great job last summer.

MATT Well, thank you. Today's service was great.

MONA Well, it was okay, but to be honest, I was not listening through it all.

MATT Is everything okay, Mona? You look, like, so tired.

MONA I am.

[*Sighs.*]

It's my son. Two nights ago, Perry had a severe asthma attack and had to be hospitalized immediately. I . . . I am an emotional mess and I came to church today to try to recollect myself. I have been worried to death just not knowing where to turn. I found myself giving a lot of thought to your offer. . . .

MATT   Mona, let us go somewhere private to discuss this.

[*They walk to a new spot on the stage.*]

MONA   Where was I? . . . Oh yes, I have been giving your offer a lot of thought, and under regular circumstances, it would not cross my mind, but I feel like such a failure knowing that my son needed a nebulizer that I could not buy because it cost too much. Now he is in the hospital. It's all my fault.

MATT   Mona, don't blame yourself You need to be strong for your son now.

MONA   But I only gave thought to your offer after this happened. Doesn't that bother you? I feel like I am making a commodity out of marriage, but I do need the money, now more than ever.

MATT   I'm sorry to hear about your son and I hope he gets better. Guilty thoughts will not help him now, though. Do you see what I mean? Emotions just take energy and prevent action. Be practical. How can you help him now? That's how you should think. It would bother me if you gave no thought to my offer at all; I am not concerned what brought you to the decision. Once you have made a decision.

MONA   I can't help that. I am a woman and that's just how we think.

MATT   You can start to change by acknowledging how emotional you are.

MONA   [*Raised voice.*] I don't need a lecture on how I should be! [*Lowers voice.*] I came here to negotiate, that is, if you are up for negotiations.

MATT   Yes, yes, I am. I have researched the requirements. All you need is a $65 registration fee forty eight hours before the actual ceremony and a witness. Then we need to prove that we are together. We could use pictures, bank statements, and proof of a common address.

MONA   That sounds like a whole lot to me. Is it really worth it when we look at the actual benefits? You get residency benefits, Social

Security benefits, tax benefits, rights over my life in case of a medical emergency, and life insurance benefits, and all I get is $15,000. That does not sound like a fair deal. What about the price of divorce if it does not work out? It would take two years for you to be granted a green card, two *whole* years. I'm thinking more along the lines of say $20,000–$25,000.

MATT Well, I see you have been doing some research and all that you say is true, but you failed to mention that I could also be made liable for your debt. You also get decisional rights over my life and tax benefits. When you look at it, there is a certain level of mutual risk that cannot be factored into cost. As with everything else, you are taking a chance. I can give you as much information as you need for you to get a sense of who I am, but in the end it all boils down to pure faith. Why should I factor mutual risk into the price?

MONA That's because I retain more risk than you. I could be placed in prison for faking marriage.

MATT And I could be deported.

MONA I have my boy to support and to protect.

MATT I never said I would harm them.

MONA I know nothing about you.

MATT That's why we do background checks.

MONA How do you do a background check on an invisible man?

MATT Well, maybe you need to give this more thought. I am serious about my offer and it still stands. It's either you are in or out. It's pointless debating with you when you have not made a decision.

MONA Wait, Matt, I have made up my mind. I want to do this; I mean, I need to do this. It would benefit me at this point in my life, but I think that you should meet me halfway on price.

MATT I only have $15,000 cash.

MONA I will take that in addition to $5,000 on credit.

MATT $15,000 cash, $3,000 credit, and I will do any repairs on your house?

MONA $15,000 cash, $4,000 credit, rights to claim you yearly on my taxes and keep the returns, and your written word.

MATT   Deal.

MONA   [*Shaking hands.*] It's a deal

• • •

Till Death Do Us

Gene Fiskin

Gene Fiskin

After producing advertising campaigns for more than 200 major corporations, Gene Fiskin joined the Orange County Playwrights Alliance, and has since written some thirty-seven plays, most of which have either been presented as staged readings or full productions. His other works include short stories, novels, and screenplays. He has also acted in and directed approximately sixty plays and videos. Fiskin's *Grandpa Was a Bachelor*, a full-length play, was produced in New York during the 2011–2012 season.

···production history···

The play is yet to be produced.

characters

HELEN, mid-40s

STEVE, 50s

···

[*An upscale Las Vegas hotel room, possibly a bridal suite. Fresh flowers and a champagne bucket stand near a king-size bed. HELEN dejectedly on the edge of the bed. STEVE, upbeat and enthusiastic enters from the bathroom.*]

STEVE   Is this a great place, or what! Did you see that tub? Eight jets!

HELEN   Ummm...

STEVE   [*Pointing out the window.*] Look at that view! Boy, Vegas is really somethin', isn't it.

HELEN   Ummmm...

STEVE   Hey, lady. C'mon, this is your wedding night. Let's see some enthusiasm.

HELEN   Yeah. Sure. Whatever.

STEVE   Okay, what's the problem?

HELEN   Problem? I don't have a problem.

STEVE   You've been Mrs. Steve Ingalls for four hours and you've had a long face the whole time. What's going on?

HELEN   [*Long beat.*] You didn't like my wedding gown!

STEVE   What are you talking about? I loved your gown.

HELEN   You didn't even notice it.

STEVE   I did, too! It was white, kind of.

HELEN   There! You don't even know what color it was. It was pale ivory.

STEVE   Isn't that white?

HELEN   NO! Pale ivory is not white. It's pale ivory!

STEVE   Looked white to me.

HELEN   You don't even care. I could have worn torn jeans and curlers and you wouldn't have even noticed.

STEVE   Helen...what's wrong with you? The truth is, I'd have been thrilled to marry you if all you had on was a smile. In fact, a smile would be very welcome right about now.

HELEN   That's right, make fun of my feelings.

STEVE   I'm not making fun of anything. I loved your dress. You looked great in it.

HELEN   You didn't tell me you liked it. You didn't say anything about it.

STEVE   I'm telling you now. What difference does it make? I love you, we got married, our whole life is ahead of us; who cares about a stupid wedding gown. You're never going to wear it again anyway.

HELEN   Don't bet on it.

STEVE   Now, what does that mean? Look, Helen, I don't want to start off our marriage taking tranquilizers. Viagra, okay. Valium, no.

HELEN   You noticed Denise's dress.

STEVE   Just because I said she looked good?

HELEN   Oh. So maybe it wasn't her *dress* you were talking about.

STEVE   No. She looked fine. You know...nice. I thought complimenting your sister would make you happy.

HELEN   *She* looked good, but you didn't even notice me.

STEVE   FOR GOD'S SAKE, HELEN...YOU WERE STANDING RIGHT THERE IN FRONT OF ME. Of course I noticed you. You looked great!

HELEN   I did not. I've got this big ugly zit coming out. And I'm bloated.

STEVE   I just thought maybe you had put on a few pounds.

HELEN   There! You think I'm a fat pig!

STEVE   No. No, I don't! I think you look terrific.

HELEN   Really...?

STEVE   Really. You've got a great look. And you carry yourself really... good.

HELEN   What does that mean? "I carry myself really good." Are you saying that for what I am, I don't look too bad? Is that it? For a wreck, I look okay?

STEVE   You're not a wreck! You're a little bloated, isn't that what you said?

HELEN   So you did notice. You stood up there in front of God and everybody and made a great sacrifice marrying a bloated, fat pig with a zit! What do want a medal?

STEVE   No. I want a divorce.

HELEN   Oh my God...!

STEVE   I'm joking, Helen. I made a joke because you're talking crazy. A little joke. My God, where's your sense of humor?

HELEN   [*Sobbing.*] Ohhhhh... he hates me. He hates me because I'm fat, with a zit, and have no sense of humor! Oh God... what did I do to get this zit?
[*Beat.*]
I should have worn lavender. I look good in lavender.

STEVE   If you keep this up, you better hope you look good in black, because you're killing me, Helen. A man should not die on his wedding night. Not without a hard-on.

HELEN   How can you even talk about sex right now? Do I look like someone you'd want to make love to? Do I... do I? Fat and bloated with a zit the size of a Buick?

STEVE   I like Buicks. My father always drove a Buick. At least until he could afford a Lexus.

HELEN   What are you talking about? Why are you bringing up cars when my heart is breaking?

STEVE   You brought it up. I just made a comment, that's all. Look, the zit doesn't remotely resemble a Buick. A Ford, maybe...

HELEN   You don't love me. You don't even care about me! I don't know why you married me!

STEVE   Helen, you're making me crazy! And if you keep this up...
[*Beat.*]
I've half a mind to give you a good spanking.

HELEN   HA...! Don't make me laugh.

STEVE   Oh, fine. That's right...go ahead, laugh at a man with half a mind.

HELEN   [*Starting to laugh despite herself.*] And that's why I married *you*, because even when I feel bad you can make me laugh.

STEVE   Well, thank God for that!

HELEN   Do you really love me, Steve?

STEVE   I married you, didn't I?

HELEN   That wasn't my question. I just want to make sure you love me despite my craziness.

STEVE   Let's get into bed and I'll show you how much I love you.

HELEN   Did you love Libby as much as you love me?

STEVE   Why bring up Libby? If I loved her, I wouldn't have divorced her. If I loved her, I wouldn't have married you.

HELEN   I'm asking...when you married Libby if you loved her as much as you love me?

STEVE   When I married her, yes, I loved her. But I wasn't in love with her. There's a difference.

HELEN   Does that mean you *love me* but you might not be in love with me...?

STEVE   I love you, crazy lady. I'm *in love* with you. And if you must know, I loved your dress...I loved your shoes and your purse. I even loved the funny thing you wore on your head. And in time,

I'm sure I will learn to love that fucking dog of yours, though that's another subject altogether. But the truth is, tonight, with you, I would like to have an erection...and I would *love* to do something with it.

HELEN   You're a sex maniac, Steven.

STEVE   When this dialogue started, that was entirely possible, now I'm not so sure.

HELEN   Are you saying we can't have a civilized conversation anymore? Does this mean if I want to talk things out, I'll stop being attractive to you? That you'll stop caring about me...or respecting my needs?

STEVE   Did I say that? Did those words come out of my mouth?

HELEN   You said you wanted me, but now you're not so sure. It's like telling me if I ask you a reasonable question, that'll be grounds for divorce.

STEVE   Helen.

    [*Beat.*]

    Helen, I don't know what to say anymore. I'm afraid to say anything. You twist it all around. We got married because we both thought it was a good idea. Foolishly, I thought it might also include some interesting thrashing around in bed.

HELEN   Don't tell me that's the only reason you married me...!

STEVE   No. That was just one of them. You're an exciting, intelligent, beautiful woman. And I admire you immensely. But would the universe be in danger if we respectfully and tastefully screwed around a little?

HELEN   I don't know you anymore, Steven. You're acting like some sex-crazed teenager.

STEVE   All things considered, there are some women who wouldn't find that so terrible.

HELEN   I'm not that kind of person. You know that, Steven.

STEVE   Well, I certainly know it now.

HELEN   You make that sound like a bad thing.

STEVE   Let's just say I'm a little surprised at the way this wedding night is shaping up.

HELEN   You're disappointed, aren't you?

[*Beat.*]

I don't know... maybe it's me.

[*Beat.*]

Or maybe you're hungry. We could go out to dinner.... Or a movie. Or, if you want to, we could go downstairs and play the slots for a while. I'm feeling lucky.

STEVE   Truthfully, when this evening started out I thought *I* might get lucky. I'm not thinking that anymore.

[*Beat.*]

Maybe I'll just go take a cold shower or something.

[*He goes off into the bathroom. When he is offstage,* HELEN *starts undressing.*]

HELEN   Don't be too long. Remember, I'll be here waiting for you.

STEVE   [*Offstage.*] Yeah. Right.

[*We hear the shower starting up.*]

HELEN   Right here, Steven. In bed. Where a bride should be on her wedding night.

STEVEN   [*Offstage.*] Helen... do me a favor. Give it a rest.

HELEN   I don't think I'll ever understand men.

[*Beat.*]

Steve use to be so romantic. Our wedding night... and he's taking a cold shower!

[*Beat.*]

I should have worn lavender....

• • •

A Number on
the Roman
Calendar

David Johnston

David Johnston

David Johnston's plays have been performed and read at the New Group, Moving Arts, the Neighborhood Playhouse, HB Playwrights Foundation, and Ensemble Studio Theatre. New York productions include working with the Blue Coyote Theater Group: Conversations on Russian Literature, a new adaptation of *The Oresteia* (*Time Out* Best of 2007), *Busted Jesus Comix* (GLAAD nominee 2005, London, Los Angeles, DC Cap Fringe), *A Bush Carol, or George Dubya and the Xmas of Evil*, and *Effie Jean in Tahiti* (both with music and lyrics by Stephen Speights). Regional credits include *The George Place* (Wellfleet Harbor Actors Theater). With director Kevin Newbury, Johnston wrote and staged *Candy & Dorothy* (GLAAD winner, 2006, WHAT, Unexpected Stage), and *The Eumenides*. Publications include *Saturday with Martin* (Short Plays to Long Remember), *The Eumenides* (Playing with Canons, New York Theatre Experience, Inc.), *Leaving Tangier* (Samuel French), and *A Funeral Home in Brooklyn*, *A Lesson* (Smith & Kraus). Current projects include the upcoming premiere of *Coney* and a film adaptation of his short play *Mothra Is Waiting*. Playwriting awards include Theater Oxford, Playwright Residency at the University of Cincinnati, Berrilla Kerr Foundation Grant, Ludwig Vogelstein Foundation, Arch & Bruce Brown Foundation, and New Dramatists. He was educated at the College of William and Mary and trained at the Circle in the Square. He's a member of Actors Equity, Dramatists Guild (publications committee), Charles Maryan's Playwrights/Directors Workshop, BMI, Blue Coyote Theater Group, and is a 2011–2012 resident artist for American Lyric Theater's Composer Librettist Development Program.

···production history···

A Number on the Roman Calendar was presented as a reading by d.i.r.t. company (Carter Jackson, Sarah Kate Jackson, co-founders and artistic directors) at the Players Club, New York City, September 12, 2011. The cast included Jonna McElrath, James Ireland, and Tom Lyons, and was directed by Carter Jackson.

characters

WILL

MARGERY

The POPE

···

[*Night. A man and a woman.* WILL *and* MARGERY. *Any age, any ethnicity. They are clothed in rags, seated on a mound of earth. It is very cold.* WILL *looks up into the stars and the sky above him.*]

WILL   This is it. The end of the world. It's the last day of earth. Our Lord and Savior Jesus Christ is coming. He will smite His foes. He will gather His children up to Him. He will wipe away all their tears and He will carry them to Heaven. He will begin his reign of a thousand years, and defeat the forces of darkness and the earth will be a memory and His kingdom will have no end.

MARGERY   I can see my breath.

WILL   It's the last day of the world. The last day of mankind.

MARGERY   It's cold.

WILL   December 31, in the year of Our Lord, nine hundred and ninety-nine.

[MARGERY *pulls her rags tighter around her body. She shivers.*]

MARGERY   Wish we had a fire.

WILL   The year nine hundred and ninety-nine. The world will end before the year one thousand. Christ is coming soon.

MARGERY   Will it be warmer then?

WILL   Shh. Quiet, my wife. My own Margery. We will wait.

[*He pulls her closer to him and continues to stare off into the night sky.*]

MARGERY   I wish we had a turnip.

WILL   It's all right, my wife. When Christ comes, there will be milk and honey.

MARGERY   I'd be happy with a turnip.

WILL   We're out of turnips.

MARGERY   I miss turnips.

WILL   We ran out of those weeks ago.

MARGERY   I don't think I could take milk and honey right now. There's nothing in my stomach. Milk and honey is too rich.

WILL   I'm sure there's other food—

MARGERY   Maybe something lighter to start—

WILL   Other food He's bringing—

MARGERY   Some kind of grain. I don't mean to sound disrespectful.

WILL   There will be something you can eat. Christ will bring—

MARGERY   Milk and honey is fine.

WILL   Something you can eat.

MARGERY   I'll just—go slow. With the milk.

WILL   We shouldn't talk about these things. It sounds frivolous. The priest would say—

MARGERY   The priest.

WILL   Would say we're being frivolous.

MARGERY   The priest would say I shouldn't think about food—

WILL   Put it out of your—

MARGERY   At a time like this. With big things. About to happen.

WILL   He will wipe away every tear. We'll be with our loved ones in glory.

MARGERY   That'll be nice. Will?

WILL   Yes?

MARGERY   Do we know what time He's coming?

[WILL *thinks for a moment.*]

WILL   Before daybreak.

MARGERY   Is He coming at midnight?

WILL   I—I don't know, Margery.

MARGERY   Because if He's coming at midnight, that's—

WILL   I don't know if it's right at midnight, Margery.

MARGERY   That would be great. But if He's coming at dawn—

WILL   We don't know the exact time. Scripture says—

MARGERY   It'll get very cold if we're here till daybreak.

WILL   It doesn't say anything about the *specific time.*

MARGERY   We could freeze.

WILL   Christ won't let us freeze. We're poor.

MARGERY   We are poor.

WILL   He loves the poor.

MARGERY   I know we're poor and He loves us, but—

WILL   What is it?

MARGERY   The cottage is right down the hill.

WILL   I know.

MARGERY   The cottage is right there.

WILL   Yes, Margery.

MARGERY   And we can see Christ coming from the cottage—we can stand at the window and—

WILL   We need to be here. We need to be awake—I want to be awake for my Lord—

MARGERY   It's right down the hill, Will. We can be awake in the cottage.

WILL   I want to be high up! I want to be high up so we can meet—

MARGERY   And it's warm. We have dung. We can burn dung.

WILL   I don't want to use up all the dung.

MARGERY   There's bits of frost in my hair.

WILL   I want to be up on a hill so we can—

MARGERY   This earth is damp. It's dry in the cottage, Will.

WILL   If we're on a hill, we can see him from a ways off—with the hordes of Satan—as He's *smiting*—

MARGERY   We're out of turnips and we're starving, but we don't have to—

WILL   Now is not the time to think about our bodies!

MARGERY   Will, I'm in my body, I can't help that.

WILL   We must be as the lilies of the field.

MARGERY   Lilies need sunshine.

WILL   Here.

[*He takes off a few of his rags and wraps them around her shoulders.*]

MARGERY   I don't want your rags.

WILL   Take them.

MARGERY   You'll get cold.

WILL   Take my rags, Margery.

MARGERY   You'll freeze.

WILL   I won't freeze. I have you.

[MARGERY *accepts his few rags, wraps them tightly around her.* WILL *nestles closer to her, and shivers a bit. They stare up into the sky.*]

MARGERY   Will?

WILL   Yes, my wife?

MARGERY   Are we sure it's December 31?

WILL   Yes.

MARGERY   We're sure?

WILL   Yes.

MARGERY   How are we sure?

WILL   Because—because—the priest said—

MARGERY   The priest.

WILL   Father Geoffrey said that on the 31st of December—

MARGERY   Do we know it's the 31st?

WILL   It is the 31st.

MARGERY   Because if it's not till Wednesday—

WILL   I'm sure Father Geoffrey—

MARGERY   We can't sit out here till Wednesday, Will. We will freeze. Christ will find us frozen.

WILL   Please don't blaspheme, Margery.

MARGERY   How is that—?

WILL   Please.

[*She crosses herself.*]

MARGERY   But we know it's tonight?

WILL   Yes.

MARGERY   We know.

WILL   I'm your husband, Margery. I will tell you the correct date.

[*He leans into her. It's clear from his face he's no longer sure if the date is correct.*]

MARGERY   Will?

WILL   Yes, my wife?

MARGERY   You know I'm slow about things.

WILL   That's not true. You're a shrewd woman.

MARGERY   So I have to have things explained to me.

WILL   A shrewd prudent helpmate blessed in husbandry and domestic crafts.

MARGERY   You're sweet. But help me with something.

WILL   All right.

MARGERY   So Christ is coming.

WILL   Yes.

MARGERY   Because it's the end of a thousand years.

WILL   Yes. His reign will last—

MARGERY   Will last a thousand years.

WILL   Yes. He is coming back in glory—

MARGERY   Because Scripture says—

WILL   Scripture says he will come again in glory after the millennia.

MARGERY   Which is a thousand years.

WILL   Yes.

MARGERY   So a thousand years since He left us.

WILL   A thousand years since He was crucified.

MARGERY   So—on the day He was crucified—

WILL   Yes—

MARGERY   On the *day* He was *crucified*. Not on the day He was *resurrected*?

[*Pause.*]

A thousand years from the day He was crucified. So—on Good Friday—right after He was crucified—that day—it automatically became January 1?

[*Pause.*]

And we're going from that day—not the day He was
resurrected—three days later. That's not January 1. And we're
not going from the time—after He was resurrected—and He said
oh I'm here—and He talked to everyone—met with them—and
then went back. In glory. That's not where we're starting from.
We're going from the crucifixion. That's January the first. Not
next week, when He was resurrected. Or whenever He went
back. In glory.

[*Pause.*]

WILL   Why are you asking so many questions?

MARGERY   I'm curious.

WILL   God is upset by curious women!

MARGERY   I just want to know where we're—

WILL   We're waiting for Christ! We're sitting here—waiting—for Him
to take us back in glory!

MARGERY   I don't mean to upset you—

WILL   We're waiting for Christ to come and take us to Heaven and
then the world will end! Why are you making it weird?

MARGERY   I want to know we're here on the right day, Will! So it's not
next Wednesday—or next Saturday—

WILL   I don't know why you can't believe!

MARGERY   So I'm not sitting at home next Saturday scraping my feet
when all of a sudden—

WILL   I don't know why you can't have faith!

MARGERY   I do have faith, Will!

WILL   Why you—

MARGERY   That is not true! I have a faithful heart!

WILL   Then why are you—

MARGERY   I have faith in you, Will. I have faith in you.

WILL   Please don't blaspheme, Margery.

MARGERY   It's not blasphemy! You're my beloved husband, and when Christ comes, He'll find me sitting next to you. Sitting next to the husband I love. Who's a good man. Who never hits me and works hard and rubs my feet when they hurt. Christ will find me with you. Here on this *cold hill*.

WILL   It's blasphemy, Margery, if you doubt that—

MARGERY   I don't doubt He's coming! I just don't want to freeze to death because the priest got the date wrong!

WILL   I have to stay, Margery. I have to. Even if it's next Wednesday. Even if it's next Saturday. I have to stay. What if I missed it?

MARGERY   Will—

WILL   I have to believe, Margery. I have to have faith. I have to believe that faith will be rewarded. We must have faith.

[*There is a loud blast of trumpets from offstage, as though proclaiming a heavenly glory. The* POPE *enters in a hurry, in full papal regalia.*]

POPE   [*Yelling offstage.*] STOP IT!
   [*The trumpets cease. The* POPE *sees* WILL *and* MARGERY.]
   Hello there.

WILL   Hello.

POPE   How are you?

MARGERY   Good.

POPE   Wonderful.

WILL   Can we help you?

POPE   I'm—a wandering merchant.

WILL   Okay.

MARGERY   [*Seeing something offstage.*] Who are all those guys?

WILL   Who?

MARGERY   The ones down the hill? The ones with all the casks and—

WILL   Horses and banners—and trumpets and chests—

MARGERY   Is that a lion?

WILL   Stretching on into—there are *hundreds of them*—

MARGERY   Is it the French?

WILL   Are we French again?

POPE   We're not French. We're merchants. All of us. Hundreds of us—wandering merchants. We have spices.

WILL   Oh. Spices.

MARGERY   We can't afford spices.

POPE   I have a question for you, humble vassal.

WILL   We hope to be of service to you, wandering merchant.

POPE   I'm looking for the poorest of the poor.

MARGERY   We're poor.

WILL   I don't think we're the poorest.

MARGERY   There's the Gowers.

WILL   Our neighbors, the Gowers. They are definitely—

POPE   I was told that the poorest of the poor in this district was a pious couple, full of—you know—fear of the Lord. Their names are Will and Margery.

MARGERY   That's our name.

WILL   We're not the poorest of the—

MARGERY   Poor—

WILL   No—the Gowers are much—

POPE   [*Agitated.*] I have it on good authority that the poorest of the poor—therefore the most deserving—before Christ comes tonight and kills those who are rich and have stored up treasure on earth etcetera—is a couple named Will and Margery. Are you Will and Margery?

MARGERY   That's our name.

POPE   You're the poorest of the poor?

WILL   I don't think we're that poor.

MARGERY   Will.

WILL   And besides, if you're a wandering merchant, why do you want us? We don't use spices.

MARGERY   Will. Let the well-dressed stranger to our province speak.

POPE   Your names are Will and Margery?

WILL   Yes.

POPE   And you're poor?

WILL   Poor we may be in worldly goods, but in our hearts, we—

POPE   Great. But can I see some proof?

WILL   Proof of what?

POPE   Proof that you're poor?

WILL   We're not that poor. We have a house right there.

POPE   Where?

WILL   [*Pointing offstage to their cottage.*] Over there. See? We have a cottage. I built it with my own hands. The sweat of my brow.

[*The* POPE *looks off in the distance, in the direction where* WILL *is pointing.*]

POPE   That's a *house*?

WILL   Where are you looking?

POPE   Right there.

WILL   Yes. That's our—

POPE   You *live* in that? That's a *house*?

WILL   Well, yes , we—

POPE   I thought it was just—something—someone *left*.

WILL   I've been doing some work on the—

POPE   I didn't think people *lived* in it. What's that thing that's leaning against the—

WILL   That's the door. The front door.

POPE   That's a *door*?

WILL   You're not getting the whole effect. When it's done, it'll—

POPE   Jesus wept. You'll do.

[*The* POPE *exits. A trumpet blast. He hurries back on with a cask.*]

WILL   The other merchants seem to treat you with a great deal of respect.

[*The* POPE *glares. He opens the cask. It is filled with gold. He sets it down hurriedly next to them on the ground.*]

POPE   Take this. You poor people. I give it to you freely. Out of the abundance of my—uh—charity. And grace. Which comes out of love of Our Father Almighty God. So—when Christ comes—and He says to me—hey, you—you with the hat—you're rich. I'm gonna kill you. I'll say—no. I'm not rich. I'm poor. Me. I'm poor. They've got the money. Those two. Will and Margery. The filthy ones over there on the hill. All right?

WILL   I don't think we can—

MARGERY   Deal.

POPE   Deal?

MARGERY   Deal.

WILL   Are you the Pope?

[*There is a blast of trumpets, which startles the* POPE.]

POPE   Yeah.

[WILL *and* MARGERY *fall on their faces in front of the* POPE.]

WILL   Oh, Prince of the Church on earth—

POPE   But you better be the poorest of the poor.

MARGERY   Not a problem.

POPE   If I find out you own stuff, you're in big trouble.

WILL   We cannot accept your gift.

POPE   You'll accept it if you know what's good for you!

MARGERY   Will, you can't argue with the Pope! Take the money!

WILL   We're not worthy of your—

POPE   You better not be worthy! That's why I'm giving you the gold, you idiot! If you're worthy, I'm taking it back! And having you killed!

MARGERY   Oh, we're very poor and not worthy, Oh, Pope—

POPE   That's more like it.

WILL   Great Pope, we—

MARGERY   Why are you in England?

POPE   Mind your own fucking business!

[*The* POPE *exits in a hurry.* MARGERY *and* WILL *slowly get up and look at the gold.*]

MARGERY   Wow.

WILL   Look at this.

MARGERY   Wow. Look at this gold. Wow.

WILL   This is a lot of gold.

MARGERY   We're rich.

WILL   Yes.

MARGERY   We're really rich.

WILL   Yes

MARGERY   We're rich like *Jews*.

WILL   We've got to get rid of it.

MARGERY   Wait a minute, Will.

WILL   We've got to give this to the poor.

MARGERY   We're poor! If you take away our gold, we're poor!

WILL   We have to get rid of the gold before Christ comes!

MARGERY   He might not get here for a few days! We could be wrong about the date!

WILL   Treasures of this world are worthless before God! They are as dross!

MARGERY   But—but—if He doesn't come till Wednesday, we can get something to eat and then unload it right before He gets here!

WILL   We have to get rid of this!

MARGERY   We can buy turnips! We can buy dung!

WILL   But He loves the poor!

MARGERY   Will. Think. Please, my husband. Think. If we have something to eat   and we have a nice fire—and we spend a night sleeping somewhere dry—why would that upset Him?
[WILL *thinks for a moment.*]
It's not like He's going to look at us and say, you've eaten in the last week, so you don't qualify! You have a turnip! You're not half frozen and covered with scabs, so you don't count!

WILL   Margery—

MARGERY   Wouldn't He still love us?
[WILL *is tormented.*]
We'll buy some food in the village—we'll share it with everybody, He likes that!—and then we'll all be together and we'll wait for Him! That doesn't make us rich, Will! Not if it just happened the hour before He got here!

WILL   I'm so afraid, Margery.

MARGERY   Will—

WILL   I'm so afraid.

MARGERY   What are you afraid of? There's nothing to be—

WILL   That He won't take us with Him. And we'll never get to see our boy again.

[*Pause.*]

If He doesn't take us with Him, we'll never get to see our boy again. I can't let that happen.

[*Pause.*]

MARGERY Will. Listen. We can go into the village. We'll buy a pig. We can buy a pig with this—

WILL Margery—

MARGERY A nice fat pig. Turnips. Too much for the two of us to eat. We can buy too much with this gold. Lots of turnips. Then—

WILL I don't like this!

MARGERY Then, Will—we'll go over to the Gowers'.

WILL The neighbors? Why are we—

MARGERY We'll go over to the Gowers'. They have seventeen children, Will.

WILL They do have a—

MARGERY They have a lot of kids. And we'll share all the pork and turnips with them. They haven't eaten either, Will. I mean, we're starving, but they've got to watch all those kids starve. That's got to be worse for them, right? So we'll take them food, and the kids will eat. And when Christ comes—if we're cooking and killing the pig and cutting up turnips for the Gowers' kids and sharing dung for the fire and we're not sitting on this hill and He says, what are you doing? Why aren't you waiting for Me out on the hill? We can say, we were taking care of these kids while you took care of ours.

[WILL *is silent.*]

He seems like the fair sort. Don't you think, Will?

WILL Father Geoffrey would say—

MARGERY We'll invite him. He likes pork. I've seen him tuck into a pig. He likes pork.

WILL But how would that—

MARGERY If we're feeding a priest when Christ comes—I mean—that reflects well on us, doesn't it? Can't hurt.

[*Pause.*]

We should start going towards the village. If we're going to buy that pig. And get back here.

WILL Everyone is asleep in the village.

MARGERY We'll throw gold at the door and see if that wakes them up. C'mon.

WILL But as soon as we get back—

MARGERY As soon as we get back—

WILL After we buy the pig and kill it and feed the kids and feed the priest—

MARGERY We'll have a little warm by the fire too.

WILL Yes.

MARGERY And we need to eat.

WILL We'll have something too.

MARGERY Yes—

WILL Then we're coming back.

MARGERY We're coming back.

WILL We'll be here. Waiting for Him.

MARGERY We're not leaving.

WILL Not till He gets here.

MARGERY Right.

WILL And you'll be with me.

MARGERY Till He gets here. Or I die. I'm here with you.

[*They hurry off to buy a pig as the lights come down.*]

• • •

Six Dead Bodies Duct-Taped to a Merry-Go-Round

Lindsay Marianna Walker
and Dawson Moore

Dawson Moore and
Lindsay Marianna Walker

Dawson Moore's plays have been produced across the United States and in Italy. He has won national awards for his short comedies *Bile in the Afterlife*, *In a Red Sea*, *The Bus*, *Burning*, *The Fears of Harold Shivvers*, and *Domestic Companion*. He is a member of the Dramatists Guild of America and New York City's Circle East. Along with Aoise Stratford, he is the founding co-artistic director of San Francisco's Three Wise Monkeys Theatre Company. He lives in Valdez, Alaska, where he coordinates the Last Frontier Theatre Conference (www.theatreconference.org) and runs an AFA program in playwriting. He is online at www.dawsonmoore.com.

Lindsay Marianna Walker earned a PhD in creative writing from the University of Southern Mississippi and currently teaches English at Auburn University. She has published widely in multiple genres. Her poetry manuscript, *The Josephine Letters*, was a finalist for the 2009 Walt Whitman Award; she has a short story forthcoming from the University of Texas's literary journal, *Bat City Review*; and her ten-minute play, *Boy Marries Hill*, is anthologized in Gary Garrison's guide to playwriting, *A More Perfect Ten*.

···production history···

Six Dead Bodies Duct-Taped to a Merry-Go-Round had its premier professional performance in Anchorage, Alaska, in October 2010 under the direction of Schatzie Schaefers for Three Wise Moose Theatre Company. The cast included Kevin Bennet as Winston and Eric Holzschuh as Toby. Also, in October 2011 it had a four-week run with Full Circle Theatre, New York; in June 2011 it was performed at the Last Frontier Theatre Conference by Three Wise Moose; in April 2011 it had a one-week run with Reader's Theatre Repertory, Portland, Oregon; in October 2010 it had four-week run at Anchorage Community Theatre; in August 2010 it had a one-week run with Salt Lake Artists League as a part of Weekend of New Works. In March 2010 it had a developmental reading with Circle East, New York.

characters

WINSTON, 50s. Grizzled truck driver.

TOBY, mid-20s. A soldier.

setting

The play begins in a Reno truck stop parking lot, then primarily takes place in the cab of WINSTON's semi-trailer truck.

costumes

WINSTON wears a greasy, faded mechanic's jumpsuit. TOBY wears camouflage fatigues and carries a large duffel bag.

time

Fall 2009.

•••

[*Lights rise on* WINSTON, *leaning out the open door of his truck's cab. He is eavesdropping on* TOBY, *who paces anxiously, talking into a cell phone, and doesn't notice* WINSTON *watching him.*]

TOBY   Come on, pick up. Pick up, Kelsey…no, I *don't* want to leave another message…uh, hey. It's Toby. Message number three.

I'm still in Reno...uh, I guess I'll just try to find another way home, and see you when I get there. Give me a call when you get this.

[*Pause.*]

This really sucks, Kels. Call me.

[*He puts the phone in his pocket, chewing the side of his thumbnail.*]

WINSTON You need a ride, soldier?

TOBY Yeah...I guess I do.

WINSTON You're not a cop, are you?

TOBY Sorry?

WINSTON Where you heading?

TOBY California. San Jose.

WINSTON Well, it's a little out of the way...I'm going to Los Angeles...

TOBY Yeah. Don't worry about it.

WINSTON No, no. I can get you there. I'm just thinking out loud about what route to take.

TOBY If you could even get me close...

WINSTON Hop in.

[TOBY *crosses around the front of the truck and gets in.*]

TOBY Thanks.

WINSTON Name's Winston.

[*Pause.*]

You're not carrying any guns, are you? I don't mean to pry, but I've got some materials in back that, uh...let's say they don't mix well with firearms. Company policy.

TOBY Don't worry about me.

WINSTON So. You like music, officer?

TOBY Yeah, I guess.

WINSTON   Yeah to the music, or yeah to the officer?

TOBY   What are you getting at?

WINSTON   Nothing. I thought you said you were a cop.

TOBY   I'm not a cop. I'm an army corporal.

WINSTON   What about before the service?

TOBY   Construction, I guess.

WINSTON   Good. That's good honest work, right there.

TOBY   I guess. I'm ready to get back to it, ready to get back anyway.

WINSTON   Coming home from Iraq?

TOBY   Afghanistan.

WINSTON   How was it?

TOBY   Awesome. It was great. Really fun.

WINSTON   Wow…really?

TOBY   No.
[*Pause.*]
Cold. It was really cold. I didn't expect that. People were burning so much garbage in Jalalabad to keep warm, the air turned black. Couldn't hardly breathe.

WINSTON   Jesus.

[WINSTON *pulls the truck out onto the highway.*]

TOBY   Coughed so hard, I gave myself a hernia. But I'm home for good. I don't have to go back. I haven't seen my wife in fourteen months, so, you know…that should be fun…she was supposed to be here.

WINSTON   Hope she's all right. Or, you know, mostly all right.

TOBY   What?

WINSTON   You don't want her to be hurt or anything, but something needs to have gone wrong, or you'll be pissed that she didn't pick you up.

TOBY Look—

WINSTON It's only human.

TOBY Can we not talk about this? I'm sure there's a good reason she wasn't there.

WINSTON Consider it dropped.

> [*Pause.*]

> Listen, you seem like a trustworthy guy, and you're not a cop, so I'm happy to drive you . . . but there's something I need for you to do for me.

TOBY Whoa. Easy, dude. I'm not going to polish your knob or whatever. I don't need a ride that bad.

WINSTON Aw, hell, that ain't what I meant. . . . Why would you think *that*? I look like some sorta sexual deviant to you?

TOBY Oh, I just . . . you know, you hear stories . . . about truckers . . .

WINSTON Happily taken for the last nine years, thank you.

TOBY I'm sorry.

WINSTON Jeez, like I'm some kind of weirdo.

TOBY I said I'm sorry. Just a misunderstanding.

WINSTON Okay. Forget it.

> [*Pause.*]

> Glad we got beyond that.

> [*Pause.*]

> Know what I'm hauling in the back of this rig?

TOBY No.

WINSTON It's a "body bus." I'm taking a load of cadavers to UCLA. Dead bodies. For research.

TOBY That doesn't scare me.

WINSTON Does me. I ain't never hauled so many bodies.

> [*Pause.*]

Actually, I've never pulled this gig before. Not bodies, never. I used to haul gas for BP. Bigger truck, less money. Go figure. The point is . . . I've never had an opportunity like this before.

TOBY   Opportunity to what?

WINSTON   I've got this idea. We'll stop in Sacramento on the way to your place. There's a park on the west side, just off the railroad tracks . . . Sam Combs Park. We'll just stop there, get the bodies out of the back—

TOBY   Pull over. Pull over. I'm not fooling around with any dead bodies, no way!

WINSTON   But I've got this idea. . . . Listen.

TOBY   Are you kidding me?

WINSTON   What are you talking about?

TOBY   Necrophilia! I'm not doing it.

WINSTON   Sex with dead bodies? That's where your mind goes first, son? Is this what posttraumatic stress is like? The first thing you think of when corpses come up is having sex with them?

TOBY   Then what are you talking about?

WINSTON   We're gonna duct-tape 'em to the merry-go-round.

TOBY   Um . . . what?

WINSTON   I got this new digital video camera. My lady and me . . . we needed money. We figured we'd be able to do something with the camera . . . you know . . . home videos.

TOBY   Oh.

WINSTON   Yeah, so that's not panning out.

TOBY   If she's not a hell of a lot better-looking than you—

WINSTON   We've been keeping our eyes open for opportunities. That's what this is, man. That's exactly what this is. We'll film it and put it on the Internet and charge people to watch it . . . five bucks a pop, maybe ten. You get a couple thousand people . . . that's millions of dollars. That's a lot of dough.

TOBY You planning on sharing the proceeds?

WINSTON You need a ride. I need a hand. Two hands. I'm on the up and up.

TOBY No way, man. Sorry.

WINSTON Someone's gonna help me. If that someone isn't you...I gotta let you off.

[*Pause*]

Your wife call you back yet?

TOBY No.

WINSTON Don't suppose she's schtupping the mailman, do you? What do you military boys call that...when a guy moves in on your girl while you're out killing the bad guys...

TOBY A Jody.

WINSTON Yeah, a Jody, that's right. I mean, for all you know, she could be banging someone—

TOBY Shut up!

WINSTON Just trying to make conversation.

TOBY [*Pause.*] You ever try to actually move a body before?

WINSTON Nope.

TOBY They're heavy. Like bags-of-concrete heavy.

WINSTON A stiff's a stiff. You look strong...hernia still bothering you?

TOBY No, surgery was over a month ago. Look, what if...what happens if we get caught?

WINSTON Listen, if you see blue lights, just run. Run, and don't look back.

TOBY I'm not saying I'll...Jesus. Who are these people anyway? And how would you like it if someone roped your dead body to a seesaw?

WINSTON   Merry-go-round. Seesaw wouldn't work…we're making a movie. We need some action.

TOBY   That makes sense. There wouldn't be any up and down with two stiffs on a teeter-totter.

WINSTON   [*Laughs.*] We don't have much of a special-effects budget.

TOBY   Winston, I can't go do this. I…I see what you're saying, and I can picture it, and I can even see a bunch of idiots paying to watch it…God help us…but it's just so, so lame…I mean… disrespectful.

WINSTON   What, to them? They don't give two shits at this point. They donated their bodies to science. Science. There's nothing we're going to do that's worse than what those doctors down at UCLA got in store. It's a chop shop down there. We're just gonna drag 'em, strap 'em, spin 'em, film 'em, and toss 'em back in the truck. Good as new.

TOBY   You should keep their faces covered, though…don't you think?

WINSTON   Maybe.

TOBY   I mean, if a family member sees it…they've got detectives for that sort of thing.

WINSTON   Oh yeah…hadn't thought…but will people pay to watch it if they can't see the dead faces?

TOBY   That's a risk we're going to have to take.

WINSTON   "We" are?

[*Pause.*]

I can live with that…hell, that's good…anonymity. Yeah. Like "we're all faceless in death…all the same." Puts a good spin on it.

TOBY   Speaking of spin…how are you planning to get the thing started?

WINSTON   I got a rope in back. I figure I'll wrap it around the base and then tie the end to the bumper. When I say action, you hit the gas and let 'em fly.

TOBY   This is insane. This is a really, really stupid idea.

WINSTON   Oh, come on…it'll take an hour, two max. You'll be home before the sun's up.

[TOBY *looks out the window, then pulls out his cell phone. He stares at it.*]

TOBY   Why do you need the money?

WINSTON   This trucking thing may look glamorous, but it barely covers rent. Mona is…well, Mona can't work any more.

TOBY   Your wife?

WINSTON   Not actually married, but for all intents, yeah, she's my life.

TOBY   What's wrong with her?

WINSTON   She swerved to miss a kid with her car. Hit a tree instead. She can't walk anymore. Her spine snapped.

TOBY   I thought you said you guys made, uh, videos…

WINSTON   Well, yeah. We still "do it," if that's what you're asking.

TOBY   How is it?

WINSTON   None of your goddamn business.

TOBY   Sorry.

WINSTON   Even though my old lady's a cripple, we're doing great. How's your marriage, huh? What's shaking with Miss San Jose? Been having troubles? Not picking you up is pretty cold.

TOBY   We got married a couple of months before I left.

WINSTON   Pregnant?

TOBY   No, no, I loved her.

WINSTON   You can have both of those.

TOBY   That's not what I'm saying…I just mean, I love her, like crazy…she sent me this care package for my birthday. It wasn't anything special, you know, of value. But there was this…coffee mug, and it looked just like this other one she'd given me when we were dating. Nothing big, but it was my favorite, until one day, she was drinking coffee, standing in the kitchen, and the mug slipped out of her hands, and smash! We both looked up at each other and yelled mazel tov!

[*Pause.*]

That was it. I knew. I mean, I'd known before, but that was the . . . the whatever-moment.

WINSTON   I know what you mean.

TOBY   So she sends me another mug, just like it, only she'd painted "Mazel Tov, Toby" on the side in gold glitter pen.

WINSTON   I get it.

TOBY   I don't know where she is. I talked to her a week ago and everything seemed fine.

WINSTON   I was just kidding before, you know.

TOBY   About the dead bodies and the merry-go-round?

WINSTON   No, that's on. All that Jody stuff. I didn't mean to say . . . lighten up, brother. She'll call. Girl like that? She'll call.

[*Pause.*]

It's not always all yellow ribbons when you get home, you know.

[*Pause.*]

I'm gonna stop at this exit up here.

TOBY   I can't.

WINSTON   Can't stop?

TOBY   The merry-go-round. I can't do it. I'm sorry. You can just let me off when we stop.

WINSTON   It's all right . . . I'll still take you home. It was a stupid idea anyway . . . you were right.

TOBY   Funny, though.

WINSTON   Yeah.

TOBY   Maybe we should just pretend that you were joking. Trying to trick me into going along with you.

WINSTON [*Pulling over.*] Yeah, I can't believe you bought that.

TOBY You sure got me!

WINSTON Like I'd do that. You're crazy. I'm going to use the head.

[TOBY *shakes his head. His cell phone goes off. He checks the caller ID. He looks up at* WINSTON, *who smiles, then gets out of the truck and exits.* TOBY *gets out, stretching as he answers.*]

TOBY Kels, thank God, are you okay?

> [*Pause.*]
>
> No, no, it's all right, I got a ride. Some weird trucker.
>
> [*Pause.*]
>
> Okay, what is it?
>
> [*Long pause; his jaw drops.*]
>
> I've got a what?
>
> [*Pause.*]
>
> Yeah . . . yeah, of course you should have told me! What if something had happened to me? I would never have known . . . it's a girl?
>
> [*Pause.*]
>
> Well, yeah, Kels, I'm kind of mad. It's been over nine months. That baby had better have teeth by now. I'm sorry, but—
>
> [*Pause.*]
>
> I don't know what to imply, all right?
>
> [*Pause.*]
>
> Yeah, of course I'm still coming home. Of course. I just . . .

[WINSTON *enters.* TOBY *turns away from him.* WINSTON *gets back in the cab of the truck, muttering.*]

WINSTON I can take a hint.

TOBY I can't talk now. . . . Look, I'll be home in a few hours.

[TOBY *hangs up and gets back in the truck.* WINSTON *pulls out.* WINSTON *finally can't hold back any longer.*]

WINSTON   Well?! What'd she say?

TOBY   I'm a father.

WINSTON   Well...I'll be damned...congratulations, Mazel Tov... there might be a cigar in the glove box...um...so are you... are you the father?

TOBY   She said she didn't tell me because she didn't want to make it harder. On me.

WINSTON   It would have.

TOBY   That's messed up, though, right? You don't wait till the night your husband's getting back after fourteen months and say, "Oh yeah, I almost forgot, we had a kid, *surprise!*"

WINSTON   You're looking at this all wrong. What do you suppose it was like for her? Better yet, think of how you would have felt, knowing you were missing the whole thing. That's the sort of worry that sucks you dry, leaves you with nothing. I can tell you from experience. It means she loves you. Making that kind of sacrifice? That's what it means.

TOBY   But...it feels wrong. *She* was wrong.

WINSTON   Maybe she was. But a wrong thing ain't always so wrong when it's done for the right reasons. She did it to protect you. Love's a pretty damn good reason to go and do something stupid.

TOBY   [*Pause.*] Her name's Caroline. She's got a tooth.

WINSTON   Wonderful.

TOBY   [*Pause.*] I'm going to do it.

WINSTON   That's the spirit.

TOBY   I mean, the dead bodies, the video...let's do it.

WINSTON   You serious?

TOBY   Let's do it, Winston. Let's go duct-tape these bastards to a merry-go-round. How I'm feeling right now...it'd be weird *not* to tape corpses to playground equipment.

WINSTON   Mona's gonna shit. We're gonna be rich.

TOBY   We should buy some antiseptic to spray it down afterward.

WINSTON   Good idea. You're a thoughtful kind of person.

TOBY   You got a title yet? You gotta have something catchy, you know. Something that'll get people's attention, without giving too much away. How about "Circle of Death"? Or…"Cadaver Carousel"!

WINSTON   [*Quietly.*] I've got a title.

TOBY   Something that gets across the essence of the thing…"Life After Death," no…"Joy in the Afterlife," no…how about "The Fun Never Ends"?

WINSTON   I've already got the perfect title.

TOBY   What?

WINSTON   I'm gonna call it "Six Dead Bodies Duct-Taped to a Merry-Go-Round."

[TOBY *stares at him, then nods and looks out the window as the lights fade.*]

TOBY   That works too.…

• • •

Starfishes

Michael Ross Albert

Michael Ross Albert

Michael Ross Albert is the author of several one-act plays, including *For the Winter* (35th Annual Samuel French Off-Off Broadway Short Play Contest), *Karenin's Anna* (Standard Deviation Theatre Company), and *Four Sons* (winner, Under 20s Playwriting Contest, Tarragon Theatre). His full-length plays include *Chagrin* (New York International Fringe Festival), *Tough Jews* (In the Beginning Festival, Harold Green Jewish Theatre Company), and *Pillars of Salt* (Holy Blossom Stagecraft). He received an MFA in playwriting from the Actors Studio Drama School. He is an associate member of the Dramatists Guild of America, and a member of the Playwright-Director Workshop at the Actors Studio in New York City.

···production history···

Starfishes received its world-premiere production Off-Broadway at the Theatre at Dance New Amsterdam as part of the Actors Studio Drama School's 2011 repertory season, featuring the following cast and creative team:

ELI, Brad Harris

CHASTITY, Shereen Macklin

Directed by Mekeva McNeil
Production Design by Shawn Lewis
Stage Manager, Joseph A. Onorato

characters

ELI, a man in his late 20s
CHASTITY, a prostitute

• • •

[*A Nova Scotia lighthouse in the late 1980s. The sitting room. A front door leading outside is upstage. On the opposite end of the upstage wall, a spiral staircase leading up. There is a window through which the maritime coast can be seen. A bookshelf, neatly stacked with books. A rotary phone. Comfortable, antiquated furniture. A rug covers a hardwood floor. Oil lanterns. A crucifix. The sound of waves crashing against the cliff. ELI is pacing the room anxiously. There is a loud, angry knock at the door. It continues throughout the following.*]

ELI   I'm sorry, I told you, this is a big misunderstanding.

[*More knocking.*]

I can't let you in.

[*More knocking.*]

This lighthouse is the property of the federal government.

[*More knocking.*]

If you continue to create a disturbance, I am required to alert the coast guard. Do you understand?

[*More knocking.*]

Argh!

[*He goes to the door and opens it a crack.*]

CHASTITY   Jesus Christ, what the hell's the matter with—

ELI   I'm sorry, this is a terrible mistake.

CHASTITY   Let me in!

ELI   No, I really can't do that.

CHASTITY   At least let me warm up for a minute!

ELI   Miss, this is federal property!

CHASTITY   I'm in the middle of nowhere. I can't see a damn thing with all the fog coming in—

ELI   I'm really sorry. . . . Good-bye.

CHASTITY   Come on, it's freezing.

ELI   I . . . listen, I can't . . .

CHASTITY   Please! It's getting dark!

> [*Beat.*]

> Hello? It's getting dark!

> [*Beat.*]

> Please, it's—

ELI   All right! Just for a minute, and that's it.

[*He steps aside.* CHASTITY *enters. She is a prostitute.*]

CHASTITY   Two hundred dollars.

ELI   Okay, listen, lady . . .

CHASTITY   Do you know how long I've been standing outside? In the freezing cold? And you can't even pay me? Uh-uh. I'm getting Rodney.

ELI   Rodney. . . . Who's . . . who's Rodney?

CHASTITY   Who do you think Rodney is? He's the man about to come inside your lighthouse and fuck you up. Understand?

ELI   Okay. Maybe we can sort this out.

CHASTITY   You wanna sort it out? Give me two hundred dollars.

ELI   Why should I have to pay you anything? We haven't...copulated.

CHASTITY   Copulated?

ELI   We haven't...you know...

CHASTITY   I know what copulated means, sweetheart. I just never heard anybody say it before in a sentence. And I'm in a line of business where there are a lot of chances for it to be said.

ELI   Yes, I can see that.

CHASTITY   Someone called. They told me to come all the way out to the edge of the cliff, to go to the lighthouse—

ELI   I'm sorry, but I don't know anything about that.

CHASTITY   Well, someone called.

ELI   It wasn't me.

CHASTITY   I don't care who it was. It took me an hour and a half to get here from the city. The fog's getting so thick, I had to walk the last kilometer in front of the headlights so Rodney could see where he was going. I expect to be paid.

ELI   I shouldn't have to pay you. We haven't—

CHASTITY   Oh, you don't have to tell me. It is painfully obvious that you and I have not *copulated*. And that you haven't copulated with anybody in a really long time. Is that true?

ELI   That's none of your business.

CHASTITY   I thought so.

[*Beat.*]

I need that money.

ELI   No, you need to leave. I have a lot of work to do. My mother will be home from Bingo soon—

CHASTITY   Bingo!?

ELI   She's not going to be too happy if she comes home and the light's not lit and I'm with a...a...

CHASTITY   A what?

ELI   Look, I'm sorry you got sent out here. But I shouldn't have to pay you.

CHASTITY   You're right. You shouldn't.

ELI   Uh...

CHASTITY   Not unless you wanna take advantage of my services.

ELI   Your... services?

CHASTITY   I mean, I'm here... you're here...

ELI   Oh no, I couldn't.

CHASTITY   Why not, stud? You don't like me?

ELI   Well, I think you're very...

CHASTITY   Why don't you like me?

ELI   I hardly know you. But. You strike me as a very... nice young lady.

CHASTITY   Oh. I get it.

[*She gathers her things.*]

ELI   What are you doing?

CHASTITY   I thought I could at least try to seduce you. I shoulda figured, though. This furniture, the *décor*. I shoulda figured you didn't like women.

ELI   What?

CHASTITY   Well, you don't, do you?

ELI   Don't what?

CHASTITY   You don't like women?

ELI   Well...

CHASTITY   You're one of those guys that's into guys, eh?

ELI   No.

CHASTITY   Oh, please.

ELI   What? Really, I'm not.

CHASTITY   All right. You don't like women, you don't like men. Who do you like?

ELI   No one.

[*Beat.*]

CHASTITY   What do you mean, no one?

ELI   Listen, I have to see if the whistle buoy's shifted its position.

CHASTITY   Wait a second. Let me get this straight.

ELI   I have serious work to do!

CHASTITY   You don't have sex with anybody?

ELI   If you don't leave right now—

CHASTITY   You're telling me you don't have sex at all?!

ELI   No, I don't! All right!? I don't have sex! Ever!

[*Beat.*]

CHASTITY   Wait. You're not a virgin, are you?
      [*Pause.*]
      Well, aren't we a match made in heaven?

ELI   This has been a lot of fun, but you are trespassing on government property.

CHASTITY   I'm sorry. It's just . . . I didn't think anyone was a virgin anymore.

ELI   Yeah, it's really funny.

CHASTITY   Even the word. *Virgin*. It sounds so . . . sacrificial. Hey, y'know, maybe that's why you live in a lighthouse.

ELI   Why?

CHASTITY   'Cuz you need to get laid.

ELI   What does that have anything to do with—

CHASTITY   It's a giant phallic symbol.

ELI   Phallic symbol?

CHASTITY   You live in a building shaped like a gigantic dildo. You live inside a shiny metal penis. Ha, this is too funny! Fucking droll is what this is.

ELI   You're pretty well-spoken for a prostitute.

CHASTITY   What did you just say?

ELI   Nothing.

CHASTITY   What the fuck did you just say? I'm pretty well-spoken for a prostitute? I know a lotta fancy words for a common whore, is that what you mean?

ELI   I wasn't trying to offend—

CHASTITY   Let me tell you something, I went to night school!

ELI   Uh-huh.

CHASTITY   I am a well-educated woman. Understand?

ELI   Sure.

CHASTITY   I'm not sucking dick for yayo. I've got a life. And an associate's degree. All right?

ELI   Okay! Would you stop pestering me? I have to light the lamp.

CHASTITY   It doesn't turn on automatically?

ELI   Not yet it doesn't. That's why I live here. Inside this giant metal phallic symbol. I turn on the light.

CHASTITY   No, you live here 'cuz you need to get some ass.

[*She picks up a book and pretends to read.*]

"There once was a virgin who lived in a dick."

ELI   This lighthouse has been in my family for—

CHASTITY   "Who desperately wanted some pussy to lick!" Ha! I'm a fucking poet!

ELI   You know what?!

CHASTITY   What?

ELI   Never mind. You're right! I live inside a dick! My grandfather, who stopped offshore oil spills, he lived inside a dick. And my great-grandfather who spent his whole life rescuing other people, he lived inside a dick. And every generation of my family for more than a hundred and eighty-five years has lived inside a giant dick!

CHASTITY   See, you're getting all angry because of your sexual repression.

ELI   Did you learn that in night school?

CHASTITY   No, I learned that by dragging my ass all the way to your goddamn lighthouse.

ELI   Did you really go to night school?

CHASTITY   What? That seems strange to you?

ELI   It's just, didn't that get in the way of... work hours?

CHASTITY   Darling, in my line of business, every hour of the day has the potential to be a working one. And when I was young and green, I worked during the afternoons so I could pay to go to school at night. Wanna see where I keep the world's smallest violin?

ELI   How long have you been doing this for?

CHASTITY   Oh, don't make me talk about that. It would ruin the mood.
[*Beat.*]
So are you planning on paying me, or do I have to get the man waiting outside in the Chevy Impala?

ELI I   I just can't, all right? It's something about me, it's just... I'm sorry.
[*She steps closer to him.*]
What are you doing?

CHASTITY   I wanted to get close to you.

ELI   Well... don't.

CHASTITY   What's your name?

ELI   Eli. What's yours?

CHASTITY   Chastity.

ELI   What's your real name?

CHASTITY   That is my real name. They named me after my grandmother.

ELI   It's a nice name.

CHASTITY   Yeah, well, it was the only nice thing about that woman. She was a nasty old Newfie who smelled like she worked at a cannery.

ELI   I was named after my father.

CHASTITY   Oh, is he at the Bingo too?

ELI   No, he drowned.

  [*Beat.*]

  When I was ten.

CHASTITY   How 'bout we sit down together?

ELI   Why?

CHASTITY   I wanna help you, Eli. You seem like a really good person. The guys around here, well . . . They're fishermen. Sailors. Wedded to the sea. Desperate for some satisfaction when their marriage hits a dry spot. It's easy work. But it's the easy work that's really hard, y'know? Makes you wonder why you do this at all. You're different, though. I can tell that about you. You're different from most men in the Maritimes. You're landlocked.

  [*Beat.*]

  So? Are you going to invite me to sit down?

ELI   Sure. . . . Hang on one second.

[*He puts a few paper towels over a segment of the couch. He motions to her to sit on the covered section. She does. He remains standing.*]

CHASTITY   You're not gonna join me?

ELI   Maybe in a minute.

CHASTITY   I want to try and figure this out.

ELI   Figure what out?

CHASTITY   I used to study the sciences.

ELI   In night school?

CHASTITY   I have an inquisitive mind.

ELI   What are you—

CHASTITY   And I wanna get to the bottom of this.

ELI   Of what?

CHASTITY   Everything in life (and this is a scientific fact), everything in life needs to fuck. Plants fuck. Sure, they get bees to carry their pollen around, but that's still fucking. Otherwise, they wouldn't reproduce. They wouldn't grow. On top of that, bees and plants would be having a hell of a dull time, rooted to the ground all their lives, or flitting about making honey instead'a making sweet love. Am I wrong?

ELI   Well—

CHASTITY   Don't contradict me. I'm right! Everything alive needs to fuck. Except you, Eli.

ELI   No, there are things, other things, that don't need to, to have sex . . . to reproduce. They just . . . it just happens.

CHASTITY   Like what?

ELI   Take starfish, for example. They don't need to have sex. Neither do I.

CHASTITY   Oh, please.

ELI   It's true. I'm just . . . one of those exceptions to the rule.

CHASTITY   So what makes you so special?

ELI   Special?

CHASTITY   Yeah. How come everyone else on this island has to go through the motions, and you get to be a starfish?

ELI   Well...

CHASTITY   I've met every other man in this province.

ELI   Every single one?

CHASTITY   That's right, every single fucking one. And I'll tell you something about them. They only think about two things. And both of them smell like fish.

ELI   Oh my God.

CHASTITY   And, unlike every other man in Nova Scotia, you don't want to have sex. At all. Why not?

ELI   I really don't know. I had to go to church a lot when I was younger?

CHASTITY   So?

ELI   My mother would drag me along with her so she'd have some company. Aside from the other women who only left their widows' walks on Sunday mornings.

CHASTITY   That's why you don't have sex?

ELI   Well... Y'know they tell you in church—are you religious? Oh, sorry, look who I'm asking.

CHASTITY   What? What!? You're saying because I'm a prostitute I can't be religious?!

ELI   No, that wasn't what I meant at all.

CHASTITY   I am a deeply religious woman!

ELI   I'm sure you are—

CHASTITY   Just because a person needs to make a living does not mean she can't be religious. You know what? I don't think I wanna help you anymore. Question my religion and make me sit on a paper towel. I'll see you in hell, starfish!

ELI   I just meant that you're studying the sciences, you probably wouldn't believe in God.

[*Beat.*]

CHASTITY   Is that really what you meant?

ELI   No. I'm sorry, I just didn't mean to upset you.

CHASTITY   Uh-huh.

ELI   Look. I may not have asked you to come here, but as long as you're my guest (and don't demand a large sum of money), I am going to try to be civil. All right? I don't want to offend you. At all.

CHASTITY   That's the sweetest thing anybody's said to me in a long time.

ELI   It is?

CHASTITY   Can I give you a hug?

ELI   A hug?

CHASTITY   Yeah, you heard of one of those? It's where you wrap your arms around another person and squeeze.

ELI   Well...

CHASTITY   Unless you're afraid it'll give you the clap or something.

ELI   I don't know....

CHASTITY   Come on, Eli. I promise I'm not gonna bite.

ELI   I guess it could be...enjoyable.

CHASTITY   So are we gonna hug?

ELI   Yeah. Sure.

[*They hug.*]

CHASTITY   Isn't that better?

ELI   It's very nice.

CHASTITY   Funny. You live inside a dick...and I think there's a lighthouse in your pants.

ELI [*Breaking away from her.*] Oh God...

CHASTITY Don't worry, Eli. No one's gonna blame you. I mean, look at me. I am one foxy lady. Don't you think so?

ELI I...I guess.

CHASTITY You guess? You've got more wood than a lumber yard.

ELI I think you should leave. I have to go record the wind speed and—

CHASTITY Can I explain something?

ELI What?

CHASTITY I'm not normally this...brazen. I'm a little upset tonight, that's all. Truth be told, I've been seriously thinking about a career change. Rodney keeps sending me out at all hours, and I get anxious when I work at night. I always told him, I hate working after dark. Sure, it makes more sense, it's better for business. But I never like doing it.

ELI Why not?

[*Beat.*]

CHASTITY Promise not to tell anyone?

ELI I promise.

CHASTITY Promise you won't laugh?

ELI Promise.

CHASTITY I'm afraid of the dark.

ELI Isn't everyone?

[*She kisses him. He breaks off.*]

CHASTITY Sorry. I know. It's just...I've never told that to anybody before. Well, except this one boy.

ELI Rodney?

CHASTITY No! It was...He lived next door to my smelly grandmother. And he was the only one that...Anyway, we're not talking about me right now.

ELI Why not?

CHASTITY Because you were trying to tell me about going to church with your mom.

ELI Oh, it's not that interesting.

CHASTITY No, please. I'm very involved.

ELI Listen, I don't want to upset your…pimp, or whatever he is. I think you should just leave and tell him—

CHASTITY Don't worry about Rodney. Tell me more about yourself.

ELI Really, the fog's getting thicker.

CHASTITY Aw, you take your job more seriously than I do. And I am a model employee.

ELI People's lives depend on this lighthouse! My father's family built it. Now the government's talking about tearing it down.

CHASTITY Really?

ELI They're firing lightkeepers all up the coast. It's easier to make these places automatic. Or just get rid of them. It's ridiculous. It—it guides lost vessels back to shore.

[*Beat.*]

Anyway, I should go upstairs.

CHASTITY Wait a second. The only woman you've talked about so far is your mother. I want to know why you've never been with a woman.

[*Pause.*]

ELI When I was younger, I used to listen to other people's conversations on the two-way radio. The lighthouse was so far away from anybody that I…And one day, I heard this girl over the radio. She must've been around my age. Pretty voice. Her name was Margaret, I think. And every Sunday, at the same time, just when I'd be getting home from church, she'd send out the same frequency.

CHASTITY What was her name again?

ELI I think it was Margaret. I started talking to her over the radio upstairs. There was something about her voice. And I think I...

CHASTITY What?

ELI It felt so...good. To have someone to talk to. Especially after my father died. *Her* father was a sailor. She used to tell me about all the exotic things he brought back with him from his voyages. Ships in a bottle from Martinique, uh...dried-out sea lions from coral reefs. But the thing she talked about most was this starfish. She said it was perfect. She said that God didn't make man in his image. He made starfish instead.

CHASTITY What happened to her?

ELI The last time I spoke to her, she was going away for the summer. Her father decided to let her travel with him. And...I heard some sailors on the radio talking about it later.... Their ship was lost at sea. It must have been a foggy night. Somebody probably forgot to light the lamp in the lighthouse. Excuse me.

[*He moves to the stairs.* CHASTITY *restrains him.*]

CHASTITY Wait.

ELI What do you want from me?

CHASTITY The way you spoke about that little girl. It sounded like you really loved her.... Did you?
[*He kisses her. He pulls away, almost in tears.*]
What is it?

ELI The sound of your voice...

CHASTITY Come here.

ELI I used to pray that I could hear her voice again.

CHASTITY Well, Eli. You finally fished your wish.

[*They kiss. They stumble to the wall. She begins to undo his pants. He stops her.*]

ELI I can't. I'm sorry, I can't.

CHASTITY What's the matter?

[*Beat.*]

ELI I called you. It was me who asked you to come here. But when you got here, I was so...nervous. And ashamed of myself.

[*Beat.*]

I'm sorry, I can't.

CHASTITY Eli.

ELI I can't, all right!? I just can't! I shouldn't have called you. I'm sorry...I'm so...Please, I...

[*He is crying. He moves to the couch and sits.*]

CHASTITY Listen. Don't worry about it, okay? I'll sort things out with Rodney. It—it'll be all right.

ELI It's not going to be all right. My lighthouse is being torn down. I have nowhere to go, and no one to, no one to even talk to. She was my only friend. Just like that boy you told me about. Margaret was the only friend I ever had. And I never even saw her face....

[*Pause.*]

CHASTITY Look, I really should get going. If Rodney's waiting outside and expecting—

ELI Don't. Please. Just...will you stay with me for a little while?

CHASTITY I can't.

ELI Just...a few more minutes. Please.

CHASTITY I'm sorry, Eli.

[*She begins collecting her things and goes to the door. She stops.*]

Can I tell you something?

[*Beat.*]

I've been doing this kind of work for too long. I know that. I've been doing this so long I didn't think there were any good people left out there. But I want you to understand. You are not like the sailors I usually fuck. You're a man, Eli. Made in God's image.

ELI If that's true, God must be so lonely. I am. I am. I...

[*She moves and sits down next to him.*]

CHASTITY I know. I am too. But one day, I'll find someone. Someone perfect for me. Someone who can make me...happy. You and I won't be alone forever. One day, Eli, I promise you, we'll find someone to love us. I know we will. There's plenty of fish in the sea.

[*She rests her head on his shoulder, as the lights fade to black.*]

• • •

St. Matilde's Malady

Kyle John Schmidt

Kyle John Schmidt

Kyle John Schmidt is a native Iowan and a recent graduate of the Michener Center for Writers. His short plays include *The Last Hat* (Actors Theatre of Louisville, Heideman Award), *Sword Play* (Actors Theatre of Louisville), *Fernando and the Killer Queen* (Theatre Masters), and St. Matilde's Malady (Frontera Short Fringe, Best of Fest). Full-length plays include *Blue Point* (UTNT), *Fernando and the Killer Queen* (David Mark Cohen New Works Festival).

···production history···

St. Matilde's Malady was produced in January 2010 as part of the Frontera Fest Short Fringe at Hyde Park Theatre in Austin, Texas, under the direction of Elizabeth C. Lay.

It was produced by Crashbox Theatre, winter 2010–2011, at the Studio Theatre on Theatre Row in New York City under the direction of Jordan Douglas Smith.

characters

MOLLY FORGE

TAMMY

CONNIE

SAMPSON

CAPTAIN TWISTER

DIRTY VICKI

• • •

[*A private sitting room on the top floor of a massive pre-industrial brothel. There are three doors: one that leads to the staircase for the rest of the building, and then two others that lead to bedrooms.* MOLLY FORGE, *a young prostitute, stands center stage, fuming, with her hands balled into fists. Behind her stands a weaving loom. Her roommate* TAMMY, *another prostitute, enters from one of the bedrooms.*]

TAMMY   Oh, fortune unfurled! I am the most ineffective prostitute in all the world. The man I got tossed last night—only because you were busy—glared and frowned the entire time. But, Molly, my friend, what was I to do? He thought he'd have you. He acted like my bed was a tomb. I resorted to juggling just to keep him in the room.

MOLLY FORGE   This is a full day of total night. Look out. The sky denies the sun and fat fog hides all the smiles. But worse, the bay is black, the water dark. SAD. SAD. SAD. Tammy, oh, Tammy, I fear I have the SAD.

TAMMY   You! Sad? You can't be sad. You're the most popular prostitute at Connie's Brothel and Rug Shop. You serviced five men, six women, and a gay couple last night. I saw your tip can. Overflowing with coinage and compliments! I only had the one, a portly teen, with neck hair, cobwebby teeth, ear jam! And he paid in coupons.

[TAMMY *picks up a coupon from her tip can.*]

"Ten coppers off wash rags." What am I to do with that! I'm sad, the saddest, most disappointing prostitute in all the town.

MOLLY FORGE   Not emotionally distressed. But a victim of SAD. A SAD.

TAMMY   A sad what?

MOLLY FORGE   S-A-D. Sexually Acquired Disease. SAD. I've got the SAD.

TAMMY   Which one?

MOLLY FORGE   I think. I fear. It seems like St. Matilde's Malady.

TAMMY   Oh no! St. Matilde's Malady! That's the worst! Are you sure?

MOLLY FORGE   Look at my hands. Clamped shut. Diseased! I can't weave with fists. And if I can't use the loom, customers will know that I am riddled with an incurable, transmittable, and debilitating infection that could leave them as locked up as I.

TAMMY   If you can move everything but your fists, you might get by.

MOLLY FORGE   Everyone checks. Which is why we are cursed with looms in our rooms. When people see she cannot weave, they know their prostitute is diseased.

TAMMY   Molly Forge, unlike a capricious man, my loyalty will never shrink or flop below the belt. I will have no daily spree until I cure your St. Matilde's Malady!

[CONNIE, *the brothel mistress, enters.*]

CONNIE   Tragedy coupled with tragedy in Connie's house of humping tragedies. We walked into happy Sandra's room this morning and she was immobile. We tried rolling her down the stairs, but St. Matilde's Malady has fastened her tight within its sickly snares.

MOLLY FORGE   She's dead?

CONNIE   Hardly. Her heart still beats tremendously within its cage. But don't grieve the poor lamb. The army came and made her a battering ram!

TAMMY   Connie, why didn't you find her a cure?

CONNIE   There's no cure for St. Matilde's Malady. But in the midnight of this tragedy, I have found daybreak. Happy Tammy, you will move into lost Sandra's room.

TAMMY   What? No! I can't.

CONNIE   It's time you were released from the feet of my deepest gorge, the formidable Molly Forge.

TAMMY   But who's going to make sure that Molly's customers sign the guest book? And take a mint. And who will take the ones who want Molly but don't want to wait and don't mind getting disappointed by my frequently heralded bedroom failures?

CONNIE   All your customers are distracted by Molly. You'll do far better on your own.

TAMMY   Clients will howl if I'm alone. Molly alleviates their disappointment. Me the pain, her the pill. She the anesthetic, me the dental drill.

MOLLY FORGE   Let Tammy stay.

CONNIE   Connie commands, everyone obeys; happy Tammy moves, handsome Molly stays. Today I need everyone to flaunt their greatest attraction. The whole harbor is completely locked up and the sailors will need distraction.

TAMMY   Why's the whole harbor stalled?

CONNIE   A tragedy, it's called.
One ship, full of oil thus,
Went beserko maximus.
With steering wheel firmly caught,
It struck every ship in th' lot.

Then, a cannon shot left this tanker doomed,
And from its shattered hull a dark yoke bloomed.
The oil made our harbor a black jail,
From which not even one ship can sail.
Thousands of sailors wait now impatient,
So we are cast to make the entertainment.
Tam and Mol, prepare your warm brothel bed,
For we have the busiest of days ahead.
To begin, my eager mares:
A young lad waits downstairs,
He has risen with the morning bands
And waits orchestration from your hands.
So we work now because we must,
Forgoing love, to conquer lust.

[CONNIE *exits.*]

TAMMY   This is the worst. The busiest day ever, you incapacitated, and me still myself.

MOLLY FORGE   This is all my fault.

TAMMY   St. Matilde's Malady is no one's fault. It could happen to anyone. I've heard it said you can't always trace the source.

MOLLY FORGE   No, I sabotaged that ship to whirl around the bay.

TAMMY   Hump what? You haven't left our room.

MOLLY FORGE   I didn't sleep alone last night. A man slept over.

TAMMY   *Molly Christine Forge!* That's forbidden!

MOLLY FORGE   He was my evening's final customer. And he fell asleep astride me, my breasts rocking in the soft hammock of his palms, my hair entangled his, his eyes locked upon mine. We bedded our armies in blissful concordance. When we awoke, he called me his star fire, I lauded him my saintly fox. Then a thousand joyful kisses without purpose or monetary remuneration. I saw my life's end on the ruby curve of his lips, and he said as much to me. It was right then that my hands froze into the puppets you see now.

TAMMY   He gave you the SAD?

MOLLY FORGE   Yes. He gave me St. Matilde's Malady. The moment he saw my hands, he bolted out of bed, discovering that he couldn't bend his knees from a similar and simultaneous disease. Frightened, he robed himself to leave, dropping his oil tanker's wheel keys. I tried halting him, but limping so to travel farther, he trundled out my window and down the trumpet vines toward the harbor.

TAMMY   You love him.

MOLLY   No. Oh no. I hate him with all the darkness and fury caught in the monstrous hurricane of my soul. In a night he has caught my dear profession from these hands and abused the morning so he can steal away. If I ever see him again, I will use every fist my body can create to tear holes across his corpse.

[*A knock at the door.*]

TAMMY   What to do! Oh, what to do! There's a man coming for reprieve and he'll know you're sick if you can't weave!

MOLLY FORGE   Bullets of rain, calamity, thunder, wind whirl, and strike! I am the worst beast the wharf ever dreamed. My staid wooden dock demonically rises plank by plank from its stale marine home and writhes viciously high above the oceanic horizons. I am the storm tornadoes flee from. I am the bluster cities bow towards. I am the devil fire no virgin sea could dream.

[*A young man*, SAMPSON, *enters.*]

SAMPSON   Hello, I'm ready for a lascivious stunt.

TAMMY   Tammy. You vile, untempered slut.

[TAMMY *slaps* MOLLY.]

MOLLY FORGE   What?

TAMMY   I told you, Tammy, to stop shouting about. Have no fear, sir, this whore, Tammy, is lamenting all the sad fates endured by the poor fellows I cannot service with my famous ten-piece band that plays lubricious carnival tunes on the vibrating accordions of the luckiest sweat-drenched thighs.

SAMPSON   Wow. I'm Sampson.

TAMMY   Hello, young sailor, I'm Molly Forge. Yes, that magical Molly Forge you always hear about. You're undisguisedly handsome. My bed is there. My tip can is there. And you can have me here, here, and here.

[TAMMY *indicates herself.*]

You're very pretty. Maybe you just want to hold my hand and talk about an imagined future we could have if you liked me and wanted to stay and live through that.

SAMPSON   I hate to hurry, but this is the first time I've ever come to land and I have to get back to my mother very soon.

TAMMY   Mother? Who's your mother?

SAMPSON   The meanest pirate to ever haul freight
And tender little me, her only mate.
She's generally a ruthless brutal queen,
But today she's the cruelest I've ever seen:
Our peaceful pirate vessel got smote
By this evil oil tanker boat,
So my irate mother never dull
Made a cannon crash into their hull.
As that ship sunk and spewed its night-colored juice,
Its feral captain swam towards the harbor sluice.
My mom leapt off our deck to sink that prey
Which gave me this great chance to steal away.
While I have my first brothel and rug shop splurge,
My mom will promptly drown that oil captain scourge.

MOLLY FORGE   But that oil captain's death is meant for my trample.

SAMPSON   Well you're too late. My mother, Dirty Vicki, the esteemed pirate queen, already executed the deed. Can we begin? For time is preciously dear. My mom would detach my arms if she found me here.

MOLLY FORGE   For plagiarizing murder from my page, this Dirty Vicki will suffer my rage. Beware, world, for what I like: my terrors unleashed, I have death at my strike!

[MOLLY *exits.*]

TAMMY   Tammy, no!

> [TAMMY *considers going for* MOLLY *but stops. Aside.*]

> To my defense, I'm not leaving her side, she has left mine, and I will help her later after I tend to the finest little bird trembling on my branch.

> [*To* SAMPSON.]

> Sampson, don't mind her. She'll return. Shall we, or do you prefer that we dream of a mutual future with a farmhouse and a pen of goats we milk together each morning dawn. Sometimes the best love is left dreamt upon.

SAMPSON   I didn't want to embarrass you in front of your friend. But I think I'd prefer her.

TAMMY   I'm more skilled. You've no doubt heard about me, Molly Forge. I'm very famous. Is it because she's prettier?

SAMPSON   No! You're undeniably lovely and I could even say that I would fall for a face that fine. But I came here because I heard this man, a portly teen, talking all about Tammy. So I want her.

TAMMY   But no one wants Tammy. She's everyone's last choice. And Molly makes innocents rejoice.

SAMPSON   I hear Tammy juggles. And I thought that would be a lovely way to spend a morning with a woman. With her juggling and me cheering her on.

TAMMY   You don't mean that. Molly is the elegant acrobat, Tammy just a dowdy clown. Let me be the bell you ring to wake the town.

SAMPSON   Why a Molly…

> [*He mimes a lascivious prostitute.*]

...when there's a Tammy!

[*He mimes a fun juggler.*]

TAMMY   If you knew how many frowns, grumbles, and crying fits
followed an experience with Tammy, you would demand Molly.
Trust me, a time with Tammy is a date with disappointment.
Your legs are too fine, your eyes too sweet a candy, for you to be
soiled with letdown Tammy.

[CAPTAIN TWISTER *enters, wet and oily, unable to bend his legs. He runs around the room.*]

CAPTAIN TWISTER   Help! Refuge. Respite! I'm being chased!

TAMMY   Who are you, if you please? And what happened to your
knees?

CAPTAIN TWISTER   When I'm not running for my life, I'm the noble
Captain Twister, but in this instant I'm willing to disguise myself
as your little sister.

[CAPTAIN TWISTER *begins putting on clothes around the room.*]
Hide me.

SAMPSON   [*Pointing to* TAMMY.] You can hide in her arms. She's
available.

TAMMY   No she's not. Who's chasing you?

CAPTAIN TWISTER   Trouble after trouble follows me today.
A cannon sunk my ship into the bay.
I fell too and was swimming to the shore
Hindered by my damn legs both stiff as oars,
Then a sea beast with a butterfly stroke
Swam up to me and grabbed by cloak.
She grappled my head between her thighs
(And so not to drown)
I gnashed the flesh her ass supplies!
This small bite that you will moan
Permitted me to free myself
From that brawny vice no man has known.

And so I escaped from a watery death,
Hoping you excuse my sea foam breath,
The pirate chases me to here and now,
So I'll hide over there if you'll allow.

SAMPSON   She's coming here? Dirty Vicki's coming here!

CAPTAIN TWISTER   Brutal creature, she won't stop until I'm bloated in barnacles at the bottom of the bay. If she finds me here, I'm doomed.

SAMPSON   If she finds me here, I'm doomed. But you deserve it. You hit our ship.

CAPTAIN TWISTER   It's not my fault, I lost my wheel key.

SAMPSON   You broke the gorgeous mermaid off the bow of our ship. My mom spent my entire childhood carving that beautiful woman with a fish tail using no other tools but her fingernails. But now that mermaid lies splintered and broke, whirling lost in the sea, leaving my poor mom bereft and angry. As much as I would like to see you mutilated for your crimes, I have to go before I face my own end times.

TAMMY   Don't leave, I'll hide you.

[*To* CAPTAIN TWISTER.]

However, I won't hide you.

CAPTAIN TWISTER   Where's Molly Forge? She'll hide me.

SAMPSON   [SAMPSON *points to* TAMMY.] She's right here.

CAPTAIN TWISTER   You've mistaken Molly Forge for an unlikely substitute.

TAMMY   No he didn't, Captain Twister. It's me, Molly Forge, or do you not recall my electric seaweed fingers, which sent you into the brightest tinctures of pleasure last night. Please, describe for young Sampson here how un-disappointing a night with Molly Forge is. He's deciding.

SAMPSON   I've decided.

TAMMY Decide again.

CAPTAIN TWISTER Sometimes it happens that you see the end of
your life looking back at you and no culminated machinations of
men's highest pleasures and imaginations can match the silent
hours nestled in the pillows of her bed. You've heard the ancient
monster Medusa who's look turned men to stone? You probably
heard it wrong. Medusa's horror was not the snakes twining
about her head, nor the mangled skin marring her face; it was her
delicate cheek, the adventure of her thighs, a glow about her shy
grin, that caught men frozen at her sight. Ugliness elicits
indifference, beauty stops.

And so I last night:

Seeing the temptation of Medusa unfold
The blightless beauty beyond the tale told,
Under the terror of that gorgeous Gorgon gaze,
Who among us wouldn't stupidly run aways.

TAMMY You love her.

SAMPSON See, I want Tammy. Molly Forge is occupied.

TAMMY Try this happy Molly fest, here between my heaving breasts!
[TAMMY *buries* SAMPSON's *head in her breasts.*]

[*A knock at the door. "Let me in! Please! Help!"*]

CAPTAIN TWISTER When people ask, I'm your visiting little sister,
who's crumpled over, blind, and shy.

[*A disguised* CAPTAIN TWISTER *runs into one of the bedrooms.*]

TAMMY Say you want Molly Forge.

SAMPSON I don't. And I never will want anything like her.

[SAMPSON *runs into the other room to hide.* DIRTY VICKI *enters in a huff.*]

DIRTY VICKI Hide me or I'll lop your head off its pedestal.

TAMMY It will be a disappointing interaction, I'm sure.

[DIRTY VICKI *puts* TAMMY *into a headlock.*]

DIRTY VICKI   I am Dirty Vicki, the most horrible pirate imperial, and you will hide me or I will grind you into a gizzard sack of digestible material.

TAMMY   Oh, Dirty Vicki, do as you wish. But if you can reprocess human bodies into new forms, please make me a silky cobweb so that I might enwrap my little angel and freeze his smile with my loving threads.

DIRTY VICKI   [DIRTY VICKI *releases* TAMMY.] This is why my boat never meets the sand.
You're all crazy or miserable on land.
I was aiming to fix a fiasco:
Avenge my sweet, sculpted mermaid torso.
A certain man cracked my only prize,
So I vowed to drown him 'tween my thighs.
While I held him down there fast,
His jaw unhinged and bit my ass!
(Look, ye, hark
There's the mark!)
I let him loose so I could scratch
And thus I lost my spiteful catch.
Giving this man chase into the streets
I meet two hammers attached to a screech.
This baleful woman with fists of hate
Blamed me for drowning her only mate.
I screamed three times, "I haven't yet,"
But fury's target was surely set.
She flung innocent me on to the ground
And let her wrecking balls go pound, pound, pound.
Had I not moved my skull here and there
I am sure that my face would share
The thousand cracks blossomed in the street,
Her rage breaking the toughest concrete.
One such punch had the force of a boulder!
Her whole arm was buried, hand to shoulder!
While she was fiercely buried

I slipped away and carried
My pirate booty to this fruity stop
Called Connie's Brothel and Rug Shop.
I knew a Connie once, a fishy maid,
But I never speak of that crusade.
So here I am,
and if you don't hide me from this unprovoked war,
I will sacrifice you to that raging two-fisted manticore.

TAMMY Do so, but know you kill a woman who wasn't good enough even when she was being someone else. You can hide behind my loom.

DIRTY VICKI You will hide me better, or I will weave your face through my thighs and crack you like a walnut. Oh no! She's come to give her pummeling. I can hear the stairs hum-hum-hum-a-ling!

[DIRTY VICKI *puts her ear to the outside door.*]

[SAMPSON *pokes his head out.*]

SAMPSON [*Sotto voce.*] Please help me.

[SAMPSON *pokes his head back in.* TAMMY *blows him an unseen kiss.*]

TAMMY Oh, my heart flutters through the pain! I can't help but try and try again.

DIRTY VICKI I must hide!

[DIRTY VICKI *tries to go into the bedroom with* SAMPSON.]

TAMMY No, you can't.

[DIRTY VICKI *opens the door, but* TAMMY *whirls her away.*]

DIRTY VICKI My son!

TAMMY No, that's my nightstand!

DIRTY VICKI Why's my son in this dirty house of caprice!

TAMMY Nay! That was a motherless furniture piece.

[DIRTY VICKI *opens the next bedroom door.*]

DIRTY VICKI   A man covered in panties.

TAMMY   No, that's my introverted sister.

[TAMMY *whirls* DIRTY VICKI *toward the outside door.* DIRTY VICKI *opens it.* CONNIE *is there.* DIRTY VICKI *stops.*]

DIRTY VICKI   Connie.

CONNIE   Dirty Vicki. My sacred enemy.

DIRTY VICKI   My dearest foe. Where have you been?

CONNIE   Here, at my brothel. It's very lucrative and I'm very happy. Much happier than I currently appear.

DIRTY VICKI   I, too, love my life and your absence from it.

[SAMPSON *and* CAPTAIN TWISTER *enter from their hiding places.*]

SAMPSON   Mother.

TAMMY   The nightstand grew a voice!

SAMPSON   [*Pointing at* CONNIE.] It's your mermaid. She walks!

CONNIE   Who is this boy?

DIRTY VICKI   No one. Get back to your room, the nightstand, before I decompartmentalize your tongue.

SAMPSON   The mermaid broke from our ship, grew legs, and walked ashore. Hello, wooden creature.

CONNIE   Is this your son?

DIRTY VICKI   Sampson, this angelic devil is not our wonderful mermaid.

SAMPSON   You said you carved her from your tears.

DIRTY VICKI   He's been drinking fish pee for years.

SAMPSON   Yes, you carved this very same figure, stuck her on our ship, and now with a little oil and water, she walks. Look here's the pose.
[SAMPSON *makes* CONNIE *cup her breasts and rearranges her face in an intimidating glance.*]

There! It is our ship's guiding force! Hello, two-legged mermaid. Now that you've been given birth, would you like to lead our sails across the earth?

DIRTY VICKI   Sampson! Who said you could come to land?

SAMPSON   I came for the love of my life, Tammy.

TAMMY   But he wants to try Molly Forge before he commits.

CONNIE   [*To* SAMPSON.] Watch out, little boy. You'll get a SAD.

TAMMY   Not from me. I'm clean, watch me weave.

CONNIE   [*To* SAMPSON.] Your mother gave me a SAD. St. Matilde's Malady. And I was locked up for months. But I got over it and am once again pure.

TAMMY   I thought St. Matilde's Malady didn't have a cure.

CONNIE   I surrounded myself with daily chores and salty whores. With my attention unblocked, my body unlocked. And the freedom . . .
[CONNIE*'s jaw locks and she begins speaking gibberish.*]
DAMNIT! I see this woman I've sworn I hate and I can't move my jaws.

DIRTY VICKI   My hands, my hands, damn these frozen claws.

[DIRTY VICKI*'s hands freeze into claws.*]

CONNIE   [*Having difficulty moving her jaws.*] I got my SAD back! I must leave.

[MOLLY FORGE *enters with her fists blazing.*]

MOLLY FORGE   Give me room to beat that hag to dust.

DIRTY VICKI   I didn't do anything!

CAPTAIN TWISTER   I'm just a terribly shy, hunkered-over little girl.

MOLLY FORGE   You musty undertow
With that camel toe:
I hereby pity your feeble crown,
For now my vengeance comes raining down.

I summon bouquets of lightning strike from high above
for killing the only man I ever dared to love.

CAPTAIN TWISTER   What?

TAMMY   My sister, who's visiting for a spell,
Cannot hear you very well.
Speak louder if your voice raises.
And maybe try repeating phrases.

MOLLY FORGE   If love means I can't move as quick or fast,
I would lose my speed to make it last.
If love means I can't run amuck,
Then I would stand forever stuck.
If love means love might die,
Then I would abandon all just to try.
But you, molting crow, drowned my stupid dream.
Now I'll pound chasms into your topography.

CAPTAIN TWISTER   Don't kill her.

TAMMY   Listen to my timid sister.

CONNIE   [*Garbled.*] Kill her.

[CONNIE *tries to leave.*]

SAMPSON   Stay, mermaid, stay!

CONNIE   You should kill her...but know you'll have to get through me.
[CONNIE *grabs* DIRTY VICKI'*s hand.*]
Though it means I lose my pride, I will not leave her side.

MOLLY   Like that will stop me, you conjoined crones,
Two lovers are as easy to mangle as one alone.

[MOLLY *advances.*]

CAPTAIN TWISTER   You never gave him a chance to return.
[MOLLY *stops.*]
Sometimes beauty-blinded people run away,
From such beds they should never stray.

In the best situation they're given a revelation
That they were not alone in their adoration.
And they return with wrenched heart ablazing
With dreams of futures beyond amazing.
Now a fearing lover dreads your rebuff.
He hopes his recurred presence is proof enough.

[CAPTAIN TWISTER *takes off his disguise.*]

CAPTAIN TWISTER   I came back.

[*Silence.*]

TAMMY   My sister is a man!

CAPTAIN TWISTER   If you'll let me.

>[MOLLY FORGE *walks up to* CAPTAIN TWISTER. *She hits him in the chest as hard as she can. She hits him again.*]
>
>Careful. You'll stop my heart.

[MOLLY FORGE *flings herself into* CAPTAIN TWISTER'*s arms.*]

SAMPSON   No, stop! I love that woman.

[*Points to* MOLLY FORGE.]

TAMMY   Oh, tragic folly, everyone loves Molly.

SAMPSON   That may be, but I love Tammy!

TAMMY   Are you sure?

SAMPSON   As sure as these balls will find tender hands.

[*An awkward moment, then he produces three juggling balls.*]

TAMMY   Sweet angel.

>[TAMMY *takes the balls and juggles.*]
>
>If this doesn't disappoint: I am sadly Tammy.

SAMPSON   Then I am happily entranced.

DIRTY VICKI   I can't release your grip.

CONNIE   That's okay. Sampson's your son?

DIRTY VICKI No. He's ours. Our only one.

CONNIE I never knew.

DIRTY VICKI And now you do.

MOLLY FORGE My elbows have locked.

CAPTAIN TWISTER So have mine. My neck bones too.

MOLLY FORGE Are we cursed together?

CAPTAIN TWISTER Not cursed. Clasped, my love, clasped together, forever.

[CAPTAIN TWISTER *and* MOLLY *sway.* DIRTY VICKI *and* CONNIE *stand hand in hand.* TAMMY *stops juggling and steps forward.*]

TAMMY Though we've sorted through this disarray,
We hope you take something from our little play:
Patrons, travel far and keep your limbs loose,
But when it happens don't let yourself refuse:
It is improbable and impossible to flee
When braced with St. Matilde's Malady.

[*Dance party! Everyone dances with frozen limbs. Slowly their entire bodies freeze up until the end when everyone freezes together. The music plays on.*]

• • •

Lobster Boy

Dan Dietz

Dan Dietz

Dan Dietz's plays include *Tilt Angel*, *tempOdyssey*, *Americamisfit*, and *The Sandreckoner*. His work has been commissioned, developed, and presented at such venues as Actors Theatre of Louisville, the Guthrie Theater, the Public Theater, the Kennedy Center, Rattlestick Playwrights Theater, the Playwrights' Center, and the Lark Play Development Center. Dietz has been an NEA/TCG Theatre Residency recipient, an NNPN Rolling World Premiere recipient, a Jerome fellow, and a James A. Michener fellow. Dietz has twice been a recipient of the Heideman Award. His latest play, *Clementine in the Lower Nine*, received its world premiere at TheatreWorks (Palo Alto, California) in October 2011.

···production history···

Lobster Boy was originally commissioned and produced by the eXchange in 2008 as part of "The Scariest," an evening of short plays. The play subsequently received the 2009–2010 Heideman Award from Actors Theatre of Louisville, and received its world premiere performance in the 2010 Humana Festival at Actors Theatre of Louisville.

characters

A **MAN** in his 30s, calm, thoughtful, intellectual, reserved.

setting

Any place suitable for a lecture with slides.

Note: It is crucial that—with the exception of the Mozart aria—no attempt be made to use actual pictures or sounds in the realization of the slides. The slides are meant to be text, letters, and symbols, nothing more.

···

[*A* MAN *stands, perhaps at a podium, a glass of water within his reach. Behind him a slide is projected that reads:* LOBSTER BOY.]

MAN   There once was a boy. He had a little brother. They were born two years apart.

> *Slide:* PICTURES IN YOUR HEAD:
> A BOY (AGE 14)
> HIS BROTHER (AGE 12)
> A LOBSTER (AGE INDETERMINATE)

They lived in a house. In a working-class neighborhood. In that kind of dead zone between the city and the suburbs.

> *Slide:* PICTURES IN YOUR HEAD:
> A HOUSE (SMALL)
> A NEIGHBORHOOD (ALSO SMALL)
> A LOBSTER (MEAL-SIZED)

Their father was a boxer. Their father was unsuccessful. He left to remedy this.

>*Slide:* PICTURES IN YOUR HEAD:
>   A MAN (TOUGH)
>   A PAIR OF BOXING GLOVES (TOUGHER)
>   A LOBSTER (CHITINOUS)

He never came back.

[*Slide out.*]

Which meant that their mother had to work day and night shifts to support them. Which meant that "the job" fell to the older brother. The job was time consuming, intimate, and went like this: the younger brother stood in his underwear, and the older brother looked at his younger brother's body, from a distance of one to three inches. Here is a brief list of what the older brother was looking for:

>*Slide:* CUTS
>   BURNS
>   PUNCTURES
>   PERHAPS A MISSING TOE
>   &c.

The reason for this was thus: the younger brother had been born beautiful, healthy, and entirely without the ability to feel pain. Thus what to us would be this:

>*Slide:* SOUNDS IN YOUR HEAD:
>   A KNIFE SLICING SOMETHING
>   A PERSON SAYING "OW!"
>   A BAND-AID BEING APPLIED

To him would be this:

>*Slide:* A KNIFE SLICING SOMETHING
>   . . .
>   . . .

Every night of every day of the older brother's life was devoted to scanning over his younger brother's body, like the way you might look up a difficult word in the dictionary.

>*Slide:* nociceptor (no•si•sep•tər) *n.* a sensory receptor for pain
>   stimuli, usually found in great bundles in the body's most
>   sensitive parts

Something was wrong with the younger boy's nociceptors. Also his brain, but the older boy never really understood that part. What he understood was that his brother's condition, combined with his father's absence and his mother's brutal work schedule, meant that any and every responsibility that placed one within any distance of a heated stove, a bladed knife, a lawnmower, etc. was up to him. So while the younger brother came home from school and did this:

> *Slide:* WATCH TV
> RIDE BIKE
> PLAY VIDEO GAMES

The older brother came home from school and did this:

> *Slide:* FIX SINK
> MOW LAWN
> COOK DINNER

And more importantly, this:

> *Slide:* HAVE NO FRIENDS

So while everyone else looked at his younger brother and saw this:

> *Slide:* BEAUTIFUL BLOND HAIR
> GOOFY BIG EARS
> AN EVER-PRESENT GRIN

More and more, he looked at his younger brother and saw this:

> *Slide:* THAT WHICH MAKES ME WORK
> THAT WHICH MAKES ME TIRED
> THAT WHICH MAKES ME ALONE

Which brings us to lobsters.

> *Slide:* PICTURE IN YOUR HEAD:
> A POT (FILLED WITH WATER [BOILING])
> A HAND (FILLED WITH A LOBSTER)
> A LOBSTER (FILLED WITH ?)

There is a bit of a debate raging over whether lobsters, upon being tossed into a pot of boiling water, feel what we as human beings with a spinal column, limbic system, and frontal cortex would recognize and categorize as "pain."

Slide: SOUNDS IN YOUR HEAD:
      A KNIFE SLICING SOMETHING
      A PERSON SAYING DAMNIT!
      A SECOND BAND-AID BEING APPLIED

It's not a new debate, and the jury seems permanently out on this one, but there is some disagreement over the gray areas. However, gray areas do not fit neatly into a ninth grade biology class, nor into a fourteen-year-old boy's mind.

Slide: PICTURES IN YOUR HEAD:
      A GRAY AREA
      A FOURTEEN-YEAR-OLD BOY'S MIND
      AN AWKWARD MOMENT

Particularly a fourteen-year-old boy who has grown extremely tired of knowing about the subtle changes in his brother's body before said brother does.

Slide: CONVERSATION IN YOUR HEAD:
      A: "Dude, you've hit puberty."
      B: "Really?"
      A: "Yep: look."
      B: "Oh yeah, thanks."

So imagine this boy's ears perking up when he hears his science teacher proclaim, without a hint of doubt, that lobsters, having evolved with only a chitinous outer shell and a few ham-fisted nerve bundles, simply do not have the physical capability to feel pain during those pre-bisque preparations.

Slide: PICTURES IN YOUR HEAD:
      A POT FILLED WITH WATER (BOILING)
      A SCIENCE TEACHER (LECTURING)
      A FOURTEEN-YEAR-OLD BOY (LISTENING)

Now imagine the same ears on the same boy perking up past what seems humanly possible upon hearing this next factoid: that lobsters, lacking an apparatus capable of sensing and processing pain, almost certainly also lack the ability to feel...fear.

Slide: PICTURE IN YOUR HEAD:
A PLAN (UNFOLDING) WITHIN A BRAIN
(BOILING) BEHIND THE EYES (DISTANT,
INTENSE) OF A FOURTEEN-YEAR-OLD-BOY

It was a simple plan that unfolded itself inside the boy's mind at that moment. One based more on a childhood sense of the tautological than on any depth of consideration. If animals that do not feel pain consequently do not feel fear, then the best and perhaps only way to give a good jolt of shock therapy to his twelve-year-old brother's nervous system and grow those prematurely burnt-out nociceptors into ones capable of experiencing the prick of a needle, the crack of a baseball in the face, the sizzling rush of okay-that-bathwater-is-gonna-give-me-second-degree-burns-now was to scare the complete and thorough Jesus out of him.

Slide: A BRAIN (BOILING) BEHIND THE EYES (DISTANT, INTENSE)

Slide: THE EYES (DISTANT, INTENSE)

Slide: THE EYES

[*Slide out.*]

Slide: A PAUSE

[*A Pause. A sip of water. Slide out.*]

The thing about drowning is, it's not about the pain.

Slide: DROWNING = PAIN?

It hurts, by all accounts, but that's really secondary to the experience. No, the thing about drowning is, it's all about the horror.

Slide: DROWNING = FEAR

It generates in one a fear that comes from a place deeper than logic, deeper even than the brain. It comes from the body itself. It's as though every organ, every cell within you recognizes that something is going horribly wrong, and if that something is not fixed, and soon...In short, it brings about absolute physical panic.

At least, this was the thought inside the fourteen-year-old boy's mind...

Slide: THOUGHT = (DROWNING = FEAR)

...as he rushed back from his school to his neighborhood...

   Slide: (NEIGHBORHOOD [HOUSE (POOL)])

...within which sat his house...within which (or just outside of which) sat its swimming pool...over which rested a simple yet crucial feature: a heavy, black, tightly fitting tarp, which snapped into place via a series of hard metal studs circling the pool.

   Slide: (NEIGHBORHOOD [HOUSE (POOL [TARP])])
            WATER

The tarp had a history of being employed in a manner not intended by its creators. For it could not help but be noticed by the two boys that their father had left behind a number of pairs of used, torn, pungent-smelling gloves.

   Slide: PICTURE IN YOUR HEAD:
            BOXING GLOVES

And it also could not help but be noticed that the tarp, once in place, etched out a space roughly analogous to that of a boxing ring.

   Slide: (TARP) = BOXING RING
            WATER

It supported the boys surprisingly well at six and eight, began to sag beneath their weight at nine and eleven, and now...well, they liked to think of it as adding an advanced level of difficulty to an otherwise rote form of entertainment. Besides, it was black, which concealed bloodstains from their mother. The snaps took a surprising amount of effort to pry loose, and in the end the boy could only uncover about a quarter of the pool before his fingers were rubbed raw and the pain forced him to stop, as it would anyone with a normal body. But a quarter, positioned directly over the deepest end of the pool, was enough. He peered for a moment at the shimmering, stale-looking water quivering just beneath the tarp's surface. Then he gently laid the corner back down onto the concrete edge of the pool, and waited for night to fall.

   Slide: PICTURE IN YOUR HEAD:
            NIGHT (FALLING)

It is astonishing to me what people assume about children. About what children are capable of.

Slide: PICTURE IN YOUR HEAD:
STARS (TWINKLING)

Mozart composed the melody to "Twinkle, Twinkle Little Star" when he was just a boy. By fourteen he'd written his first opera.

[*Suddenly, "Nel sen mi palpita dolente il core" from Mozart's* Mitridate, Re di Ponte *bursts into our ears—perhaps starting at the intense, terror-filled final thirty seconds.*]

Slide: PICTURE IN YOUR HEAD:
A FOURTEEN-YEAR-OLD BOY WITH AN OPERA
IN HIS EYES

An opera. At fourteen. It ends with a suicide.

[*A moment, as the* MAN *stares beyond us, through us, into something unseen. Then the music ceases, and the* MAN's *eyes refocus.*]

Slide: PICTURE IN YOUR HEAD:
NIGHT (FALLEN)

When it was dark out, and the tarp's surface nothing more than a black blob in the backyard, the older brother entered the younger brother's room and tossed a pair of boxing gloves onto his bed. It was a gesture in need of no words. The routine was understood. The younger boy donned his gloves and the older boy helped him lace up. Tightly. Then the two boys raced down the stairs together, rushed through the living room, and out the back door. With a howl of joy…

Slide: SOUND IN YOUR HEAD:
JOY

…the younger boy leapt onto the surface of the tarp, while the older boy, for the first time ever in the history of their game, stopped short. The second the younger boy's feet hit the tarp, the undone corner sank beneath his weight and the water sucked him right under.

Slide: SOUND IN YOUR HEAD:
A SPLASH

The older boy's goal had always only been to instigate fear within the younger boy. He saw it (and he knows now, believe me he knows this must seem at best bizarre and at worst rather sick) but he saw it as a sort of gift.

> *Slide:* PICTURES IN YOUR HEAD:
> A CORNER OF A TARP (SINKING)
> A BODY UNDER THE TARP (FLAILING)
> A PAIR OF LUNGS (CONSTRICTING)

A gift given, as many gifts are, that it might benefit not only the receiver but the giver as well.

> *Slide:* PICTURES IN YOUR HEAD:
> A YOUNGER BOY (PANICKING)
> AN OLDER BOY (WATCHING)
> STARS (TWINKLING)

For if the younger brother were to be scared deeply enough, he might regain his ability to feel pain.

> *Slide:* SOUNDS IN YOUR HEAD:
> CRYING
> GURGLING
> SMACKING (GLOVED FISTS AGAINST
> UNDERSIDE OF TARP?)

And if he regained his ability to feel pain, he could be as afraid of it as the rest of us.

> *Slide:* PICTURES IN YOUR HEAD:
> AN OLDER BOY (BY THE POOL)
> BOXING GLOVES (REMOVED)
> BARE HANDS (REVEALED)

And if he was as afraid of pain as the rest of us, he would seek to avoid injury.

> *Slide:* PICTURES IN YOUR HEAD:
> AN OLDER BOY (KNEELING)
> BARE HANDS (SWEATING)
> BLACK TARP (WAITING)

And if he sought to avoid injury, it would no longer be necessary for the older brother to carry the entire load of the house upon his back, take care of everything, all without a mother or father around to guide, to assist, to encourage, to offer more than a symbolic presence in his already ancient-feeling life.

Slide: SOUNDS IN YOUR HEAD:
    CRYING
    GURGLING
    MUFFLED SCREAM (A BOY'S NAME?)

And then, as if adding one last insult to the labor of his days, to check for injuries every night upon a body that ought to know its own damn surfaces by now.

Slide: PICTURE IN YOUR HEAD:
    STARS (TWINKLING)

A gift. To them all. But the factor the older brother had failed to account for was the sheer disorientation that occurs when one is submerged underwater with no air and no light. Meaning that, once he slipped under the tarp, the younger boy had no way to judge which direction to swim in toward safety.

Slide: PICTURES IN YOUR HEAD:
    HANDS (SUBMERGING)
    FINGERS (GRASPING)
    TARP (RISING)

So when it came time to lift the corner and pull it back, to expose the younger brother to the darkness and stars and above all air, when he finally pulled it back...his brother wasn't there.

Slide: SOUNDS IN YOUR HEAD:
    AS BEFORE, BUT SUBSIDING

He reached into the black water then, frantically searching for something, a blond head of hair, a goofy ear, a gloved fist.

Slide: SOUNDS IN YOUR HEAD:
    SUBSIDING

He strained until it hurt, until every fiber of his arm, from the shoulder blade to the fingertips, was alight with what all but perhaps the lobster would recognize and categorize as pain. Nothing.

Slide: SOUNDS IN YOUR HEAD:
    . . .

There was nothing he could reach.

[*Slide out.*]

Slide: A PAUSE

[*A pause. No water this time. Slide out.*]

In studies of the subject, the distinction is often made between two different components of pain: the physical and the emotional. The physical component is where the sensation comes from, but it is the emotional component that makes the sensation a bad one. A lobster in a pot may struggle and slam itself repeatedly against the sides, the lid . . . but we do not know whether the slamming and struggling comes from the experience of a bad sensation, or simply from the automatic response of its muscle fiber to a substance that is rapidly enveloping and destroying it. You will notice that nowhere in there does anyone so much as mention the third possibility: that the lobster might actually be afraid.

> *Slide:* PICTURES IN YOUR HEAD:
> POOL
> POLICE
> POLICE LIGHTS

This is what the older boy reminded himself as the police hauled back the black tarp and shone their lights down on the body of his little brother, floating facedown, gloved hands red and weirdly reminiscent of those of a smaller, more chitinous animal with whom he seemed to share a few things in common.

> *Slide:* PICTURE IN YOUR HEAD:
> BOXING GLOVES

The older brother reminded himself that he had almost certainly failed. That his kid brother, who had always been so brave, so reckless, moving through the world with the eager abandon of a child giant . . . that his brother probably didn't feel a thing. And was, up to and including the final moment of his life, almost certainly not scared.

[*Slide out.*]

Remarkably (or perhaps not so) the word "deliberate" was never used.

> *Slide:* **ACCIDENT** (ak•si•dent) *n.* an unfortunate incident that happens unexpectedly and unintentionally, usually resulting in damage or injury

The older brother was assumed not to have committed the crime on purpose, in much the same way that he was assumed not to have written an opera. And the events of that autumn fell away, brushed slowly aside to rest beneath the category of "neighborhood tragedy." Which all had a strange effect on the older brother.

Slide: PICTURE IN YOUR HEAD:
      A LOBSTER

He found himself unable to feel anything about the situation. One way or the other. He recognized the absence of his brother. He recognized that at one time he had both adored and despised the little boy in an ever-shifting, ever-churning mixture. But now, he could feel nothing. No guilt. No sadness. And though it probably goes without saying, certainly no pain. [*Slide out.*]

The older brother grew up to be a teacher, and now, in a choice bit of irony, works in the very same high school he attended back in those days. He stands in a classroom all day, five days a week, and lectures on mathematics to a group of bored and vaguely angry-looking kids. Sometimes for complicated equations, he uses slides or an overhead. But lately. Lately, he's started doing something new. Something probably not quite legal, though it would be difficult to define the crime in it exactly. Lately, he sneaks in at night.

Slide: PICTURE IN YOUR HEAD:
      STARS (TWINKLING)

When all but the janitors are gone. Sneaks into the classroom he'd sat in long ago when that magical plan had unfolded itself inside his mind. He sets up his slides, fills a glass of water…and he lectures. The lecture he gives at night is to nobody at all, and concerns nothing anyone would understand. Pots and lobsters and a pair of young boys. If pressed, he could not adequately explain why he does it. If pressed, he would simply stare at you, silently, with a pair of eyes not quite his own.

Slide: A FOURTEEN-YEAR-OLD BOY WITH AN OPERA
      IN HIS EYES
Slide: AN OPERA IN HIS EYES
Slide: HIS EYES

[*Slide out.*]

If you ask me, though . . . if you want to know what I think . . . I'd say he is actively attempting, on a nightly basis, to scare the complete and thorough Jesus out of himself.

[*The final few moments of Mozart's "Nel sen mi palpita dolente il core" rush in to fill our ears. The* MAN *simply stares at us, expressionless.*]

      Slide: BLACKOUT

[*Everything, including the slide, cuts out.*]

• • •

You're Invited!

Darren Canady

Darren Canady

Darren Canady hails from Topeka, Kansas. His play *False Creeds* was named the winner of the Alliance Theater's Kendeda Graduate Playwriting Competition and was also workshopped at the O'Neill Playwrights Conference in 2006. *False Creeds* was also a finalist for the Abingdon Theatre Company's Christopher Brian Wolk Award and the Goldberg Prize in Playwriting. Another play, *Brothers of the Dust*, has received recognition in the Lorraine Hansberry Playwriting Competition, the Theodore Ward Prize for African American Playwriting, and the James W. Rodgers Playwriting Competition, and will be produced by Congo Square Theatre in Spring 2011 (Black Excellence Award, BTAA Award, Jeff Award nomination). His ten-minute play *He Was Mine but Then You Took Him* received a production at NYU and competed at the Region II Festival of the Kennedy Center American College Theatre Festival. *He Was Mine* was also a finalist for the Actors Theatre of Louisville's 2006 Heideman Playwriting Award. How *Theo Changed His Name*, an opera for which Canady provided the libretto, had its premiere through the Pittsburgh (Pennsylvania) Symphony Orchestra. His work has been seen at the Quo Vadimus Arts' ID America Festival, the Fremont Centre Theatre, Chicago's Congo Square Theatre, and the BE Company. Canady holds a BA in creative writing from Carnegie Mellon University and an MFA in dramatic writing from New York University. He was a 2006–2007 fellow in the Juilliard School's Lila Acheson Wallace American Playwrights Program, and is a former member of Primary Stages' Dorothy Strelsin New Writers Group. He is a member of the Old Vic Theatre's Old Vic New Voices Network, where he participated in the 2010 T. S. Eliot US/UK Exchange. He currently teaches playwriting at the University of Kansas.

···production history···

You're Invited! was originally developed as part of the Old Vic Theatre's 2010 T. S. Eliot US/UK Exchange partnership with the Public Theatre. It was subsequently produced in May 2010 at the Old Vic in London, UK.

characters

PAUL

JEREMY

WILL, Paul's partner

TERRI, Jeremy's wife, black

MAGGIE

All characters are late 20s/early 30s.

setting

The kitchen of PAUL and WILL's upscale home. An upscale kitchen.

• • •

[*From offstage, we hear "Happy Birthday to You" being sung. Mid-song, the voices suddenly cut off. Quick moment of silence, then shouts of "Mikey!" "Ohmigod!" "Stop! Stop!" Kids crying. Moments later,* PAUL *enters carrying the remnants of a birthday cake.* JEREMY *is fast behind him.*]

JEREMY Paul! Oh my God, I—I—I—I'm so sorry!

PAUL Look. You didn't do it. It's . . . it's fine.

JEREMY No, no, no—it's not. Oh God. I'm so really sorry—I don't know what got into him!

[WILL *enters carrying the rest of the cake.*]

PAUL Too much punch, I guess.

JEREMY Really. I'm really sorry!

PAUL Listen. It's fine.

WILL Are you nuts?! His kid pissed on Logan's birthday cake!

PAUL Will. Please.

JEREMY   Will. I'm really sorry—

WILL   I mean, what the hell are we supposed to do with chocolate ice cream piss cake?!

JEREMY   We'll make it up to you. I swear.

WILL   Are you gonna make it up to my kid?

PAUL   Okay Will, you can dial down the dramatics.

[TERRI *enters, checkbook in hand.*]

TERRI   Okay. How much was the cake?

JEREMY   Right, right. The least we can do is pay for the cake.

WILL   Well, I mean, you gonna pay for the entire party? 'Cuz the whole thing is ruined!

JEREMY   Sure, sure, just name a price—

TERRI   Whoa, whoa, whoa, wait a minute, Jeremy. Look, I'm sorry for Mikey's accident—

WILL   "Accident"?!

TERRI   But I'm not footing the entire bill for this Prada and Gucci dog-and-pony show you're passing off as a toddler's birthday party.

JEREMY   Terri—

WILL   Excuse us for having a little class. We didn't know we were inviting the neighborhood golden shower machine to our son's birthday party.

PAUL   Will!

TERRI   Hold up—what did you just call our son?!

PAUL   The party is not ruined, Will. There's still the—balloon artist guy coming—and that magician—

WILL   Of course it's ruined! I mean, do you hear that out there?! We've got a fucking Mormon Tabernacle Choir's worth of crying kids 'cuz there's no cake. Correction: there's a cake—it's just marinating in piss at the moment.

JEREMY   Where'd you get it from? Cold Stone Creamery or something? We can run down right now and get another…

PAUL   No, it was a special order. That new bakery downtown. Listen—

TERRI   Well, we won't be running anywhere until I get an apology from Will.

JEREMY   C'mon, Terri.

WILL   Apologize for what?!

TERRI   "Golden shower machine"?! Let me tell you something—

[MAGGIE *enters. She's carrying a bottle of beer with her.*]

MAGGIE   Hey, guys, just wanted to let you know, it's gettin' a little tense out there between Logan and the pee-pee kid—

TERRI   His name is Mikey.

PAUL   Umm—is that a beer?

MAGGIE   Oh. Yeah. I brought it in my cooler, if you guys want—

PAUL   No, thanks. Uh, Maggie, we don't allow drinking around Logan.

MAGGIE   Oh. Okay. Just so you know, I'm not, like, giving it to him.

PAUL   It's just a rule we have—

MAGGIE   Cool, whatever, but you've got bigger problems. Logan's trying to mow Mikey down with the tricycle you bought him.

JEREMY   What?!

TERRI   Great. Now he's trying to kill my son.

WILL   He was clearly provoked. I'll go break it up.

[WILL *dashes out.*]

JEREMY   I better go help.

[JEREMY *exits.*]

PAUL   Listen, Terri, I'm sorry about what Will said. He just—wanted this to be a good time for Logan.

TERRI   I get that, but the kid's four years old. He won't even remember half of it.

MAGGIE   He sure will remember the fresh smell of piss and chocolate ice cream, though.

TERRI   You're not helping.

MAGGIE   Aw, c'mon—laugh a little. I mean, did you see Logan's face?! That shit's a YouTube sensation waiting to happen.

PAUL   Okay, I'm all for not blowing this out of proportion, but I don't find anything funny about it.

MAGGIE   My kid laughed.

PAUL   And don't you think that was pretty mean?

MAGGIE   Eh, Brian's a little prick—I never take it personal.

PAUL   My God, he's a toddler.

TERRI   Exactly. Which means they're going to cry and pee at parties and pick fights, and we just come behind and clean up. So, anyway, this check for the cake. How much was it?

PAUL   Don't worry about it.

TERRI   No, lemme have it. If I don't write this check, Jeremy will never let me hear the end of it.

PAUL   No. It's all right—

MAGGIE   Dude. Just take the money.

PAUL   Look, y'know, maybe you guys...can...have us over for dinner or something...

TERRI   Or you can just tell me how much the cake was and we can be done with it.

PAUL   Fine!...Four twenty-five.

[*Beat.*]

TERRI   Shut the front door—!

MAGGIE   Are you fucking kidding me?!

TERRI   Tell me you mean four dollars and twenty-five cents.

PAUL   I told you we wanted it to be special—

MAGGIE Ohmigod—you're serious!

TERRI For four hundred and twenty-five dollars, that damn cake shoulda been able to wash off Mike's pee and follow it up with a tap dance and a Vegas floor show!

PAUL Look! We just wanted to show Logan how much we love him—

MAGGIE Oh, and if you don't spend money like water, you don't love your kid?

PAUL That's not what I'm saying—

TERRI Swear to God, that's almost as much as our wedding cake! Do you seriously expect me to fork that over?

PAUL No, which is why I said to drop it!

[JEREMY *and* WILL *re-enter.*]

JEREMY Crisis averted—the magician's here!

MAGGIE And what're his rates—a grand an hour?

PAUL Great. This is why I didn't want to say anything.

TERRI Well, I hope you're happy, Jeremy. We now own a one-of-a-kind, three-tiered, chocolate pee-pee monument to Will and Paul's love for Logan that's only gonna set us back four hundred and twenty-five dollars.

JEREMY Four hundred and twenty-five dollars?!

WILL It was a special order.

JEREMY From where—the Magical Land of Fairy Cakes?

WILL "Fairy Cakes"?! What's that supposed to mean?!

JEREMY Oh—oh—oh no—oh my God—n-n-no—that's not what I—I would never! No, I just meant—oh God—my stupid mouth—

TERRI No, your stupid guilt! You keep it up, they'll have us paying their mortgage too.

WILL Well, clearly you owe us something since you failed at potty training.

MAGGIE I'll drink to that.

TERRI Why are you even in here?!

MAGGIE Cheap entertainment.

PAUL Okay, look, look, look—we can settle this. Terri, if you don't want to pay us, then don't.

JEREMY No, no, I mean—we should—we have to give you *something*.

PAUL Fine, whatever, just write a random number on the check, hand it over, and we'll be done.

TERRI Fine.

[*She begins to write.*]

Just so we're clear, it's not that we can't afford it, y'know. We're not broke. It's—it's principle. I mean, it's a flippin' cake. You can get one at Dairy Queen for like thirty bucks.

WILL Did it ever occur to you that maybe some people prefer their purchases to be slightly above bargain basement?

TERRI Are you calling me cheap?

PAUL No, no, that's not what he meant—

TERRI Because clearly, I spend money on things that matter. That daycare our kids go to costs an arm and a leg!

WILL It sure does, but Mikey being there makes me think they're not screening their candidates close enough.

TERRI Lucky for you, since no one would take a spoiled crybaby like Logan.

JEREMY Okay, okay, okay—that's enough! This is supposed to be a party, right? I mean, we're friends, right? Or—at least—our kids are. Not thirty minutes ago we were joking and having a good time. Can we please just … go back to that? We're the adults here, okay? We're cool. We can talk—or—chat—I mean, someday we're gonna really laugh about this. This could be the beginning of a great—circle of friends! Yeah … ?

[*There is a pause. Perhaps this will work?*]

MAGGIE   Eh—I think you all are bitch-asses.

PAUL   What?!

MAGGIE   Yeah, y'know, I didn't really want to come over here to the party in the first place, but I thought, what the hell—I'm goin' bass-ackwards broke payin' for my kid's daycare, he oughta at least get to hang out with his friends. Tell ya the truth, as soon as I saw you guys lived over here I was like, "Shit man, that neighborhood's crawling with rich snobs and their McClaren strollers and organic soy baby milk and hybrid cars." And like, the piss cake was entertaining and all, but y'all really are douches.

JEREMY   Well, I don't think that's very fair. I mean, we've been really nice to you.

WILL   Exactly. And don't think I didn't notice you didn't bring a present.

TERRI   Yeah, and I went out of my way to talk to you at the orientation last month.

MAGGIE   That doesn't mean you're not assholes. And you'll probably turn your kids in to assholes. I mean, maybe Mikey stands a chance. Anyone who'll piss on the birthday kid's cake gets a thumbs-up in my book.

[*Beat.*]

PAUL   Oh—oh my God—you . . . you really think I'm an asshole—!

WILL   Don't listen to this nut job.

PAUL   N-n-no, Maggie—I'm the one people like—people like me. I'm not an asshole. Other people—like—like *them*—they're assholes, but not me!

JEREMY   No, now wait a minute. I—I'm no asshole! I'm—I'm a good guy! I mean, Mikey did his thing and whatever, but I'm being nice! I'm offering to pay you back—

WILL   How novel—being responsible for your spawn.

JEREMY   Well, we don't have to!

TERRI   Exactly.

MAGGIE   And if you don't want to, you shouldn't pay—

JEREMY   Right.

MAGGIE   But then you'd be an asshole.

JEREMY   What?! No, I just—don't want people to think—

MAGGIE   What people? Will? Will's an asshole.

WILL   Paul, this is why I said not to invite her.

PAUL   I was trying to be nice!

TERRI   So you're good without the check? Because I mean—seriously—four twenty-five—you were sorta asking for it.

JEREMY   Terri, stop that. Be nice.

TERRI   Fuck "nice."

MAGGIE   That's right—fuck "nice"!

PAUL   And what is so wrong with being nice? What is so wrong with a few nice people getting together, eating some damn cake, and pretending for just a few hours that they actually enjoy each other's company? I don't think it's asking too much for people to put on a happy fucking face, haul out some manners and good breeding, and do it all in the name of a four-year-old having a happy goddamned birthday. Pretend, damnit! Nice people do it all the time. I'm nice—I do it! I pretend that I want you here, in my house, choking down my four-hundred-dollar cake and guzzling down the summer punch I made from mint leaves from my own garden. Because that's what nice queers do! We invite the half-Jew, half-black family and the antisocial single mom to the party because they're oughta be some goddamned solidarity even if you're all raging jackasses and vicious bitches, which I can't tell you, you are because I'm the nice one, and could a few other people please join me in being fucking nice?!

[*Awkward beat.* JEREMY *crosses to* PAUL.]

JEREMY   Oh. So. You want nice?

PAUL   Um—well—I just meant—

[PAUL *is cut off by* JEREMY *smearing his face with piss cake.*]

JEREMY   Fuck "nice."

[MAGGIE *and* TERRI *cheer.*]

PAUL   Oh my God!

WILL   What the fuck, man, I mean, what the—

TERRI   Do it, baby!

WILL   Oh, you think that's cute?!

[WILL *tries to smear* TERRI *while* MAGGIE *moves to rescue her beer.*]

MAGGIE   Watch the Bud Light!
[MAGGIE *gets caked.*]
Motherfucker!

TERRI   [*To* WILL.] Bring it!

PAUL   Stop—everybody, stop!

WILL   Oh no! Terri's gonna be wearin' this cake!

JEREMY   Your husband started this! Leave her alone!

PAUL   Let he who is blameless cast the first baked good, asshole!

MAGGIE   Oh God—I'm gonna throw up—

TERRI   Swear to God, Will, you hit me with that cake, you will put
forth a hand and draw back a stump!

PAUL   Stop running in the house!

JEREMY   Now who isn't nice?!

[*Pandemonium. The couples bicker. Then—*]

MAGGIE   Hey, hey, hey! EVERYBODY, SHUT THE HELL UP!!!
[*Stunned silence.*]
Listen! Do you hear that?!

[MAGGIE *goes to one of the windows.*]

JEREMY   Do I hear what?

MAGGIE   [*Pointing out the window.*] Look! Look at 'em!

[*We hear the children brightly singing "Happy Birthday" to Logan again. As the kids keep singing.*]

Oh my God, look at 'em. They're pattin' Logan on the back, givin' him hi-fives and stuff. Wow! Hugs and kisses—the whole nine yards. Like they're actually having fun. Isn't that just like kids? The second we leave 'em alone, they actually start acting like humans. Like seriously. My Brian was a real dumb ass the whole car ride over here. And he was like Mikey's lead cheerleader with the cake. But look at him now. I think Brian just kissed Logan on the forehead. He only acts likes an ass when I'm around. I think it's on purpose.

WILL Wow. Mikey's—like—leading the celebration out there.

JEREMY I think—I think I'm actually moved.

TERRI It's good to see Logan not—y'know—crying and whining.

PAUL They all look—really...nice...

[*Gentle beat as they take in the celebration.* PAUL *hands* JEREMY *a washcloth.* WILL *scoops some of the cake off* TERRI.]

TERRI Ahm, Will, I'm—I'm really sorry. It was a rough week at the firm and—

WILL No, Terri. I should never treat a guest like that—really!

PAUL Jeremy, listen, you're right, you're nice—and nice is not bad—

JEREMY C'mon, Paul—no sweat—we're totally cool!

MAGGIE [*Still at the window.*] How come you guys didn't mention you had a spare cake?

WILL There's no spare cake. There's just the last part of the one Mikey peed on.

MAGGIE Oh. 'Cuz Logan is serving it to everyone else.

[*Pause. The parents spring to action yelling at Logan to stop as they charge out of the kitchen.*]

[*Blackout.*]

• • •

acknowledgments

I would like to thank John Cerullo of Hal Leonard Publishing Group and June Clark, my agent, for supporting this project. Thanks, too, to Bernadette Malavarca and Carol Flannery for helping in-house with this book.

Loads of folks helped round up the finest short plays around the country for this volume. I'd like to thank especially my colleagues in the American Theatre and Drama Society, who answered the call by sending names and plays from every corner of the country. Those who spread the word so nicely include John Patrick Bray, Steve Feffer, James Fisher, Iris Smith Fischer, Oyamo, Jorge Huerta, Susan Harris Smith, John Fleming, Chris Wheatley, Gary Harrison, Beth Lincks, Robin Bernstein, Lauren Friesen, Megan Jones, Cassandra Medley, Bethany Whitehead, Eric Eberwein, and Lisa Reinke. Special thanks to Stephanie Ward. And thanks to everyone who submitted their work for me to read and review, making this project such a joyful but also challenging undertaking.

THE BEST AMERICAN SHORT PLAYS SERIES